She Who Struggles

'An exhilarating and immensely valuable collection of the stories of revolutionary women across the globe – a much-needed addition to our histories of resistance.'

—Priyamvada Gopal, Professor of Postcolonial Studies,
University of Cambridge

'Captures the resolute vision of revolutionary women in twentieth-century anti-colonial, anti-capitalist and anti-imperialist struggles. This captivating collection chronicles individual accounts of remarkable women, though it tells their collective global fight for socialism, communism and internationalism. The book is a corrective to the crucial silences and absences in the historiography of revolutionary movements.'

—Shahrzad Mojab, Professor, co-author of *Revolutionary Learning: Marxism, Feminism and Knowledge*

'This powerful collection, complex and compassionate, is a meaningful intervention – not only in women's and revolutionary history, but in world history. Learning from struggling women's labour, sacrifice and imagination is fundamental for internationalist horizons in the twenty-first century.'

—Dilar Dirik, author of *The Kurdish Women's Movement: History, Theory, Practice*

She Who Struggles

Revolutionary Women
Who Shaped the World

Edited by
Marral Shamshiri and Sorcha Thomson

PLUTO PRESS

First published 2023 by Pluto Press
New Wing, Somerset House, Strand, London WC2R 1LA
and Pluto Press, Inc.
1930 Village Center Circle, 3-834, Las Vegas, NV 89134

www.plutobooks.com

A previous version of Chapter 7 was published in *Cold War Camera*. See Thy Phu, Evyn Lê Espiritu Gandhi, and Donya Ziaee, 'Icon of Solidarity: The Revolutionary Vietnamese Woman in Vietnam, Palestine, and Iran', in *Cold War Camera*, eds. Thy Phu, Andrea Noble, and Erina Duganne (Durham, NC: Duke University Press, 2023), 67–112. The authors thank Duke University Press for the permission to revise and reprint this chapter.

British Library Cataloguing in Publication Data
A catalogue record for this book is available from the British Library

ISBN 978 0 7453 4824 7 Paperback
ISBN 978 0 7453 4825 4 PDF
ISBN 978 0 7453 4826 1 EPUB

Typeset by Stanford DTP Services, Northampton, England

Simultaneously printed in the United Kingdom and United States of America

Contents

List of Figures

Acknowledgements

The idea for this book project emerged from conversations between friends at what felt like a moment of political defeat for a progressive mass movement in the UK in 2019. Our conversations were inspired by continued popular struggles at home and internationally against racism, settler colonialism, and capitalist extraction and exploitation. Within these struggles, there was revived interest in radical histories and education, and the role that they must play in understanding and changing the world today. At the same time, gender and sexual liberties across the globe continued to be attacked, reminding us that feminist struggles remain as urgent as ever, and that freedoms once won are never guaranteed. These setbacks and ongoing struggles of a world in crisis prompted us to look to the past as a source of inspiration and learning.

In our work as historians, the university has provided a forum for making sense of these contemporary issues alongside other academics working on histories of revolution, internationalism and solidarity. From this, in political communion with feminist scholars, past and present, we found ourselves questioning the absence of women in these histories. Believing in the need to take these conversations beyond the university, we invited academics and activists who work on and with women in revolutionary movements to take part in this collection. The outcome is a collective endeavour and we are grateful to the brilliant contributors to this collection who have brought profiles of revolutionary women and their struggles to life in fierce and inspiring ways: Mahvish Ahmad, Maurice J. Casey, Evyn Lê Espiritu Gandhi, Kanwal Hameed, Karen Buenavista Hanna, Jehan Helou, Yatta Kiazolu, Marvi Latifi, Kebotlhale Motseothata, Thy Phu, Jeremy Randall, Sara Salem, Elif Sarican, Ismat Shahjahan, Tooba Syed, Madina Thiam, Molly Todd and Donya Ziaee. We are especially grateful to Jehan Helou and the Women Democratic

Front (WDF) in Pakistan for enriching this collection by sharing their first-hand testimonies and experiences. We would also like to thank Roba Salibi for recording, transcribing and translating part of the testimony of Jehan Helou from Arabic to English, and to Mohid Rehman for transcribing and translating the WDF interview from Urdu to English.

We would like to acknowledge the difficulties that were faced in the writing of this book. We greatly appreciate the work of all the contributors who amidst the conditions of a global pandemic chose to contribute to this book project. The WDF conducted their interview while floods devastated Pakistan in 2022, and we are grateful for their willingness to take part while organising critical flood relief. Kebotlhale Motseothata researched and wrote her chapter while experiencing internet problems from load-shedding in South Africa. Many of our contributors also juggled this project with care work at home, in their communities and in their workplaces.

Thank you to Neda Tehrani, our commissioning editor at Pluto Press, for your guidance, editorial work and trust in us throughout this process, and to the rest of the Pluto team. We also thank those who engaged generously and intellectually with this work, including the anonymous reviewers, Shahrzad Mojab, Rosa Campbell, Lucien Begault, James Hoctor, Mana Shamshiri and the countless other people who played a role in taking this project from an idea to a book.

List of Abbreviations

ANC	African National Congress
AWP	Awami Workers Party
CPP	Convention People's Party
CRIPDES	Christian Committee for the Displaced of El Salvador
CTC	Workers Central Union of Cuba
EWCP	Egyptian Workers Communist Party
FLN	(Algerian) National Liberation Front
FMC	Federation of Cuban Women
FMLN	Farabundo Martí National Liberation Front
GUPW	General Union of Palestinian Women
ILD	International Labour Defence
IUS	International Union of Students
JRA	Japanese Red Army
KALAYAAN	Organisation of Women For Freedom
KWM	Kurdish Women's Movement
MK	Umkhonto we Sizwe
MPLA	Popular Movement for the Liberation of Angola
NAACP	National Association for the Advancement of Colored People
NAM	Non-Aligned Movement
NCNW	National Council of Negro Women
OIPFG	Organisation of Iranian People's Fada'i Guerrillas
OSPAAAL	Organisation of Solidarity with the Peoples of Africa, Asia and Latin America
PAC	Pan-African Congress
PCC	Cuban Communist Party
PFLP	Popular Front for the Liberation of Palestine
PKK	Kurdistan Workers' Party
PLO	Palestine Liberation Organisation

RAF	(Japanese) Red Army Faction
RAWA	Revolutionary Association of the Women of Afghanistan
RDA	Rassemblement Démocratique Africain
ROTPI	Revolutionary Organisation of the Tudeh Party of Iran
SWC	Soviet Women's Committee
UFOA	West African Women's Union
VWU	Vietnam Women's Union
WDF	Women Democratic Front
WFTU	World Federation of Trade Unions
WIDF	Women's International Democratic Federation

Introduction: She Who Struggles

Marral Shamshiri and Sorcha Thomson

When we think of revolutionaries who shaped the twentieth century, who comes to mind? For many, it is the names of men who appear most readily, stirring different reactions depending on where, and on what political ground, you stand. Lenin, Che Guevara, Amílcar Cabral, Hồ Chí Minh, Malcolm X, Mao Zedong, Yasser Arafat and Nelson Mandela exist in the established canon of revolutionary history. Their names evoke distinct organisations and theories, places and tactics, moments of victory and defeat. They are the protagonists of a revolutionary story that features landmark speeches, intellectual legacies and valorised acts. This book asks: where are the women in this story? How can we know them when their lives and political activities have been overshadowed by the iconographies of male revolutionary leaders?

The question of where women's liberation, sexual and gender politics, and feminism lie in transformative movements – often known as the 'woman question' – has been grappled with by social and political movements throughout history and should be on the agenda of any truly transformative politics today. However, this question has often been treated as a secondary concern, both by the movements these women were part of and in the histories written about them. Within these movements, women's liberation was often placed as subsequent to the achievement of national and social transformation, and women faced gendered and sexualised forms of oppression. In addition, revolutionary movements have been written about and remembered in ways that overlook the roles that women played and the place of gendered politics within them. The ongoing neglect of women in these histories is a reproduction of the patriarchal politics experienced by these women historically. Revolutionary women need to be written into history so that we

1

can learn more about their multi-faceted struggles, their radical traditions, and the ways in which the woman question was grappled with. However, this isn't just women's history, in fact, we learn more about revolutionary movements as a whole when we pay attention to the women in the story.

In this collection, we feature revolutionary women from Cuba, Ghana, Mali, Ireland, Palestine, Japan, Iran, Vietnam, Kurdistan, South Africa, Egypt, the Philippines and El Salvador whose political activities stretch from the 1930s to the present. These women were engaged in transformative anticolonial, anti-imperialist and socialist projects that crossed borders in the twentieth century. The women in this volume are presented together not to showcase a number of individuals who single-handedly championed causes, but rather, in placing these women side by side, we can see a bigger and connected story about the collective struggles they took part in from different corners of the world. Their activities were rooted in the politics of solidarity and internationalism which shaped the twentieth century: revolutionary women mobilised liberation movements, forged networks of solidarity, and presented and acted on radical visions of the world – a world which continues to be struggled for. Most of the women featured in this book identified as communist or socialist women and were anchored in anticolonial and anti-imperial revolutionary struggles in Asia, Africa and the Americas. These political traditions are often obscured in contemporary institutionalised commemorations of women's struggle which tend to focus on bourgeois women from Western Europe and North America. For example, International Women's Day, celebrated on 8 March, has been stripped of its radical origins in international socialism. In 1922, German communist Clara Zetkin presented the idea of an International Women's Day to the Third International, the international communist organisation founded in 1919. Zetkin, who organised socialist women against poverty, high rents and exploitative conditions, did not identify as a feminist, which she saw as a bourgeois project for elite women.[1] Half a century later, when the Day was institutionalised by the United Nations (UN) in 1976 it was the outcome of an initiative by the Women's International

Democratic Federation (WIDF). The WIDF was founded as an anti-fascist organisation in Paris in 1945 and became an important pro-Soviet international platform where representatives from women's organisations in the socialist countries and Africa, Asia and Latin America debated, learned from each other, and built alliances that pushed forward a liberatory agenda for women of the world.[2]

Remembering these neglected histories allows us to ask pertinent political questions today. How does our knowledge of imperialism, understood here as an ongoing system of capitalist relations rather than a distinct historical era, change when we centre women's lives in relation to it? The twentieth century witnessed the demise of European empires which had ruled the majority of the world and their replacement by a system of nation states. In the post-war period and cold war that followed, dozens of anticolonial national liberation movements won political independence and self-determination, and a process of formal decolonisation took place. Yet, the so-called 'end of empire' in this way did not mark the end of imperialism. As Lenin theorised in 1917, imperialism was a system of economic domination of monopolies and the export of finance capital that carved the world up in different spheres of influence.[3] This system of capitalist imperialism was not limited by national borders and took new shape in relation to the shifting dynamics of the twentieth century and beyond. Our understanding of capitalist imperialism expands when viewed through a lens that is both Marxist *and* feminist. A Marxist-feminist analysis allows us to recognise how capitalist imperialism organises social relations not only of class in the traditional sense, but also gender, race and sexuality.[4] Marxist-feminist scholars Sara Carpenter and Shahrzad Mojab question if 'consciousness about capitalist imperialism as *social relations,* connecting peoples and communities through a myriad of complex and contradictory relations, lags behind its omnipresence throughout the world'.[5] Recovering a hidden history of women's struggle reveals some of these complex and contradictory relations and can be a feminist step towards reactivating a revolutionary consciousness about capitalist imperialism today.

* * *

Presenting these women's lives would not be possible without the existing works of scholars, feminists and activists who have grappled with writing women into history. We follow the tradition of 'history from below', which emerged in the second half of the twentieth century partially from the interests and figures of the British Communist Party Historians' Group, the journal *Past & Present* and the History Workshop movement, which called for the democratisation of history.[6] The Women's Liberation Movement in the late 1960s also engaged with history from below by writing women's active roles in history. This tradition tells us that History is shaped not only by the ruling classes, political elites and leaders, but the lives, experiences, practices and ideas of ordinary individuals and less powerful groups found beneath and in the margins of the hegemonic narratives of the 'great men' of history.

We build on these approaches, and early pioneering work in feminist historiography of radical movements, in seeking to further democratise and decolonise history with women at the centre.[7] To do this, we take inspiration from a growing literature of radical women's biographies. The women's lives we feature here can be added to a list of other women – such as Claudia Jones, Leila Khaled, Beatriz Allende and Ella Baker – who are more recently being remembered and written about as historical revolutionaries.[8] Kristen Ghodsee's *Red Valkyries* (2022) introduces us to another five Soviet and Eastern European women, highlighting a tradition of socialist feminism rather than that of liberal feminism which, she argues, remains dominant in popular culture today.[9] Likewise, Francisca de Haan has published a collection of 25 communist women's lives from across the world. Such work is a challenge to the 'double-blind spot' that obscures women in histories of communism, and communism in histories of the women's movement.[10] In the same spirit, this collection features short profiles of revolutionary women from across the world, with the aim of reviving a revolutionary consciousness and popular memory about the radical traditions to which they belonged.

All the contributors to this collection share the feminist concern of making women visible in history. We start with a feminist curiosity: we know that women took and take part in revolutionary movements, so we must retrieve, archive and write their histories. When researching this history, it becomes clear that it is not enough to use political archives, movement archives or official records, if women have been underrepresented or are absent in those sources. Rather than a focus on intellectual histories of revolution typically concerned with theorists and ideas – areas where women have been historically underrepresented – we turn to the broader terrain of political work, in everyday spaces and sites where women were involved and can be made visible through their actions.[11]

The chapters in this collection combine feminist methodologies and social history that expand and diversify the archive. The feminist practice of using auto/biography and memoir uncovers women's life histories, in their own words or in the words of those who knew them.[12] Similarly, oral history is used to allow individuals to share their experiences, memories and perspectives first-hand, and to narrate their own stories. With their diverse geographic and linguistic expertise, the brilliant authors in this book use previously untranslated memoirs, biographies, oral histories, publications, records and archival ephemera. Many have a background in academic disciplines across the humanities and social sciences; many are engaged in contemporary movement work and political activism.

Writing revolutionary women into history is a collective endeavour. We recognise that this collection presents only a small sample of countless revolutionary women. There are more well-known women who might feature in such a collection, for instance, Algeria's Djamila Bouhired or Paula Fortes and Ana Maria Cabral of Cape Verde and Guinea-Bissau. The women featured in this collection do not reflect the full spectrum of diverse gender identities and sexualities, nor are these questions, or those of queer revolutionary struggles more broadly, addressed in this book. There are many women whose names we may never know but who have shaped the world in their various revolutionary struggles.

*   *   *

How revolutionary women navigated the central political questions of their era while defying and challenging perceptions and limitations on what it meant to be a woman did not follow one path. Several of the chapters offer biographical profiles of revolutionary women whose legacies are prominent in their national or movement context. **Melba Hernández** (1921–2014) in Chapter 1 is regarded as a revolutionary heroine in Cuba. Her life spanned the different eras of the Cuban Revolution: from the underground struggle against the Fulgencio Batista regime in the 1950s, to becoming a driving force behind Cuba's campaign of solidarity with the people of Vietnam, the anti-imperial cause célèbre of the 1960s and 1970s, and a leading figure in the Organisation of Solidarity with the Peoples of Africa, Asia and Latin America (OSPAAAL). Her life directs us to the work of solidarity – even on grand intercontinental scales – as grounded in everyday activities, in the times of abeyance between landmark moments, where women played an essential role in the sustenance of the revolutionary movement.

Like Hernández, some women gained international prominence through their roles as diplomats, government officials and campaigners. The tensions between women's liberation and national liberation are demonstrated in the internationalist political activities of **Mabel Dove Danquah** (1905–1984) and **Aoua Kéita** (1912–1980), before, during and after Ghana and Mali's national liberation struggles in the 1950s and 1960s in Chapter 2. Dove built transatlantic and pan-African solidarity with the Black freedom struggle in the US through women's organisations, which ended up costing her an elected seat in the newly independent Ghanaian parliament. Kéita's political work as a nurse and a trade unionist centred women's health and maternal issues across French Soudan (later Mali). When she became a founding member of a leftist, pan-African political party, she encouraged women's participation through her midwifery networks, ultimately leading to her political exile. Seen together, these African women appear as visionaries who centred the liberation of women in their quests for their nations' independence.

Others found themselves at the centre of political campaigns by more unusual or unexpected routes. The life of **Mary Mooney** (c. 1848–1934), known in her political activism as Mother Mooney, shows us a working-class woman on a journey across continents in the inter-war period, from the rural west coast of Ireland under British colonialism to the US in Chapter 3. Mooney was part of a campaign for justice for her imprisoned communist son and the African American Scottsboro Boys, which unexpectedly brought together the Irish and African diaspora communities in the US in a defining moment of solidarity.

Allowing us to see solidarity work on an international scale, Chapter 4 presents a testimony from Palestinian revolutionary **Jehan Helou** (b. 1943). Helou was uprooted from Palestine with her family in the 1948 Nakba to Lebanon. In Lebanon, she joined the Palestinian Revolution in 1967, where her revolutionary work focused on the liberation of women at the grassroots level in the refugee camps and in organising and mobilising women in the liberation movement. She quickly rose to a leadership position in Fatah, the largest Palestinian resistance organisation, and played an instrumental role in the General Union of Palestinian Women (GUPW). Her testimony sheds light on one aspect of Helou's prolific revolutionary life: the power of women's cooperation in international solidarity activities, which took her to many countries around the world including India, Vietnam, the USSR and Latin America, and the struggles she faced in the pursuit of both women's and national liberation.

The Palestinian Revolution inspired and resonated with several other women in this collection, perhaps none more so than **Shigenobu Fusako** (b. 1945) in Chapter 5. Shaped by her upbringing in post-Second World War Japan, and the capitalist, imperialist and patriarchal boundaries of her society, she pursued political activism that challenged existing frameworks of the Japanese student movement and sought to forge global revolution – with Palestine at its centre, and Beirut as a base. Sexualised in her portrayal in the media and faced with misogynist stereotypes about women's place in the revolution, Fusako's release from prison in 2022 has brought new reflection on her role as a revolutionary leader, not just within the Japanese Red Army (JRA) but as a writer, theorist and activist of world revolution.

Militancy and the idea of world revolution is a common theme amongst the revolutionary women in this book. Chapter 6 features **Marziyeh Ahmadi Osku'i** (1945–1974), a guerrilla poet and member of the Organisation of the Iranian People's Fada'i Guerrillas (OIPFG), Iran's foremost Marxist revolutionary organisation in the 1970s. She was murdered by the Iranian secret police at just 29 years old, during a courageous attempt to protect her comrade. Her short revolutionary life presents a window into the anti-imperialist politics and revolutionary consciousness of a generation of left-wing Iranian revolutionaries – and her legacy has unexpectedly extended to Afghanistan and India through poetry and street theatre. The visual icon of the militant, often arm-bearing revolutionary woman became an important symbol of anticolonial revolution and circulated far and wide between movements. Chapter 7 shows how the iconic image of the revolutionary Vietnamese woman travelled into different contexts of revolutionary struggle. Between North and South Vietnam, the competing projects of communism and anti-communist republicanism were symbolised in the images of **Madame Bình** (b. 1927) and **Madame Nhu** (1924–2011), who symbolised different traditions of women's political participation. The chapter reveals why the figure of the revolutionary woman became so symbolic in the heyday of revolution and how the Vietnamese image inspired women in Iranian and Palestinian movements, although not without limits.

Other legacies of militant women provide urgent inspiration in the present. In Chapter 8, we learn about **Sakine Cansız** (1958–2013), nom de guerre **Sara**, who was a founder of the Kurdistan freedom movement. Sakine Cansız was assassinated in 2013, yet her presence continues to be felt. Sara's revolutionary life began with her upbringing amidst genocide and Turkish state repression, to the imprisonment that was central to her politicisation. Her role in the establishment of the first autonomous women's armed force of the Kurdistan Workers' Party has a lasting legacy in the Kurdish women's movement and the ongoing struggle in Rojava today.

The forms of revolutionary militancy that these women engaged in were never isolated from other political strategies and tactics. Most of them combined their militant struggle with other forms of intellectual and cultural work. One such revolutionary was **Lindiwe Mabuza** (1934–2021). In Chapter 9, her life shows the extraordinary cultural politics of a Black South African woman in the anti-apartheid struggle from exile. Her poetry serves as an archive of women's voices that are often left out of narratives of national liberation. Mabuza's political activities in exile later included representing the African National Congress (ANC) in Scandinavia before her eventual role in the first democratic parliament in South Africa under Nelson Mandela.

In addition to poetry as a weapon of cultural resistance, women used film and memoir to document and theorise their struggles. In Chapter 10, **Arwa Salih** (1953–1997) features as a leader of the Egyptian student movement in the 1970s; her memoir *The Stillborn* documents the challenges of being a communist and feminist intellectual during those days, as well as the struggles of theorising in the aftermath of revolution, in a context of defeat and nostalgia. Through film, we learn about the multiple practices of resistance by Palestinian and Egyptian women including **Widad Mitri** (1927–2007), **Aisha Odeh** (b. 1944), **Therese Halassa** (1948–2020) and several others. Together, these stories reveal to us a hidden world of feminist theorising in North Africa and West Asia, and the need to diversify and expand our archives.

Women's revolutionary theorising sometimes took place in universities, but also in their letter writing, study groups and creative practices. Chapter 11 introduces **Delia Aguilar** (b. 1938), a revolutionary woman from the Philippines in the US whose prolific academic intellect pushed back against both orthodox Marxism and Western Marxist feminism. Through her body of written work from her position in the US we see the multi-directional flow of ideas, theory and practice that were developed through dissident friendships cultivated with feminist revolutionaries in the Philippines.

The ability to communicate across borders and determine independent networks of information were extremely important to establishing these revolutionary women's connections. Chapter 12 takes us to the networks of solidarity between women in El Salvador and migrant communities in the US, through the work of the **Sister Cities** campaign. Salvadoran campesinas – 'peasants' – such as Domitila Ayala Mejía (b. c.1958) contributed to revolutionary efforts in the country with particular focus on developing connections with comrades in the US. The Sister Cities movement speaks to the belief of the Salvadoran campesinas that a better world is possible, and their continued commitment to bring that world into being.

Chapter 13 includes a conversation with the **Women Democratic Front** (WDF) of Pakistan, a collective who not only form part of this history but continue to forge a tradition of socialist feminism in their revolutionary work today. Mahvish Ahmad, a member of the WDF based in London and professor at LSE, interviewed Marvi Latifi, Ismat Shahjahan and Tooba Syed. The interview allows us to learn about the history and activities of the WDF, bringing the political practice of existing movements into conversation with the histories written in academic institutions. It disrupts male-centred politics by centring the experiences and analyses of four socialist feminists and reveals how many of the historical tensions between women's liberation and socialist revolution remain present to this day.

* * *

Retrieving the stories of these women's lives does more than simply correct the male-centric historical record or address the geographical imbalance towards Western, white feminisms in Europe and North America. Their lives contain within them universal lessons about what it was, and can be, like to be a part of revolutionary movements, and why it was and remains necessary to form internationalist connections. These revolutionary women took part in international conferences and political tours; took up arms in direct struggles against dictatorships and colonial occupations;

they formed solidarity committees; engaged in cultural and literary work; and worked in hospitals and universities. Some held leadership roles in high-profile organisations, others were less visible to the public, working behind-the-scenes to sustain and nurture the movements to which they belonged. They became politically active in refugee camps, in family homes, classrooms, prison cells, and their journeys across borders into new worlds. Some of their diverse practices included care roles within their communities and families, communication and campaigning activities, writing and translation, delivering and distributing messages underground, and diplomatic work.

If we focus on these women not as individual figures but as strugglers in community with one another – despite their specific political tendencies – we can see that they were responding to a shared set of world conditions. While these women operated primarily in their national contexts, they were consciously responding to the material conditions that manifested in different forms across the world. In Iran and the Philippines, for example, the revolutionary movements struggled against the dictatorships of Mohammad Reza Pahlavi and Ferdinand Marcos, which were seen as sub-imperialist powers backed and funded by the US. Likewise, the Zionist occupation of Palestine was seen as an extension of US and world imperialism. Reading these chapters alongside one another, it becomes apparent that the women featured in this book sought not reformist approaches to achieving equality with men, but a dismantling of the imperialist system and capitalist mode of social relations that oppressed not only women but the majority of humanity.

Many of these women made connections amongst themselves and looked to one another's struggles for inspiration and support. They learned from other movements, and read from a shared revolutionary canon, not only of Lenin to Mao, and Zetkin to Luxemburg, but also movement produced studies of revolutionary experiences in Vietnam, Cuba, Algeria and elsewhere. In many liberation struggles, women were combatants who raised arms alongside their male counterparts. But at the same time, women's roles were often not on the frontlines but in gendered support roles as nurses, carers, message carriers, cooks or uniform sewers.

The notion of militancy is important in itself – what characteristics defined the militant woman? Militant is a term that these women may or may not have identified with. As Lindiwe Mabuza, Sara, Melba Hernández and Marziyeh Ahmadi Osku'i's lives show us, the militant woman was not only a fighter in combat but a poet, writer, diplomat and organiser. Ideas of armed struggle that these women adhered to were not a blind embrace of violence, but rooted in theories of world revolution, as Shigenobu Fusako shows us, which was common to the era of anticolonial struggle. Amongst these women and movements, there were different conceptions of the strategies and tactics for revolutionary violence. With this in mind we might question how the arm-bearing revolutionary woman became an iconic symbol of resistance, when revolutionary women were not only those who took up arms. Through the variety of women's practices, we gain new vocabularies for tangible revolutionary practices beyond armed struggle. The Sister Cities campaign shows us how 'sistering' is a form of transnational grassroots social justice activism that links war-displaced Salvadorans with US-based groups. The idea of 'dissident friendships', seen in Delia Aguilar's work, is based on revolutionary love and produces deep relationships of commitment necessary for anti-imperialist and socialist futures. And, as Lindiwe Mabuza's anti-apartheid poetry shows us, culture can be a 'weapon of resistance'.

The experiences of these revolutionary women also reveal how the violent counter-revolutionary practices of the state, in the service of capitalist imperialism, have been used – but not unchallenged – across borders. Many of these women were subjected to counterinsurgent tactics of surveillance and imprisonment because of their political activities, including Melba Hernández, Marziyeh Ahmadi Osku'i, Shigenobu Fusako, and Palestinian women such as Aisha Odeh and Therese Halassa, who faced torture and physical and mental abuse. Inside these prisons, multiple forms of resistance, from hunger strikes, death fasts, political education through illicit books, and the transfer of secret messages, have been central to revolutionary political movements. Many of these women were also killed by the state because of their political activities, such as Sara and Marziyeh Ahmadi Osku'i. As Sara's life in the Kurdistan freedom movement shows us, universal emotions of belief, hope and the joy to participate in the struggle for humanity underpin the motivations of revolutionary women, even when facing the full force of the carceral state. And as the Women Democratic Front of Pakistan highlight, it is necessary to remember the sacrifices of assassinated peasant women like Mai Bakhtawar for popular socialist-feminist movement-building today.

For some, the question of women's liberation was a primary reference point in their political struggles, as self-proclaimed feminists. Others did not self-define as 'feminists', as they understood feminism to be a white, bourgeois concept from a Western tradition and language different from their own, and instead subscribed to a leftist politics which often saw women's liberation as secondary to first overcoming imperialism or capitalism. These women maintained that their adoption of socialist theory and practice contained within it a framework of liberation for women and for all. Rather than accepting the idea that Marxism and feminism contain inherent oppositional qualities (with categories of class and gender competing for primacy), making an historically 'unhappy marriage'[13] as some Western feminists claimed in the 1970s, many of these women grappled with questions of how such categories interacted in their everyday lives. The participation of women in these male-dominated struggles on equal footing was not without opposition: for Mabel Dove and Aoua Kéita in Ghana and Mali, pursuing women's interests ultimately found them at odds with and expelled from their national parties; for the Women Democratic Front in Pakistan, similar tensions remain until today.

Most of these women lived during the cold war. Here, we choose not to capitalise this term, to acknowledge that the cold war was not a singular event of US-USSR superpower conflict but was made up of and shaped by the multi-faceted experiences of a wide range of movements, actors and nations across the world. This era was shaped by infrastructures of internationalism tied to the Soviet

Union and Third Worldism, whereby nations in the Global South self-defined as a 'Third World' political bloc that was neither Western nor Eastern, but in reality leant towards the Soviet Union and ideas of communism. Soviet-supported organisations such as the International Union of Students (IUS), the World Federation of Trade Unions (WFTU), and especially the Women's International Democratic Federation (WIDF) feature in these chapters as avenues through which many of these women – particularly those representing liberation movements and revolutionary states – met face to face (often for the first time). The Havana-based Organisation of Solidarity with the Peoples of Africa, Asia and Latin America (OSPAAAL) published a magazine, designed iconic posters, hosted meetings and facilitated networks of Third World support for national liberation movements around the world. However, the influence of institutions such as the WIDF was in decline by the mid-1980s. OSPAAAL only closed its doors in 2019, a decision made as part of a reorientation of foreign policy under Cuban President Miguel Díaz-Canel, yet also the result of longer-term reduced capacity related to the redirection of limited resources in the political and economic reality for the country since the 1990s.[14]

The decline of socialist infrastructures connected to state-led projects, whether Maoist China or the Soviet Union, and the fragmentation of the Third World project was devastating for anticolonial and liberation movements that relied on their financial and diplomatic support. At the same time, these very movements were contradictory for women in the tension between women's liberation as a celebrated aspect of these struggles and the reality of their experiences and the priorities of political agendas. These contradictions took new shape as the twentieth century of radical struggle changed but, in multiple ways, women had been let down on questions of political and personal agency in state-led socialist and anticolonial nation-building projects. As many of these projects proved, when national liberation movements transformed into state-building projects, women's liberation and demands were sidelined, co-opted and actively suppressed, before, during and after – in some cases – national liberation was achieved. Some of the women in this collection continued their political activism in different arenas or in ways that spoke to the new unipolar international political order.

* * *

The following chapters introduce readers to important figures from anti-imperial, anticolonial and socialist movements from across the world – women who shaped the world, even if not always in the most visible or traceable way. Each chapter stands alone as a story of women's revolutionary action. Read together, these stories can be instructive in illuminating new paths for today's activism. As Angela Davis writes, historical movements are 'unfinished activisms',[15] and socialist politics and movements exist beyond the failures of state-led socialist experiments. This collection does not take the defeat of the twentieth century socialist project as its starting point, but instead asks what we can learn about the political strategies, networks and imaginations of revolutionary women from this era without reading their activities through the lens of failure.

Women's contributions to social and political movements are not subsidiary or merely complementary, but essential to an understanding of the radical history of the twentieth century. Crucially, the women in this book were not singularly interested in the issue of overcoming women's oppression. Women faced a double oppression in two positions – as women in relation to men; and as women in relation to the economic system – and in order to truly transform the material conditions of women's lives, fixing the former would not be enough. They were interested in dismantling the unequal structures that oppressed the people of the world: a solidarity that was not based on shared traits and the intersectionality of identities, but an intersectionality of struggles – rooted in an awareness of interlocking structures of oppression under capitalist imperialism.

Together, the chapters reveal a tradition of women engaged in anti-imperialist, internationalist socialist praxis that speaks to contemporary politics and movements today. We hope that as you read this book, these women become known to you – not as extraordinary characters of a distant world – but as people who might be connected to you by virtue of the struggles we share.

NOTES

1. Temma Kaplan, 'On the Socialist Origins of International Women's Day', *Feminist Studies* 11, no. 1 (1985): 163–71; The Editors, 'The Socialist Origins of International Women's Day', *JSTOR Daily*, 8 March 2019, https://daily.jstor.org/the-socialist-origins-of-international-womens-day/ (accessed 1 June 2022).

2. See Francisca de Haan, 'Continuing Cold War Paradigms in the Western Historiography of Transnational Women's Organisations: The Case of the Women's International Democratic Federation (WIDF)', *Women's History* Review 19, no. 4 (2010): 547–73; Yulia Gradskova, *The Women's International Democratic Federation, the Global South, and the Cold War: Defending the Rights of Women of the 'Whole World?'* (London: Routledge, 2021); Jocelyn Olcott, *International Women's Year: The Greatest Consciousness-Raising Event in History* (Oxford: Oxford University Press), 197.

3. Vladimir Ilyich Lenin, *Imperialism, the Highest Stage of Capitalism* (1917), Lenin Internet Archive, Marxists Internet Archive.

4. Shahrzad Mojab, 'Adult Education in/and Imperialism', in *Educating from Marx: Race, Gender, and Learning*, eds. Shahrzad Mojab and Sara Carpenter (New York: Palgrave Macmillan, 2011), 171.

5. Sara Carpenter and Shahrzad Mojab, *Revolutionary Learning: Marxism, Feminism and Knowledge* (London: Pluto Press, 2017), 112.

6. Luke Parks and Anna Davin, 'An Introduction & Index to the Material', *History Workshop*, 5 November 2012.

7. See Sheila Rowbotham, *Women, Resistance and Revolution: A History of Women and Revolution in the Modern World* (London: Verso, 2013 [1974]); Miranda Davies, *Third World, Second Sex (Volume 1): Women's Struggles and National Liberation* (London: Zed Books, 1984); Kumari Jayawardena, *Feminism and Nationalism in the Third World* (London: Verso, 1986); Miranda Davies, *Third World, Second Sex (Volume 2)* (London: Zed Books, 1987); Margaret Ward, *Unmanageable Revolutionaries: Women and Irish Nationalism* (London: Pluto Press, 1995); Judy Cox, *The Women's Revolution: Russia 1905–1917* (London: Haymarket Books, 2019); Andrea D'Atri, *Bread and Roses: Gender and Class under Capitalism* (London: Pluto Press, 2020); Dilar Dirik, The Kurdish Women's Movement: History, Theory, Practice (London: Pluto Press, 2022).

8. See Carole Boyce Davies, *Left of Karl Marx: The Political Life of Black Communist Claudia Jones* (Durham, NC: Duke University Press, 2008); Barbara Ransby, *Ella Baker and the Black Freedom Movement* (Chapel Hill, NC: University of North Carolina Press, 2003); Tanya

Harmer, *Beatriz Allende: A Revolutionary Life in Cold War Latin America* (Chapel Hill, NC: University of North Carolina Press, 2020); Sarah Irving, *Leila Khaled: Icon of Palestinian Liberation* (London: Pluto Press, 2012).

9. Kristen Ghodsee, *Red Valkyries: Feminist Lessons from Five Revolutionary Women* (London: Pluto Press, 2022).

10. Francisca de Haan, ed., *The Palgrave Handbook of Communist Women Activists around the World* (London: Palgrave Macmillan, 2023); Victor Strazzeri, 'Beyond the Double Blind Spot: Relocating Communist Women as Transgressive Subjects in Contemporary Historiography', *Gender & History* (2022), advance online publication, https://doi.org/10.1111/1468-0424.12675.

11. Naghmeh Sohrabi, 'Writing Revolution as if Women Mattered', *Comparative Studies of South Asia, Africa and the Middle East* 42, no. 2 (2022): 546–50. More broadly, on the sexual division of labour, see Maria Mies, *Patriarchy and Accumulation on a World Scale: Women in the International Division of Labour* (London: Zed Books, 1986).

12. There are many memoirs and autobiographies written by revolutionary women available in English, for example: Leila Khaled, *My People Shall Live: The Autobiography of a Revolutionary* (London: Hodder & Stoughton, 1973); Ashraf Dehghani, *Torture and Resistance in Iran* (1973), Ashraf Dehghani Website; Angela Davis, *Angela Davis: An Autobiography* (New York: Random House, 1974); Assata Shakur, *Assata: An Autobiography* (Chicago: Lawrence Hill Books, 1999); Gioconda Belli, *The Country under My Skin: A Memoir of Love and War*, trans. Kristina Cordero (New York: Knopf, 2002); Sakine Cansız, *Sara: My Whole Life Was a Struggle, Vol. 1* (London: Pluto Press, 2018); Sakine Cansız, *Sara: Prison Memoir of a Kurdish Revolutionary, Vol. 2* (London: Pluto Press, 2019); Elaine Mokhtefi, *Algiers, Third World Capital: Freedom Fighters, Revolutionaries, Black Panthers* (London: Verso, 2020); Houzan Mahmoud, ed., *Kurdish Women's Stories* (London: Pluto Press, 2021); Jehan Helou, *Making Palestine's History: Women's Testimonies* (Nottingham: Spokesman Books, 2022).

13. Heidi I. Hartmann, 'The Unhappy Marriage of Marxism and Feminism: Towards a More Progressive Union', *Capital & Class* 2, no. 1 (1978): 1–33.

14. Fernando Camacho Padilla and Eugenia Palieraki, 'Hasta Siempre, OSPAAAL!' *NACLA Report on the Americas* 51, no. 4 (2019): 410–421.

15. Angela Davis, '17th Annual Steve Biko Memorial Lecture', 9 September 2016, University of South Africa (UNISA), Pretoria, YouTube, www.youtube.com/watch?v=Fb_TpOTjmM8 (accessed 2 December 2021).

1

Melba Hernández: From Cuba to Vietnam, under One Roof

Sorcha Thomson

On 20 December 1963, the Cuban campaign of solidarity with Vietnam was officially constituted in the theatre of the Workers Central Union of Cuba (Central de Trabajadores de Cuba, CTC) in Havana. The event was presided over by Ernesto 'Che' Guevara, who shared with the audience the instruction of Commander in Chief Fidel Castro that Melba Hernández, heroine of the 1959 Cuban Revolution, was to be responsible for organising and developing the Solidarity Committee with South Vietnam. The committee brought together comrades from political, student, worker's and state organisations, as well as intellectual and cultural figures within Cuba. Their objective was to delve into all aspects of the United States' imperialist aggression against Southeast Asia, and organise Cuban and international support to the Vietnamese people.[1] The campaign led by Melba, when Vietnam was the cause par excellence for a generation of revolutionaries in the 1960s and 1970s, can be added to the record of Cuba's illustrious history of international solidarity, which includes the sending of military and medical aid to the National Liberation Front (NLF) of Algeria in their struggle against French colonial rule, and the tens of thousands of Cuban soldiers who fought with the Popular Movement for the Liberation of Angola (MPLA) to end apartheid in South Africa.[2] Yet, despite her position at the forefront of this globally significant campaign, Melba is known less widely than the revolutionary men she worked alongside. Her extraordinary life (1921–2014), spanning and taking part in the various stages of the Cuban Revolution, through its era of underground preparation, armed struggle, and in the institutions of the post-1959 revolutionary state, shines a light on the many contributions of women to the Cuban Revolution and its international solidarity with the world.

RAISING A REVOLUTION(ARY)

Manuel Hernández Vidaurreta and Elena Rodríguez del Rey Rodríguez were married on 18 October 1920 in Cruces (in the Cuban province now known as Cienfuegos). Nine months later, Melba, their first and only child, was born. Manuel was a union representative and a 'man of studies', graduating with a degree in agricultural technology from the University of Santa Clara and becoming a co-founder of the Cuban Society of Botanicals at the University of Havana.[3] Elena, whose graduate studies were stopped short by the need to care for an ill Melba in the early years, remained known amongst their peers as a compañera (comrade) of progressive ideas. Their new family home was open to visitors, mostly young and politically engaged people, who would gather to listen to the views of Manuel and debate the diverse problems that afflicted the country. Elena always participated, and Melba – too young to understand – would sit on her father's lap while the issues of corruption and exploitation by the Gerardo Machado government (1925–33) were dissected. Melba attributed her early political education to her parents, who inculcated in her, she said, the values of justice and a knowledge of the people who had struggled for the liberation of Cuba from the Spanish in the late nineteenth century wars of independence.[4]

When Melba was in high school, her father was arrested for his union activities, the family house came under surveillance, and the threat of political persecution from the forces of military officer Fulgencio Batista loomed. Batista participated in a coup that overthrew the Machado government in 1933, and since then had led the repression against socialist and communist groups in Cuba with a heavy hand. The family decided to leave the province and emigrate to Havana in 1935. Manuel, after some time, found a job in the Ministry of Agriculture, and Elena worked to maintain the family home as they were forced to move multiple times before finding a secure base. With the encouragement of her parents, Melba continued her studies until she graduated with a law degree from the University of Havana in 1943. When she began to practise her profession in a consultancy, she didn't seek cases that would bring the most financial reward but instead directed her efforts towards the clients that most needed her support: the exploited peasants and workers.[5]

Melba gained her first experience of party politics as a member of the Party of the Cuban People (Orthodox), founded by Eduardo Chibás in 1947. The party aimed to create a youth vanguard in the fight against corruption and campaigned for economic and social reforms. Alongside Melba, the party counted Fidel Castro amongst its active young members. The party were favourites to win the 1952 general election, but Batista, who had held the presidency between 1940 and 1944, staged a coup on 10 March 1952 and established a military dictatorship. With financial, military and logistical support from the United States, exploitation, corruption and repression of political opposition increased, including the revocation of political rights such as the right to strike, and the torture and assassination of left-wing activists. In response, demonstrations spread across the streets, parks and university campuses of the country, while anti-government and socialist activities were forced further underground.

When the coup happened, Manuel, Elena and Melba, aged 31, were living in an apartment in central Havana at the address Jovellar 107. Melba's friend came to visit her with news of a brother and sister, Abel and Haydée Santamaría, who lived nearby and were organising politically. That night, Melba and her friend visited this apartment. Here, Melba was impressed by the brother and sister before her, 'two young people intoxicated with dreams, romantic idealists like me', speaking of patriotic duty and the need for change. In that meeting, Melba expressed her decision to do everything possible for the revolutionary cause, and joined the group, called 25 y O after the intersection of streets at the apartment where they met.[6] Amongst their first acts was a commemoration for an assassinated worker, on 1 May, where Abel Santamaría and Fidel Castro met for the first time. At once, the group of 25 y O was incorporated into the underground apparatus of a still nameless revolutionary movement being led by Fidel. The first task appointed to Melba was the distribution of the newspaper that was being clandestinely published by the 25 y O, to make sure it reached students at the University of Havana. The group began to multiply its contacts and there was enthusiasm – especially from Fidel – for building a more militant front.

Melba's parents never objected to the activities of their daughter, but rather provided a space for the development of the group's political plans. After the Santamaría household was reported to the authorities, the group moved their activities to Melba's family home at Jovellar 107. The house became a hub of activity where her father, Manuel, transmitted his vast historical knowledge and experience of clandestine struggle from an earlier generation to the small cohort of soon-to-be world renowned revolutionaries.[7] Elena, meanwhile, ensured the home was a welcoming space for those who would pass through, her contributions to the movement fondly remembered later in life by those she hosted. From Jovellar 107, the group debated the strategic direction of the movement, established contacts with militant groups from the different provinces, prepared logistics, organised the appropriation of arms, and collected the uniforms – Melba hand sewing on the military insignia – that they would wear to launch an attack against the Batista regime.[8] The house was used as a preparation base, until the day came for Melba and her comrades to leave Havana and embark on a journey that would cement their names in history.

GUERRILLERAS

On 26 July 1953, a small group of around 140 revolutionaries launched an attack on the Moncada military barracks in Santiago de Cuba. Melba and her close friend Haydée were the only two women to participate in the attack. The fighters were driven back by the Batista troops, scores were killed and the rest imprisoned or exiled.[9] Fidel was sentenced to 15 years in prison. The operation itself was a military disaster yet the 26 July Moncada attack is arguably the most commemorated event in Cuban revolutionary history, widely recognised as marking the beginning of the armed struggle that would result in the victory of the Cuban revolutionary movement over the Batista regime on 1 January 1959.

Once captured, Melba and Haydée were separated from their male comrades and taken to Guanjay women's prison. Inside the prison, the women were prevented from interacting with other prisoners, receiving visitors or seeing sunlight.[10] They were shown evidence of the torture taking place against their captured male comrades but refused to give up names and information that could incriminate others. In an act of subversion, an iconic picture of the women was taken by Marta Rojas, a Cuban journalist who visited the prison under the pretext of writing an article about children born behind bars. Meanwhile, Melba's colleagues from her days at the law consultancy began a campaign for her release. The women defied the tyranny of their isolated imprisonment by organising resistance activities within the prison – including protesting the assassination of a student and winning the sympathy of the ordinary guards who admired their principles.[11] After seven months, they were released on 20 February 1954. Asked by a reporter waiting outside – 'now what?' the women replied, 'We start again ... we owe it to our dead brothers and sisters'.[12]

Rather than being warned off further revolutionary activity, Melba and Haydée continued to organise on behalf of their imprisoned comrades. The house at Jovellar 107 had become a place of frequent visitors of families of the disappeared or arrested, and people interested in political issues. After her release, Melba rose to serve on the National Directorate of the underground July 26th Movement (M-26-7), the revolutionary movement named after the date of the Moncada attack. She maintained communication with Fidel, who remained in prison, through smuggled letters. Fidel instructed Melba to maintain the propaganda efforts of the group by collecting, editing and distributing the notes from his courtroom speech. Melba and Haydée collected money to print over 10,000 copies of the text and distributed it around the island in a rented car.

The text evoked the name of nineteenth century Cuban national leader José Martí in connection to the ongoing Cuban struggle against exploitation by US capitalism and regime corruption. The published manifesto, which became known by the title *History Will Absolve Me*, gave details of the 'five revolutionary laws' Fidel wished to see implemented on the island, including the reformation of land rights, the distribution of company profits among workers, and the introduction of universal healthcare. It is considered one of the most important documents of the Cuban Revolution, containing the revolution's early programme and acting as an organising tool for a movement while many of its leaders remained imprisoned.[13]

The group of people now operating from Jovellar 107 worked tirelessly to communicate with the press and pressure the government in a campaign for the freedom of the Moncada prisoners. Finally, on 2 May 1955 an amnesty law was passed, and the captured male comrades were released. Melba and the others of the July 26th Movement fled to Mexico. Here, they prepared, with the assistance of Latin American comrades – including an Argentinian called Ernesto 'Che' Guevara – the next landmark operation of the Cuban Revolution, the Granma yacht attack. Their surprise arrival by yacht was set to coincide with mass actions by workers and others in the southern city of Santiago de Cuba.[14]

Melba's desire to form part of the expedition team did not materialise – the limited capacity of the yacht was one given reason, the other that the expedition itself was not the only vital task, and her role was to be in the organisational, logistical and propaganda work that surrounded it. On 2 December 1956 the Granma yacht transported 82 male fighters – including Fidel, his brother, Raúl, Guevara and Camilo Cienfuegos – to the western shores of Cuba. Melba began work on her precise instructions: to eliminate all traces of the clandestine life they had been leading to minimise the risk to those involved, and to pay any outstanding debts to those who had helped in the preparation stage. She had to work with immense caution, as the Mexican police, Batista's esbirros (henchmen), and the FBI were closing in on the movement, and Melba in particular was well known because of her involvement in the Moncada attack.[15]

The Granma yacht fighters were met by helicopter and airplane bombardment from Batista troops. Only around a dozen men survived the counterattack. Those survivors fled on foot to the mountains of the Sierra Maestra from where they regrouped and continued the insurgent revolutionary struggle. Over the next two years, the revolutionaries were in constant contact with the cities and built links with workers and farmers. Together, a programme was developed to address the chronic issues caused by the subjugation of the economy to imperatives dictated by corporations based in the US.[16] Melba had returned to Cuba from Mexico in early 1957. In Havana, her family home continued to offer a space where revolutionaries could meet, and where Melba organised funds and coordinated information in support of the revolution. Because of this activity, the house came under increasing surveillance, with tapped phone lines and regular night raids from Batista's esbirros. During one search, in Melba's absence, they dared to tell her mother Elena to collaborate with the government and stop helping the revolutionaries. The response of Elena, who had been fighting for decades with her husband and later her daughter, was a quick and sharp no. However, operating from the house became impossible and, after the entire family were arrested and released within 24 hours, Elena, Manuel and Melba moved to a new, safer location.[17]

Melba displayed her untiring commitment to supporting the revolution from the city. The leadership assigned her tasks such as organising strikes in coordination with military plans, until, with an awareness that Melba's life was increasingly in danger the longer she stayed in Havana, she was invited to join the M-26-7 Rebel Army in summer 1958.[18] Women were active in the Cuban armed struggle, making up a significant number of the Rebel Army forces and holding leadership positions. At the same time, their roles – as described in a Cuban strategy document shared with the Palestinian Revolution – were often gendered support positions such as teaching children and soldiers, cooking, nursing and sewing military uniforms. Women were viewed as useful in developing 'revolutionary willpower' and in carrying secret messages, believed to be treated less harshly than men if captured by the enemy.[19]

In September 1958, an exclusively female military squadron was formed of 12 women. The women's squadron was the outcome of a request from female fighters to have their own unit. Following a debate amongst the leaders of the Rebel Army the request was authorised. While there remained voices of opposition, Fidel maintained that these women were to be armed equally. Following the announcement of revolutionary victory over Batista's troops from Santa Clara on 1 January 1959, the Women's Platoon joined the M-26-7 Freedom Caravan on 2 January 1959 that entered Havana on 8 January.[20] Several of these female fighters went on to have prominent roles in the post-1959 revolutionary state. As well as these leading militant women, the story of women in the Cuban Revolution directs us to the times and spaces in between the large-scale military operations, the moments of abeyance. The early inclusion of women in the preparation and organisation of the movement – partially due to the imprisonment of so many of the men – was essential to its survival and success.[21] The lives of these women, including Melba, tell a history of revolutionary struggle not of intermittent periods of armed conflict, but of continuous and collective work in many forms.

TWO, THREE, MANY VIETNAMS

The victory of the Cuban Revolution on 1 January 1959 brought dramatic improvement to the lives of women and girls in Cuba. During the Batista dictatorship, women were under-employed, underpaid, mostly illiterate, and – although granted the right to vote in 1934 – hugely underrepresented in political life. In 1960, the Federation of Cuban Women (Federación de Mujeres Cubanas, FMC) was founded to defend equal rights, end discrimination and support women in the building of a new society. Castro emphasised the importance of this: 'Cuban women, doubly humiliated and repressed by a semi-colonial society, required their own organisation, one that would represent their specific interests and work to achieve their greater participation in the economic, political and social life of the Revolution'.[22]

Although Fidel's triumphant claim that women's emancipation was handed to them as a 'revolution within the revolution', women's activism and leadership, as historian Michelle Chase has argued, was critical at every stage of transforming society.[23] One example of this is the work of the FMC in the fight against the exploitation of sex workers, including the around 100,000 female sex workers of Batista-era Cuba. The aim was to involve these women in building the new society. Their social rehabilitation was facilitated by the creation of new opportunities for women, with the introduction of free 'Children's Circles' (day care centres or nurseries) to allow mothers access to training, work and participation in the country's economic life. Internationally, the FMC also played a pioneering role in promoting women's reproductive rights – in 1965 Cuba became the first Latin American country to legalise abortion.[24] Reproductive justice and 'women's issues' were, due in part to the activism of the FMC, seen as an integral part of a wider politics of transformation. But women's activism in the new Cuba went beyond the work of the FMC on specific women's issues. Cuban women, like Melba, were politicised by the revolution, not just as wives, sisters or mothers, but also as fighters, organisers and leaders with agency which was not defined by their relationship to men.

Melba held several high-profile positions that shaped the post-revolution Cuban state, as a member of the Cuban Communist Party (Partido Comunista de Cuba PCC) especially in the country's extension of its support to national liberation movements and revolutionary groups elsewhere in the world. The most significant of these was her role as president of the Committee of Solidarity with South Vietnam that was formed on 25 September 1963. The National Liberation Front (NLF) of South Vietnam had been formed two years earlier, in December 1961, and was leading the fight against US imperialism in Southeast Asia. The committee headed by Melba was the first in the world dedicated to mobilising solidarity and support on behalf of the Vietnamese people. Her nomination to its presidency by the Cuban Institute of Friendship with the Peoples (Instituto Cubano de Amistad con los Pueblos, ICAP, formed 1961) and Castro was a sign of the prominence of this cause for the Cuban leadership – appointing one of its most accomplished revolutionaries – and of Melba's determination to continue the fight against imperialism for those still struggling against it.

The state provided her with a house from which to operate in Havana, where prominent journalists, scientists, jurors, historians, militants, and leaders of youth and mass organisations met. Melba had experience of hosting a revolutionary house from her parents, and the years at Jovellar 107. Here, discussions took place about the aggressions being committed against the north and south of Vietnam, of the bombings that were devastating the country, and of the historic resistance of the Vietnamese people against French, Japanese and North American occupations.[25] In the early years of the Committee, Melba spoke alongside Guevara in public forums about the need for Cuba to commit to the defence of the Vietnamese people.

Such discussions with the Cuban people were rehearsals for Che's 1966 'Message to the Tricontinental' – delivered to an international conference of anti-imperial leaders from Africa, Asia and Latin America held in Havana in 1966. The conference declared itself as the coming together of two historic currents of world revolution – that which started with the 1917 October Revolution in Russia and the parallel current of the revolution for national liberation.[26] More than 500 representatives from 82 countries came together to discuss anti-imperialist strategy, resulting in the foundation of the Organisation of Solidarity with the Peoples of Asia, Africa and Latin America (OSPAAAL). The meeting was also attended by observers from a range of socialist countries, progressive European and North American groups, and international organisations such as the Women's International Democratic Federation (WIDF), the International Union of Students (IUS) and the World Federation of Trade Unions (WFTU). The gathering connected anticolonial struggles across the Tricontinental world with socialist countries and progressive movements in the West in a coordinated project.[27] The US State Department called the meeting the 'biggest threat that international communism had ever posed to the free people of the world'.[28] The issue of Vietnam, and how to support the Vietnamese people through coordinated action, was central. As Guevara wrote in his message to the conference, in words that reverberated across continents, 'How close we could look into a bright future should *two, three or many Vietnams* flourish throughout the world'.[29]

With a very limited budget, Melba worked towards this vision. She mobilised solidarity for Vietnam on political, journalistic and cultural fronts, in the form of donations, conferences and delegations. Under her leadership, women were put at the forefront of delegations to Vietnam. One of the first cultural acts of the committee was the organisation of a delegation of Cuban ballerinas to Hanoi headed by the Director of the Cuban National Ballet, Alicia Alonso, where they were met by Hồ Chí Minh.[30] The first Cuban press delegation to South Vietnam was led by Marta Rojas, the journalist who had taken Melba's picture in prison and was later appointed vice president of the Vietnam Solidarity Committee. Rojas returned to Vietnam yearly to report on the anti-imperial struggle. Her work in collaboration with Cuban cinema legend Santiago Alvarez produced a number of noticieros (newsreels) that presented the Vietnamese woman as an icon of revolutionary solidarity and an example of the militant role that women could play.[31] These short newsreels were shown at cinemas throughout the country before film screenings, and were distributed regionally and internationally in mobile cinemas, film festivals, youth meetings and communist congresses.

Melba's position as head of the committee allowed her to travel to several international conferences and forums. In 1967, accompanied by Rojas, she went on a tour of Europe, meeting with Black Panther Party leader Stokely Carmichael at a Vietnam rally in Paris, and taking part in the Russell Tribunal in Sweden and Denmark, sponsored by British philosopher Bertrand Russell. The tribunal brought together a range of activists from anticolonial movements and the New Left, who collectively condemned the crimes of US imperialism in Vietnam. Based on her travels, Melba wrote, in Spanish, several reports and books about the struggle of the Vietnamese people, such as *En Vietnam* (1969), *Embajada en la selva* (1969) and *La Educacion de Vietnam: Documentos del II simposio contra el genocidio yanqui* (1969). Melba's campaigning in the international arena is attributed by her Vietnamese comrades as having allowed the rest of the world to see that the issue of Vietnam was not 'local' as Washington proclaimed, but central to the global struggle for peace and socialism.[32] In the early 1970s, Melba made many trips to Southeast Asia to organise support for the communist forces. These forces claimed victory in 1975, with the liberation of the South Vietnamese capital Saigon from US forces on 20 April. Melba was appointed as the first Cuban Ambassador to the liberated Vietnam in February 1977, from where she coordinated hundreds of Cuban engineers, architects and builders in the rebuilding of the nation destroyed by the war. The solidarity committee became the Cuba-Vietnam Friendship Association which is active to this day.

A TRICONTINENTAL LEGACY

Melba's dedication and experience in solidarity with Vietnam made her the obvious candidate for general secretary of OSPAAAL in 1980. Since its foundation in 1966, the organisation had been headed by Osmany Cienfuegos, another participant in the armed struggle of the Cuban Revolution. A second Tricontinental conference was set to take place, in Cairo, within five years of the 1966 conference, where a new general secretary and headquarters for the organisation were to be chosen by the delegates. But events in the Middle East, including the June 1967 Arab-Israeli War (Naksa) meant this second conference never took place.[33] At the Second Congress of the Cuban Communist Party in December 1980, it was decided – with much enthusiasm – that Melba should become the organisation's new general secretary.[34]

Under her leadership, OSPAAAL continued to work across multiple platforms – its magazines, posters, statements and events – to promote anti-imperial, anti-capitalist and anti-racist solidarity with the exploited and oppressed of the world. As the majority of the national liberation movements championed by OSPAAAL throughout the 1960s and 1970s won independence, Melba ensured that the organisation continued its commitment to support ongoing movements against colonialism and racism, including the Palestinian liberation movement. As the Palestine Liberation Organisation

(PLO) was attacked by the Israeli army during the 1982 invasion of Lebanon, Melba visited Beirut and spoke on behalf of the Tricontinental movement, offering their moral and material support to the Palestinian people in their struggle to return to their homeland. Her other focus was neo-colonialism in Africa, with an emphasis on ending the apartheid regime in South Africa.[35] Apartheid in South Africa was ended in 1994; the liberation of Palestine remains amongst the causes championed by OSPAAAL that did not come to fruition before the organisation officially closed its doors in 2019. After her three-year leadership of OSPAAAL came to an end, Melba continued international work, in the World Council of Peace and as head of the Ministry of Foreign Relations South Asia Studies department. When she became too elderly to continue her work with the ministry, she continued to meet visiting journalists, students and delegations in her home, particularly from Vietnam, where she would warmly welcome a new generation with stories of their shared revolutionary traditions. During her lifetime, she received numerous awards, and was uniquely decorated with the Heroine of the Republic of Cuba, Heroine of Labour of the Republic of Cuba, and the Hồ Chí Minh Order. Melba died on 9 March 2014, aged 92, in Havana. Her life was honoured around the world, including in Vietnam, Lebanon and Palestine, for her exemplary commitment to the Tricontinental project. She is remembered for this, by Raúl Castro, as an untiring 'luchadora' (struggler) for the people of her homeland and the world.[36]

One of the features of the Tricontinental movement that OSPAAAL and Melba championed, as told in the life-stories of activists from the 1970s, was the way it helped people to understand 'oppression at home' as connected to 'imperialism everywhere'. Its legacies can be seen in the tactics and visual repertoires of transnational solidarity movements today.[37] Melba's contributions to this hugely influential historical movement show how a grand vision of global solidarity was sustained by the everyday work of people like her. The enduring visibility of OSPAAAL's magazines and posters and the legacy that the organisation has left behind is only possible because of the work done, in offices in Havana, Beirut, Hanoi and elsewhere, by not only the movement leaders but the writers, translators, designers and myriad other roles of support, many of which were the domain of women.

Melba's own role within OSPAAAL was the outcome of a revolutionary life shaped by her practical experience of the Cuban Revolution. By revisiting her revolutionary life, we can see the not-so-small things that often evade valorised accounts of revolutions – the households that raised and sheltered activists, the preparation and logistical work of operations, and the friendships that survived repression and sustained hope – where women played a central role. Her life and legacy of bringing people together under one roof – whether in her family house in Jovellar 107, sheltering activists and organising operations, or in solidarity committees and organisations, extending an understanding of collective liberation beyond national borders – is part of the vast history of everyday, continuous work of revolution in which women have played a yet to be fully recognised role.

NOTES

1. Margarita Ilisástigui Avilés and Gladys Rosa Álvarez Porro, *Melba: Mujer de Todos Los Tiempos* (La Habana: Ediciones Verde Olivo, 2005), 184.
2. Piero Gleijeses, 'Cuba's First Venture in Africa: Algeria, 1961–1965', *Journal of Latin American Studies* 28, no. 1 (February, 1996): 159–95; Piero Gleijeses, *Visions of Freedom Havana, Washington, Pretoria, and the Struggle for Southern Africa, 1976–1991* (Chapel Hill, NC: University of North Carolina Press, 2013).
3. Ilisástigui Avilés and Álvarez Porro, *Melba*, 11.
4. Ibid., 18.
5. Ibid., 21–3.
6. Ibid., 36–7.
7. Ibid., 40.
8. For a history of the house at Jovellar 107, see Alcídes Iznaga, *La Casa de Melba* (La Habana: Editorial de Ciencias Sociales, 1978).
9. Lorraine Bayard de Volo, *Women and the Cuban Insurrection: How Gender Shaped Castro's Victory* (Cambridge: Cambridge University Press, 2018), 65.

10. Ilisástigui Avilés and Álvarez Porro, *Melba*, 83.
11. Ibid., 87.
12. Pedro Antonio García, 'The Fearless Haydée and Melba', *Granma*, 28 July 2016.
13. Ilisástigui Avilés and Álvarez Porro, *Melba*, 101.
14. Bernard Regan, 'Defending the Revolution: History, Activism and the Cuba Solidarity Campaign', *History Workshop*, 13 August 2018.
15. Ilisástigui Avilés and Álvarez Porro, *Melba*, 131–41.
16. Regan, 'Defending the Revolution'.
17. Ilisástigui Avilés and Álvarez Porro, *Melba*, 144–5.
18. Ibid., 156–7.
19. Fateh, *The Chinese, Vietnamese, and Cuban Experiences* (Arabic) (Kuwait, n.d.).
20. Luis Hernández Serrano, 'Revelaciones sobre Las Marianas', *Juventud Rebelde*, 3 September 2018.
21. Bayard de Volo, *Women and the Cuban Insurrection*, 65.
22. Salim Lamrani, 'Women in Cuba: The Emancipatory Revolution', *International Journal of Cuban Studies* 8, no. 1 (2016): 110–11.
23. Michelle Chase, *Revolution within the Revolution: Women and Gender Politics in Cuba, 1952–1962* (Chapel Hill, NC: University of North Carolina Press, 2015).
24. Lamrani, 'Women in Cuba', 111.
25. 'Honor y gloria a la heroína Melba Hernández en su Centenario', *Ministerio de Cultura Republica de Cuba*, 28 July 2021.
26. *First Solidarity Conference of the Peoples of Africa, Asia and Latin America Proceedings* (Havana, 1967).
27. Ibid., 187.
28. Subcommittee to Investigate the Administration of the Internal Security Act and other Internal Security Laws of the Committee on the Judiciary United States Senate, *The Tricontinental Conference of African, Asian, and Latin American Peoples, A Staff Study* (Washington, DC, 1966).
29. Che Guevara, 'Message to the Tricontinental' (Havana: OSPAAAL, 16 April 1967), Che Guevara Internet Archive.
30. Liurka Rodríguez Barrios, 'Nosotras, las cubanas, en frentes de solidaridad con Vietnam', *Cubadebate*, 15 September 2018.
31. Santiago Álvarez Index, National Library José Martí, Havana.
32. Mariela Pérez Valenzuela, 'A 45 años de la histórica visita de Fidel a Vietnam', *Vietnam+*, 13 September 2018; René Montes de Oca Ruiz, 'Imposible olvidar la historia de Melba', *Cubadebate*, 28 July 2021.
33. Fernando Camacho Padilla and Eugenia Palieraki, 'Hasta Siempre, OSPAAAL!' *NACLA Report on the Americas* 51, no. 4 (2019): 410–421.

34. Author interview with Santiago Rony Feliu (the last director of OSPAAAL before it closed in 2019), Havana.

35. Ilisástigui Avilés and Álvarez Porro, *Melba*, 211.

36. Raúl Castro, 'Preface', in ibid., 7.

37. Anne Garland Mahler, *From the Tricontinental to the Global South: Race, Radicalism, and Transnational Solidarity* (Durham, NC: Duke University Press, 2018).

2

Mabel Dove and Aoua Kéita: Feminist and Internationalist Struggles from Ghana to Mali

Yatta Kiazolu and Madina Thiam

Gold Coast women have played a glorious part in this political struggle and it is time the men showed some appreciation ...[1]

—Mabel Dove, 1952

Political independence was the great crowning of our efforts and of our martyrs' sacrifices. But the struggle was far from over. It continues, and will continue for a long time to come, for liberty, democracy and universal peace.[2]

—Aoua Kéita, 1975

On 6 March 1957 the Gold Coast (colonial Ghana) became the first African state to seize independence from European colonial rule. Anti-imperial activists, leaders and intellectuals from all over the world, including Coretta Scott King and Martin Luther King Jr from the United States, Julius Nyerere from Tanzania, and George Padmore from Trinidad, were present to witness the historic event: a culmination of internationalist decolonial struggle that had risen over the previous decades.[3] Three years after Ghana, the colonial French Soudan won its independence in 1960 as the Republic of Mali, alongside 17 other African states.[4] While connected in many ways, the decolonisation of English-speaking Ghana and French-speaking Mali are rarely viewed together, because of the disconnect in historical scholarship along linguistic lines reflecting the division and partition of the African continent by competing European empires.

Yet, Ghana and Mali bear a number of parallels. They are both entry points into Africa's liberation movements against British and French imperialism. Kwame Nkrumah, Ghana's first prime minister (1957–60) and president (1960–66), was a pan-Africanist who believed that the establishment of strong socialist African states could usher in the transformation of a global political order otherwise dependent on the subjugation of people of African descent. Towards these ends, Nkrumah positioned Ghana as a significant player in African decolonisation, supporting liberation movements across the continent as well as enlisting the cooperation of Black diasporas in his nation-building agenda. Likewise, Mali's first government under Modibo Keïta (1960–68) opted for decidedly socialist and anti-imperial policies, and played a central role on the international stage. Mali threw its support behind the Algerian National Liberation Front (FLN), prompting a visit from Algiers-based Caribbean psychiatrist and revolutionary Frantz Fanon. Within just two years of achieving independence, Mali ordered all French troops to be removed from its national territory and created its own independent currency. In 1966, Mali joined the Non-Aligned Movement (NAM), and was elected a member of the United Nations Security Council. From the outset, both countries centred internationalism and transnational solidarity as key aspects of their postcolonial political trajectories: they provided refuge and support to liberation movements from other nations, including Algeria and South Africa, and were even briefly united under the short-lived Union of African States (also known as the Ghana-Guinea-Mali union), with the goal of further reducing economic and political dependence upon their former colonial powers, Britain and France.

Though fewer African women participated in internationalist struggles in comparison to their male counterparts – those traditionally dubbed the 'fathers of independence' – the profiles of those women who did are lesser known.[5] As a consequence of the processes of postcolonial state construction, women's movements in Ghana and Mali were co-opted by the male elites of their countries. Yet, African women identified and challenged the gendered colonial oppression they encountered in their daily lives, particularly as it eroded their livelihood and economic power. For these women, the fight for independence did not represent an end in itself, but an opportunity to overturn colonialism's gendered forms of subjugation.

The lives of Ghanaian journalist Mabel Dove Danquah (1905–1984), and Malian nurse Aoua Kéita (1912–1980) are examples of how both Ghana and Mali's anti-imperial internationalism in the 1960s stemmed in part from Gold Coast and Soudanese women in the 1950s. Since any possibility of women's liberation was bound to the realisation of self-governance, Mabel Dove and Aoua Kéita developed their own ideas about what a postcolonial future would look like, and ardently worked to incorporate these ideas into the nation-building process.

Both women produced writings, notably Dove's journalism and creative works and Kéita's autobiography. Dove and Kéita were also pioneers, as the first elected women legislators on the continent and in French West Africa, respectively. Their status and their writings have contributed to their visibility, though still limited, within memories of national independence. Together, Dove and Kéita's political lives offer a window into African women's varied decolonial visions, their role in the achievement of national independence, and the persistence of patriarchal dominance after decolonisation.

MABEL DOVE: GHANAIAN INDEPENDENCE AND WOMEN'S (INTER)NATIONAL LEADERSHIP

'The discrimination against the dark peoples of the world especially the Negro has continued far too long and it must be uprooted and entirely destroyed in this enlightened age' wrote the Gold Coast's Mabel Dove Danquah in the *Accra Evening News*.[6] The anticolonial feminist critic was enraged by the Sharpeville Massacre in South Africa, where police opened fire on protesters challenging apartheid laws in 1960. For Dove, the experiences of Black South Africans were linked to the structures of white domination that plagued the entire continent. Even more, these structures were responsible for the racial oppression experienced by 'dark peoples of the world' everywhere, and needed to be eradicated. In this way, Dove echoed the sentiments of anticolonialists across the African continent and around the world who actively struggled to bring an end to colonial rule in favour of determining their own futures. As a pan-Africanist, she linked the political destinies of not just continental Africans, but also diaspora communities abroad.

At the cusp of Gold Coast independence, just four years prior, Dove sought to forge these linkages at a critical moment of political opportunity. The Convention People's Party (CPP), a socialist political party under the leadership of Kwame Nkrumah, successfully mobilised mass support in a series of direct-action campaigns and subsequent elections which ultimately delivered independence in 1957. In one of these elections leading to independence, under the CPP ticket and representing the Ga district, Mabel Dove became the first democratically elected woman legislator in the Gold Coast, and the first democratically elected woman legislator on the African continent.[7]

In the summer of 1956, Dove, of her own volition, set out on a three-month tour of the US with special interest in both the experiences of Black Americans and women's civic and political organisations. However, the timing of the trip was risky. CPP pressure on the colonial administration accelerated the West African colony on its desired path of self-governance and another impending election on the horizon would formally deliver Gold Coast independence. For these reasons, Nkrumah discouraged Dove's tour, and yet, against his advice, she ventured on. Considering the long struggle and high stakes of independence, why did Dove view this trip as politically necessary and what were its potential gains?

Mabel Dove's vision for post-independent Ghana and its role in the struggle for global Black freedom came from her pan-African and feminist grounding shaped by her personal and professional background. Dove belonged to an elite family with roots in both Ghana and Sierra Leone. Educated in Sierra Leone and later London, Dove eventually returned to Accra where she began a career as a creative writer and journalist and wrote under pseudonyms with a focus on women's issues. As the struggle for self-governance advanced, Dove expanded her advocacy for women's rights by embracing direct action as well as writing. After Nkrumah's break from the conservative United Gold Coast Convention (UGCC) in 1949, he established the CPP, which partially found its strength in its willingness to mobilise Ghanaian women in visible positions as propaganda secretaries and grassroots organisers.[8] Dove officially joined the CPP in 1950 aligning with Nkrumah's vision of liberation for Africans everywhere.

The following year, just as Gold Coast women gained the right to vote in 1951, Dove intensified the pursuit of her decolonial vision. Serving as a primer for her investment in melding the expansion of women's rights with national liberation, she collaborated with her cousin Constance Cummings-John to establish the Sierra Leone Women's Movement (SLWM).[9] Like many African women nationalists, she anticipated national liberation would open new opportunities for women. She critiqued women's subjugation, admonishing the Gold Coast colonial legislator in 1952 for its lack of representation of women:

> Gold Coast women have played a glorious part in this political struggle and it is time the men showed some appreciation. The sister of Pandit Nehru [Jawaharlal] was once ambassador in America and there are now two women [of] Cabinet rank in the Indian Assembly. The time is past when the male swaggers in front and the female with a baby on her back, a bundle on her head and another bundle on her arm, walks timidly behind her lord and master. If the men of Ghana want to gain the respect of the modern world, they must walk side by side with their women folk.[10]

Her nod to the leadership of India's Nehru and fellow women cabinet members anticipated the possibilities she foresaw for women as nation builders. Known for her concern for women's issues, upon election in 1954, Dove embraced the experiences of Black diaspora women abroad in her own formulation of the meaning of decolonisation, just as Nkrumah welcomed the cooperation of the diaspora in his pan-Africanist nation-building agenda.

Her determination to bring women's interests to the independence struggle ultimately cost her the 1954 elected seat when, in 1956, she travelled to the US as a participant of the US State Department's Foreign Leaders Exchange programme. With keen interest in the state of women's organising abroad, Dove's application to the programme expressed an interest in seeing US women's organisations, 'both political and non-political' and believed that the 'inter-racial problems are of great concern.'[11] As a pan-Africanist, a journalist, and a representative of a soon-to-be independent Black nation, gaining a deeper understanding of the Black freedom struggle in the US was an opportunity for her to strengthen pan-African ties.

Dove arrived in the US in a political environment immersed in an increasingly intensifying civil rights movement. She was supported by the National Council of Negro Women (NCNW) and their extensive national network to advocate for racial solidarity throughout her time in the US. At a public meeting hosted by the Norfolk, Virginia chapter of NCNW, Dove, joined by Sierra Leone's Carmela Renner, delivered critiques of US global leadership and its hypocrisy considering the treatment of African Americans.[12] Dove expressed admiration for African Americans' fight for full freedom and declared, 'No one of the Negro race should go to sleep again on the struggle for full equality', connecting the civil rights movement to liberation movements abroad.[13] Towards this end, Dove insisted on visiting Montgomery, Alabama, at the height of the then six-month bus boycott of the city's racially segregated public transport.

Montgomery was a centre of Black American women's leadership in the civil rights movement. Rosa Parks, secretary of the Montgomery chapter of the National Association for the Advancement of Colored People (NAACP), was the face of the movement, and backed by the organisational work of Joanne Robinson and the Women's Political Council. In this way, Montgomery well matched Dove's interests of women's participation in Black liberation. For Dove, the audacious protest of the city's Black residents was an episode in a shared and protracted history of global Black struggle. She shared these sentiments in a letter addressed to Martin Luther King, Jr and 'to the warriors of Alabama Montgomery' acknowledging the intrepidness of the Black race and encouraging the resilience and demand for freedom of Black people in the US.[14]

Aside from the letter's existence, it is unclear whether Dove managed to visit Montgomery in person. A significant contribution to this ambiguity is the fact that by the time she wrote the letter to Martin Luther King, Jr, the tour had begun to receive negative press. The news coverage reported that the State Department cancelled her tour after 4 July, labelling it a 'complete flop'. Press reports also included personal references to Dove as 'cynical and sullen' after she resisted the Department's interference in the tour's locations.[15] In fact, the government explicitly discouraged her from going to the southern city citing she would be 'insulted and humiliated' if she went to Montgomery.[16] Dove's acute attention to the city's political developments as expressed in her letter show that the experiences of Black Americans were intimately linked to the fight against white domination at home and across the continent 'that must be uprooted and entirely destroyed', as she would come to mandate just four years later.

Dove returned home shortly after the tour's conclusion in August and lost her elected seat, due to being abroad during the election. It is unclear from available historical material what Dove's own reflections were on the tour's success or potential lessons. However, as a Black African woman representative of a foreign administration, her tour carried political significance, even if that significance was partially unrealised. Determined to make the tour, she defied a warning from Nkrumah not to travel to the US because the course to independence was unfolding quickly. During her absence, the CPP organised a general election for mid-July of 1956 and nominated C.T. Nylander in her place. Her defeat, historian LaRay Denzer suggests, came as a result of her 'political naïveté' or the fact that candidates were required to submit their registration in person.[17]

The loss of Dove's elected seat imparts larger questions about women's leadership in relation to the national project. Participating in the tour represented an important step in advancing her mission to expand the growing women's movement in soon-to-be independent Ghana. While Dove supported CPP goals for independence, she also pursued her own vision of making Black women's interests central to the nation-building project as the only woman legislator. Women's decision-making, choices and ability to set a programme rested upon their cooperation with an often predetermined agenda made by male-dominated party leadership – an agenda of which they were not equal partners in establishing.

AOUA KÉITA: THE GLOBAL LEFT, AND WOMEN'S RIGHTS IN MALI

In the late 1950s, as Mabel Dove waged anticolonial struggles in the Gold Coast and forged transatlantic Black solidarities, Aoua Kéita organised women and mobilised the power of international trade union networks in the fight against colonisation in her native French Soudan. Born in Bamako in 1912, Kéita became one of a handful of students attending the city's only girls' school: her father, a veteran employed as a janitor, decided to send her to French school so that she could financially support her mother in the future. Upon completing her primary education, Kéita travelled to Dakar, Senegal. There, she studied in the medicine school, one of the only options available to African women in the federation at the time. By 1931, Kéita, now a degree-holding midwife and nurse, and a member of an emerging Western-educated class of Africans in French colonies, returned to the French Soudan.

Through the 1930s, Kéita's overlapping experiences of daily European racism, structural health neglect for colonised Soudanese people, and poor working conditions for health personnel led her towards organised collective action. In 1931, for her very first assignment, the colonial administration assigned her to a posting in the northern city of Gao, on the Sahara desert's edge. Upon settling, Kéita addressed a letter to the colony's French governor, to request the opening of a women's reproductive health facility in the city. As her request was met with silence, she kept writing for three consecutive years, and by July 1934, set up Gao's very first maternity ward. Kéita's sustained advocacy and health services allowed her to build strong connections with various segments of the population. She wrote: 'after six months, the inhabitants of the city's three quarters had fully adopted me. I was welcomed in all families, be it farmers, traders, herders, fishermen or public servants'. After Gao, Kéita intimately embedded herself in her assigned local communities, including reaching women in remote villages by bicycle or horse from her post to the southeastern town of Kita in 1937, until the administration finally provided them with a car in 1939. Kéita's activities as a nurse stationed in various towns throughout the colony (after Gao and Kita, she would end up in Kayes, then Niono) allowed her to refine her understanding of the struggles people shared, and the local issues they faced, across the Soudan's diverse territory and population. It also made her acutely aware of the structural health neglect African practitioners and patients experienced. By 1945, she took part alongside fellow African health professionals throughout French West Africa in the three-month long strike of the Symevétopharsa union.[18] Beyond Kéita's local-level advocacy for Soudanese women's health, global developments ultimately buttressed her political engagements and activism.

The main turning point in Kéita's internationalist and anticolonial ideologies were cemented in the decade between the mid-1930s and the mid-1940s. First, she experienced Italy's 1935–37 invasion of Ethiopia as a watershed event. Next, following the outbreak of the Second World War in 1939, she witnessed the great suffering of the people around her: 'atrocious domination, oppression and all sorts of humiliations made up the bulk of our day to day life'.[19] The years 1941–42 were particularly arduous: as the colonial administration cut gas and cash subsidies to funnel funds towards the war, Kéita had to curtail her services to patients in rural areas.

In 1946, political parties emerged throughout French West Africa, ushering in a post-war movement that ultimately led to decolonisation. Kéita elected to join the Rassemblement Démocratique Africain (RDA), a pan-African party with chapters throughout several colonies. She became a founding member of the RDA's Soudan branch, the US-RDA. A leftist, pan-African, anticolonial party with chapters throughout French Africa, the RDA was an internationalist organisation by nature. From the onset, the party's leadership clearly aimed to transcend colonial borders and reach as many colonised African peoples as possible. Upon publishing the party's founding manifesto in 1946, its authors penned a letter addressed to 'all political parties, associations and organisations, trade unions, and major individual figures of French West and East Africa, Cameroon, Togo, French Somaliland, Madagascar, and French islands of the Indian ocean'. They encouraged the letter's recipients to relay the RDA manifesto to the local press, and to spread the news of the upcoming Bamako meeting – where the RDA was to be formally inaugurated – as far and wide as possible, 'by any means necessary'.[20]

The letter's call was taken up. In Dakar, newspapers wrote about the upcoming founding meeting. In Conakry, organisers of the Communist Study Group prepared to travel to Bamako. Across Côte d'Ivoire, political leaders in urban and rural areas sent delegates: a caravan of some 50 trucks ferried waves of attendees from various Ivorian regions to Bamako. Now part of this large pan-African and anticolonial organisation, Kéita fused her activities as a midwife with her political activism, leveraging her labour with women and rural populations to keep making connections and elicit party memberships. Doing so, she faced numerous confrontations, stemming from Soudanese political opponents, French colonial administrators deeply fearful of the US-RDA's seditious potential, and Soudanese men, including political allies, who merely opposed women's political participation. Soudanese political officials condescendingly referred to her as the 'little midwife of Gao'. In Niono, a man who overheard Kéita discussing politics with his pregnant wife during a health check abruptly shut down the conversation: 'politics', he asserted, 'is men's business!' In the same town, Kéita chose to renounce an extra allowance she qualified for, which France granted to European employees and certain African public servants, but not to other African workers. This act of solidarity and protest, along with her increasingly visible political activism, made her the object of French suspicion and surveillance. Growing increasingly wary of her influence, the colonial administration tried to subdue it by assigning her postings in remote locations in the Soudan, and eventually transferring her to Senegal.[21]

By the mid-1950s, as decolonisation was underway in French West Africa, Kéita returned to the Soudan. These were the early Cold War years, in the immediate aftermath of the 1955 Bandung Conference that heralded the Non-Aligned Movement. Soudanese women tapped into the energy of transnational trade union networks to learn from others about their shared experiences, build unity and solidarities, and strengthen their struggles at home. In 1956, Kéita and teacher and union leader Aissata Sow founded Bamako's Union of Working Women. One of their chief demands was income equality between women and men. Kéita then participated in the foundation of the Federation of Black African Workers in Cotonou, Dahomey. The following year, Sow and Kéita travelled to Leipzig, East Germany, to represent Soudanese women workers at the World Federation of Trade Unions (WFTU), being the only two Black women in attendance. Kéita was particularly galvanised by the rallying call of all women delegates at the conference, to fuse the women's movement and labour movement into one:

> Women delegates ... called upon all the women workers of the world, in the cities and in the countryside, to help bring about a vast women's movement. Their efforts within this movement, combined with that of progressive forces all over the world, will facilitate new victories for the working class.[22]

In 1958, Soudanese trade unionist Bassata Djiré, one of five African attendees at the Fourth Congress of the Women's International Democratic Federation in Vienna, developed along with others the idea for the creation of the West African Women's Union (Union des femmes de l'Ouest africain, UFOA). Sira Diop, also a member of the Women's Workers' Union, presided over the West African Women's Union's first Congress, held in Bamako in July 1959. This Congress marked the apex of the women's movement in the Soudan. It also heralded its downfall, as sharp tensions emerged between the women's rights and trade union movement, on the one hand, and the male-led political struggle for national liberation, on the other.

On 20 July 1959, the West African Women's Union's Congress opened in Bamako. Over the course of three days, women delegates from Dahomey, Haute-Volta (today's Burkina-Faso) Guinea, Senegal and Soudan, the host country, gathered to imagine, discuss and debate the postcolonial future they envisioned, and drafted a series of resolutions. Aoua Kéita, who was overseas at the time, was unable to attend, but wrote to express her support for the initiative.[23] At the Congress, the delegates insisted on the importance of pan-African unity in working women's emancipation, aiming to break the connected yokes of colonialism and patriarchy. In her welcoming speech, Sira Diop stressed African women's determination 'to take an interest in all social, cultural, and political activities', and 'to fight for the construction of the African Nation'.[24] The meeting garnered a large mobilisation: Radio-Soudan reported that 'almost a thousand women gathered this afternoon at the Technical College for the opening of the First Congress of the West African Women's Union'.[25]

But within a few months, the US-RDA instead annihilated the women's movement in the Soudan. The male US-RDA leadership leveraged disagreements that had occurred along class lines during the 1959 Congress, over the issue of the abolition of polygyny – a demand amplified by the minority of Western-educated women but rejected by the majority of women who feared this would result in a loss of economic security. Ignoring the women's attempts to work these divisions out through compromise and further dialogue (in fact women organisations promptly dropped the resolution on polygyny), the male US-RDA leadership sowed more mistrust between the two groups, using rumours and divisive methods to co-opt all Soudanese women's mobilising power under the wing of the party. The US-RDA leadership resorted to 'colonial tactics' to silence some of the most vocal women leaders, including Djiré and Diop, who were assigned professional postings away from Bamako as a form of political exile – as had happened to Kéita under the French. By November 1959 the US-RDA leadership ordered the dismantling of all women's organisations. And in the period leading up to independence in September 1960, it was a man, Mamadou Béchir Gologo, whom the party tasked with delivering a speech on the role of women in the construction of the nation.[26]

As for Aoua Kéita, she tried to maintain a tenuous political line that straddled both the vindication of 'women's legitimate demands' and the defence of the party's efforts towards national liberation.[27] Eventually, she was elected as the only female parliament representative of the new independent government. However, she was sacked in 1967. Her removal occurred as part of a wider purge within the party (labelled the 'Active Revolution'), during which the US-RDA leaders sacked opponents as well as partisans deemed insufficiently radical.

* * *

Despite sharing the liberation ideals of unity, freedom and justice, the Pan-African Movement and the African feminist movements have been like two ships passing in the night, primarily following parallel paths with only tenuous points of intersection.[28]

—Sylvia Tamale, 2019

The political lives of Dove and Kéita make African women's leadership visible within national liberation movements. These activists served their movements in different capacities: Dove as a journalist and Kéita as a nurse and trade unionist. They both found a political home in their respective national parties in which they supported the struggle for national liberation not only towards the end of colonial rule, but towards the revolutionary agendas envisioned by their party leadership. By tracing their lives, these women appear not only as national party members, but as ascendant nation builders.

Dove and Kéita's visions of a postcolonial future and the means by which they sought to achieve these ends demonstrate a keen awareness of the reality that their own liberation as women depended on both the formal end of colonialism, and of its induced forms of women's marginalisation. They pursued guarantees on women's abilities to participate in public life and improve women's material conditions. In centring this agenda as a key element of their visions for nation building, their efforts to connect women's experiences through international networks both on the continent and abroad underscores their expansive sphere of engagement. However, the pursuit of women's interests ultimately found them in tension with their national parties.

Dove and Kéita's fight to incorporate their own visions into the nation-building process, and their ultimate failure, provides a revealing foray into the relationship between patriarchy, gender and the national question. Their decolonial visions challenged the patriarchal nature of colonial domination and its preservation within national liberation movements. While women's roles were encouraged within the parties in Ghana and Mali, they would only be tolerated to the extent that their activities aligned with the agenda of the national party's male-dominated leadership. By positioning women as auxiliary agents of the national parties own predetermined agenda, women's interests were designated as matters to be dealt with *after* the movement's success. This minimisation of the woman question advanced under the pretence that the success of national liberation would automatically usher in women's liberation. Dove and Kéita's experiences not only counter this assumed inevitably, but demonstrate that women's liberation cannot be achieved if placed as a secondary aspect of decolonisation.

NOTES

1. Mabel Dove, 'Women in Politics', *Daily Graphics*, 5 September 1952, in *Selected Writings of a Pioneer West African Feminist: Mabel Dove*, eds. Stephanie Newell and Audrey Gadzekpo (Nottingham: Trent Editions, 2004), 112.
2. Aoua Kéita, *Femme d'Afrique: La vie d'Aoua Kéita racontée par elle-même* (Paris: Présence Africaine, 1975), 395.
3. Adom Getachew, *Worldmaking after Empire: The Rise and Fall of Self-determination* (Princeton, NJ: Princeton University Press, 2019), 2–4.

4. The name 'French Soudan' and adjective 'Soudanese' are used in historical literature to refer to colonial Mali, West Africa, not to be confused with the East African country, Sudan.

5. Ricci Shryock, 'There Is No Fight without the Women', *Africa Is a Country*, 20 January 2022.

6. Mabel Dove, 'Racial Discrimination – a Crime: Commonwealth Must Act Now', 11 May 1960, *Evening News (Accra)* in *West African Feminist*, 115.

7. Dove's position as an elected official was distinct from the women's section of the CPP.

8. Wilhelmina J. Donkoh, 'Nkrumah and His "Chicks:" An Examination of Women and the Organizational Strategies of the CPP', in *Africa's Many Divides and Africa's Future: Pursuing Nkrumah's Vision of Pan-Africanism in an Era of Globalization*, eds. Yvette M.Alex-Assensoh, Charles Quist-Adade, and Vincent Dodoo (Tyne, UK: Cambridge Scholars Publishing, 2015), 106.

9. LaRay Denzer, 'Women in Freetown Politics, 1914–61: A Preliminary Study', in *Sierra Leone, 1787–1987: Two Centuries of Intellectual Life*, eds. Murray Last, Paul Richards, and Christopher Fyfe (Manchester, UK: Manchester University Press, 1987), 447–8.

10. Dove, 'Women in Politics', 112.

11. Biographical Information on Miss Mabel Dove of Accra, n.d., Series 7, Box 1, Folder 1, NCNW Papers, National Archives for Black Women's History (NABWH), Washington, DC.

12. 'Tell Negroes to Join with Other Peoples of the World', *Alabama Tribune*, 22 June 1956, 4.

13. Ibid.

14. 'To the Warriors of Alabama Montgomery', 27 July 1956, Box 25, Folder 1, Dr. Martin Luther King, Jr. Archive, Boston University, Howard Gotlieb Archival Research Center, Boston, MA.

15. 'From the Diplomatic Pouch', *The Chicago Defender (National Edition) (1921–1967)*, 21 July 1956, 2.

16. Bettye Collier and V.P. Franklin, *My Soul Is a Witness: A Chronology of the Civil Rights Era, 1954–1965* (New York: Henry Holt & Co., 1999), 47.

17. LaRay Denzer, 'Gender & Decolonization: A Study of Three Women in West African Public Life', in *Readings in Gender in Africa*, ed. Andrea Cornwall (Bloomington and Indianapolis, IN: Indiana University Press, 2005), 222.

18. Kéita, *Femme d'Afrique*, 44–7 and 252.

19. Ibid., 47.

20. Pierre Kipré, *Le congrès de Bamako ou la naissance du RDA* (Paris: Afrique Contemporaine, 1989), 89–90.

21. Kéita, *Femme d'Afrique*, 360 and 56–9.

22. Ibid., 357–8. Kéita kept forging international solidarity in the years that followed: Tatiana Smirnova and Ophélie Rillon, 'Quand des Maliennes regardaient vers l'URSS (1961–1991) Enjeux d'une coopération éducative au féminin', *Cahiers d'Études Africaines* 226 (2017): 331–54.

23. Rosa de Jorio, 'Of Rumors and Transfers: The Short Life of Western-Educated Women's Associations in French Sudan (1955–1960)', *kritisk etnografi – Swedish Journal of Anthropology* 3, no. 1 (2020): 76.

24. Sira Diop, 'Madame Sira Diop, présidente de l'U.F.S. ouvre le 1er Congrès Des Femmes de l'Ouest Africain', *Rencontres africaines*, 23 July 1959. As cited in ibid., 63–82.

25. de Jorio, 'Of Rumors and Transfers', 71.

26. Ibid., 77–8; and Bintou Sanankoua, 'Femmes et parlement au Mali', *Afrique Contemporaine* 210, no. 2 (2004): 147–8.

27. de Jorio, 'Of Rumors and Transfers', 76.

28. Sylvia Tamale, 'Towards Feminist Pan Africanism and Pan-African Feminism', *Nyerere Dialogue Lecture*, October 2019 (Dar es Salaam: Nyerere Resource Centre).

3

Mary Mooney: A Story of Irish and African Diaspora Solidarity

Maurice J. Casey

In September 1934, thousands gathered in San Francisco to pay their respects at the funeral of a working-class Irish woman, Mary Mooney, known to those who followed her cause as 'Mother Mooney'. Born in Ireland amidst a cataclysmic famine more than eight decades before, Mary Mooney's life (c.1848–1934) had been fraught with difficulties. Yet it was also marked by extraordinary events, not least her elaborate funeral ceremony, held in the prestigious surroundings of the San Francisco Civic Auditorium. It was the kind of honour that few Irish immigrants of her generation could have ever expected to receive. Above Mary Mooney's open casket was a banner that spoke of her extraordinary life: 'Mother Mooney, We Will Finish Your Fight'.[1]

This is the story of Mary Mooney's 'fight', the unlikely history of an Irish woman's journey from a childhood on Ireland's impoverished western seaboard to involvement in an international campaign on behalf of political prisoners. Her story moves through a pivotal and little-known moment in 1932, when Mary Mooney's campaign to have her son freed from a San Francisco prison became intertwined with the fate of the 'Scottsboro Boys', a group of African Americans on Alabama's death row.

Less than two years before her death, Mary Mooney toured the US and Europe as the star attraction in a global campaign known as the Scottsboro-Mooney tour. Her tour itinerary included trade union halls, sports grounds and open squares, from the west coast of the United States to the crucible of the world revolution in Soviet Moscow. Mary Mooney, an octogenarian former paper-mill worker from rural Ireland without a formal education, may seem an unlikely protagonist for a history of global anti-racist organising in the inter-war world. Yet, by the time she had completed her tour of the US and Europe in 1932, Mary Mooney had come to symbolise a movement that could overcome the divides of racial prejudice.

The broader history of relations between Irish and African American communities in the US is often perceived as a history of ambivalence or antipathy – usually with good reason. From the early nineteenth century onwards, intellectuals and campaigners discussed and denounced the anti-Black racism of Irish migrants in the US. It was precisely the Irish populations' suffering at the hands of imperialism and their often-impoverished conditions in emigration that baffled social reformers when it came to Irish attitudes towards the Black population in the US. Surely the Irish and Black working classes made for a natural coalition? Yet, from their moment of arrival in the US, the Irish were set apart from the Black population by merit of how they were racialised and legislated by the host state.[2] This division in law – and the decision made by many Irish Americans to benefit from the status quo rather than challenge it – shaped inter-community histories in profound ways.

Yet there were moments when the current of this story flowed in another direction. Histories of inter-communal romantic relations, shared cultures and mutual political inspiration provide examples of a remarkable number of common spaces and causes shared by the African and Irish diasporas.[3] The story of the Scottsboro-Mooney campaign, an ambitious and impactful alliance between African American and Irish American radicals, is rarely mentioned within Irish diaspora history or wider histories of Scottsboro.[4] As a depression-era tour organised by avowedly communist radicals that built a coalition of Irish and African American activists, the Scottsboro-Mooney tour does not slide easily into the usual historical grooves.

THE MOONEY FAMILY

How did a working-class woman from rural Ireland, who never learned to read nor write, become a central figure in an Irish and

African diaspora coalition? Although her final decades proved exceptional, Mary Mooney's early life was typical of her class, gender, nationality and era. Born Mary Heffernan around 1848 in Belmullet, County Mayo, young Mary's life would have almost certainly been one of deprivation and difficulty. Raised in an Irish-speaking region on Ireland's western coast in the aftermath of a catastrophic famine, the Heffernan children were destined to seek opportunities far from home. Aged 17, Mary Heffernan emigrated to the United States, where she eventually met and married Bernard Mooney, an Irish American mine worker from Indiana who became an organiser for the Knights of Labor, a movement that sought to organise skilled and unskilled labourers.[5] Three of the couple's five children survived beyond childhood; their eldest Tom, born in Chicago in 1882, along with Tom's siblings Anna and John. When the Mooney siblings were still children, their father Bernard was shot in the leg by a strike breaker. Although he survived this incident, Bernard succumbed to tuberculosis not long after Tom's tenth birthday.[6]

After her husband's death, Mary Mooney settled with her children in Holyoke, Massachusetts, where her sisters already resided.[7] Young Tom left school at 14 and found a job at the same paper mill where his mother worked. This was his first introduction to the world of labour and one that would ultimately set him on the road to becoming an international cause célèbre. In his late teens and early twenties, Tom Mooney became immersed within the socialist currents of the early 1900s US political scene. In 1908, aged 25, he joined Eugene V. Debs' Socialist Party and travelled country-wide promoting Debs' bid for US president.[8] Tom met and married Rena Brink Hermann, a music teacher from Kansas, and together they settled in San Francisco.[9] The wider Mooney family – his mother Mary and his siblings John and Anna – eventually joined the young couple in the Californian city, living together in the Mission District.[10] After a life of toil and transience, this must have seemed like a form of retirement for Mary Mooney. But the Mooneys had relocated into the eye of a storm.

On 22 July 1916, a bomb exploded in San Francisco, killing 10 people and wounding 40 others. The bomb, contained within a suitcase, was placed alongside the marching route for the city's 'Preparedness Day' parade, a march advocating US involvement in the First World War. The city's militants – and particularly the militantly anti-war, such as anarchists and other labour radicals – came under suspicion. With much of the city still reeling from the attack, Martin Swanson, a private detective working for large companies in California, began zeroing in on his prime suspect: Thomas J. Mooney.

Before the July 1916 bombing, Tom Mooney had already been tried and acquitted on several occasions for alleged crimes involving dynamite. Specific charges included accusations of transporting explosives with the purpose of destroying infrastructure belonging to the Pacific Gas and Electric Company.[11] Mooney's connections to people such as the anarchist Alexander Berkman only made him more suspicious to authorities. On 26 July, Tom and Rena's home was raided. They were arrested the next day. While Rena was eventually acquitted, Tom was sentenced to be hanged on 24 February 1917. The execution was scheduled for the following May. The global fight to prove his innocence and save his life had begun. From the outset, Mary Mooney believed in her son's innocence and fought to prove it. Estolv Ward, a biographer of Tom, noted that Mary was so assured of her son's innocence that she purchased flowers for the family home before her son's sentence was announced to welcome him home.[12]

Was Tom Mooney responsible for the Preparedness Day bomb? Modern conclusions rest close to where popular opinion settled shortly after Mooney's conviction: he was not responsible for the bomb. One of the more remarkable pieces of evidence to emerge was an image captured by an amateur photographer, Wade Hamilton, which provided the Mooneys with a photographic alibi. One of Hamilton's photos captured Tom Mooney and his wife Rena around the time of the explosion, watching the parade from a rooftop more than a mile away from where they were alleged to have planted the bomb.[13] A 1918 pamphlet published by the Tom Mooney Molders Defense Committee highlighted the image, drawing attention to the clockface in the photo's background with the precise timing of Hamilton's photograph.[14] By 1929, even Judge Franklin Griffin, the judge who originally sentenced Mooney, was publicly advocating for his release.[15] The real culprit behind the 1916 bombing has never been found.

For many with intimate knowledge of the US justice system's relationship with organised labour, Tom Mooney's innocence was axiomatic. A prominent early defender of Mooney was 'Mother Jones', the famous US labour leader born in Cork, Ireland, whose epithet 'Mother' would later be taken up by Mary Mooney herself. In the final chapter of her life, Mother Jones campaigned for a pardon for Tom Mooney, raising money for his defence and delivering petitions to California governors.[16]

Anarchist networks proved particularly rapid in responding to the Mooney case. In revolutionary Petrograd in April 1917, an anarchist group marched towards the US embassy demanding Tom Mooney's release. The protest appears to have been set in motion by the San Francisco-based Irish American anarchist Eleanor M. Fitzgerald, who sent a message to a Russian anarchist comrade suggesting he should 'raise a clamor for Mooney's freedom'.[17] Later retellings of this story in the US communist press and in Tom Mooney's own writings omitted to mention its anarchist organisers and even went so far as to count Lenin among the protestors.[18] By early 1918, an article in Max Eastman's paper *The Liberator* saw fit to claim that discussion of Mooney's case was 'stock conversation in American working-class homes' and had 'gone as far as the trenches of the European armies'.[19] The author even asserted that there is 'hardly a Russian village where the name of "Tom Muni" has not been heard'.[20] Although surely exaggerations, these statements reflected the real and immediate internationalisation of the Mooney case. Over the next decade, his case became emblematic of the struggle for justice under capitalism.

Following the sentencing, the Mooney family became part of a campaigning network and the heart of a movement that ebbed and flowed over the decades. By the onset of the Great Depression, Tom remained imprisoned. His campaign was already in the doldrums and the economic downturn brought with it financial difficulties for all. Mary Gallagher, an Irish American activist who became secretary of Tom Mooney's defence committee in 1928, remembered that by the time she started working for Mooney his case 'had been dormant for about seven years'.[21] It took an alliance with the International Labour Defence (ILD), a Communist Party-aligned legal defence organisation, to reinvigorate the Mooney movement. The renewed vibrancy of the campaign in the 1930s was rooted in an alliance with those intent on saving the Scottsboro Boys from execution.

THE SCOTTSBORO BOYS

In March 1931, nine young African Americans were pulled from a Southern Railroad freight train 20 miles outside of Scottsboro, Alabama, and arrested. The nine – Haywood Patterson, Andy and Roy Wright, Eugene Williams, Charlie Weems, Clarence Norris, Olen Montgomery, Willie Roberson and Ozie Powell – were travelling in search of work amid the dismal economic prospects of the depression. All were brought to Scottsboro jail, where they were charged with the rape of two white women who had been travelling on the same train. As news of the accusation spread, a lynch mob gathered outside the jail and the National Guard was called in to defend the building. Injustice was soon served with four trials in four days in April 1931 resulting in all-white juries finding the defendants guilty of the rape accusations. Eight of the accused – who would come to be known as the 'Scottsboro Boys' – were sentenced to death. The case of the youngest of the accused, 13-year-old Roy Wright, was deemed a mistrial.[22] Just as in Mooney's case, the sentence sparked a global movement.[23] It would take eight decades for the Alabama parole board to finally grant (posthumous) pardons to the final three Scottsboro Boys, who did not live to see their exoneration.[24]

Soon after the arrests outside Scottsboro, an organisation that would prove pivotal to the campaign to free the Scottsboro Boys entered the fray. The Communist Party-aligned ILD was the US section of the Communist International's political prisoner defence organisation International Red Aid.[25] The May edition of *Labor Defender*, journal of the ILD, carried an article by leading

Black communist and lawyer William Patterson on the Scottsboro case. Patterson wrote that the ILD 'has already sent two lawyers to the South to represent the boys'.[26] ILD support was profoundly impactful. As Clarence Norris, one of the 'Scottsboro Boys', later remembered: '"Propaganda!" I didn't know the word. But I believe the spotlight the "reds" put on Alabama saved all our lives. The ILD was working everywhere on all levels'.[27]

The ILD became a vital conduit linking the Mooney and Scottsboro campaigns together. A shared struggle between Irish Americans, white political prisoners and Black Americans facing a racist justice system was not something that Tom Mooney himself imagined nor emphasised as part of his campaign prior to Scottsboro. The aforementioned radical lawyer William Patterson, who would later accompany Mary Mooney to the 1932 Scottsboro Supreme Court ruling, recalled in his autobiography that although 'the attack on Mooney was an attack on the trade unions and on all oppressed people, [Tom Mooney] did not associate his persecution with the injustices perpetrated on Black people'.[28] Ward notes that in accepting ILD support for his own campaign, Tom Mooney conceded his previously 'ironclad position' that his case should not be 'intermingled with any other cause'.[29] The political imagination required to initiate the Scottsboro-Mooney coalition belonged to the radical legal minds guiding the ILD. Once the link was created, however, many of those prominent within the Mooney movement, and Mary Mooney in particular, became steadfast in their articulation of a common cause with the Scottsboro Boys.

THE TOUR

In April 1932, Tom Mooney sent a letter from San Quentin prison to leading African American intellectual W.E.B. Du Bois. In the letter, Mooney recalled a 1918 article about a lynching which Mooney had read 'in my condemned cell awaiting execution'.[30] Mooney wanted Du Bois to know that 'all my adult life, I have been keenly, warmly and sympathetically interested in the problems that confront your race and that I hate the hundreds of wrongs they have suffered with all of my being.[31] The reason for the timing of Mooney's missive to Du Bois is easy to discern. As Tom Mooney wrote from his San Quentin cell, his mother Mary was already on a tour that would take her across the US and Europe calling for the release of her son and the Scottsboro Boys. For several months in 1932, thousands of people gathered in squares and meeting halls across the US and Europe to hear a woman from rural Ireland talk about her son.

Mary Mooney's journey began with an appearance at the New York Coliseum on 24 February 1932. Declared 'International Scottsboro-Mooney Day' by the ILD, the date marked the 15th anniversary of Tom Mooney's sentencing.[32] One reporter described an audience of 10,000 people, who started cheering loudly when '"Mother" Mooney' arrived on stage.[33] B.D. Amis, an African American labour organiser and secretary of the League of Struggle for Negro Rights, joined her on the platform to assist her in reading out her speech.[34] Mary Alice Montgomery, the six-year-old sister of Scottsboro defendant Olen Montgomery, also stood on stage.[35] The Communist Party newspaper the *Daily Worker* described Mary Mooney as 'deeply moved' by the meeting and quoted her as stating with 'deep emotion': 'I know how the mothers of the Scottsboro boys feel … And I want the fight for my boy Tom, to be a fight for the Scottsboro boys, too.'[36] As the tour crossed the US, the accompanying speakers joining Mary Mooney sometimes changed, but the demand remained the same: freedom for Tom Mooney, the Scottsboro Boys and all political prisoners.[37]

Articulating the aims of the tour, the International Red Aid, the ILD's Comintern parent organisation, encouraged its world sections to explicitly link the Mooney and Scottsboro campaign. 'The traditions and prestige of Mooney's fight for liberty tied up with the Scottsboro case are of incalculable value in breaking the walls of racial prejudice', the International Red Aid noted.[38] An anti-communist journal of the Ohio Left saw a more cynical rationale. Describing the 'pathetic sight' of Mary Mooney, the paper argued that the communists were using the 'tragedy of her son's life to sell the membership of the Communist Party.'[39] The tour organisers knew, of course, that in foregrounding mothers they had struck on a 'universal motif', with one party leader noting that mothers were 'a weapon' to be utilised in building 'this mass movement'.[40] Regardless of the motives at play, there is no evidence to suggest Mary Mooney felt compelled to undertake the tour against her will. Indeed, her dedication to the tour is evident. Despite her enthusiasm for taking to the stage in defence of her son, the tour took its toll on Mary Mooney. Several months into her tour, while visiting Chicago, Mary Mooney became severely weak and lost much of her eyesight. Nonetheless, she recovered and was ready to sail for the European leg of the tour in October 1932.

But before she set sail for Europe, Mary Mooney was scheduled to visit the US Supreme Court. The Afro-Caribbean radical Cyril Briggs reported from the Supreme Court where an audience awaited the Court's latest ruling on the sentences delivered to the Scottsboro Boys. 'The solidarity of the white workers of the whole world with the persecuted Negro masses was dramatically demonstrated', Briggs reported, when 'Mother Mooney, victim of another notorious frame-up by the American ruling-class', entered the court room.[41]

The journalist Dorothy Parker was among those onboard the ship that carried Mary Mooney and her ILD entourage to Europe in late 1932. Parker witnessed Mooney delivering a short speech to ILD passengers who gathered regularly in a dining hall for political meetings. According to Parker's account, Mary Mooney spoke in 'pure Synge', describing how 'they've had my boy in the dungeon for something he didn't do'.[42] The international tour took Mary Mooney through Germany, Russia, the Netherlands, France and England. Moscow, capital of the world revolution, was designated with a special place on the itinerary. Yet 84-year-old Mary Mooney, impacted by the Moscow winter, was seemingly too weak to undertake much public speaking. Mary Leder, daughter of US political migrants in Soviet Russia, recalled Mary Mooney's visit in her memoir. 'A tentative understanding existed that Stalin would see Mother Mooney', Leder noted. However, the arrangements did not come to fruition.[43] 'She was a frail old woman', Leder remembered, 'rather bewildered, who seldom left her hotel'.[44]

As Mary Mooney struggled to see through the tour, despite ill-health and a hectic itinerary, the symbolism of the tour itself fostered moments of solidarity. In May 1932 in Los Angeles, *Scottsboro, Limited*, an agit-prop play written by the radical Harlem Renaissance playwright Langston Hughes, was performed.[45] It was accompanied by a participatory poem that was designed to fill the auditorium with chants calling for Tom Mooney's release.[46] In Chicago in March 1932, a Free Mooney-Scottsboro cross-city running match was organised. Reporting on the sporting events, organised by the Labor Sports Union, the *Chicago Defender* reported that there would be a national 'counter Olympics' held in the city in 1933 to protest against 'unfair treatment of Black and working class athletes'.[47] Tom Mooney was the honorary chairman.[48] In August 1932, four men and two women invaded the track at the closing ceremony of the Los Angeles Olympics carrying 'Free Tom Mooney' signs.[49] The spirit of cooperation across the US racial divide even made it to the dancefloor. In early 1933, an Irish American judge in Baltimore sought to have the city's 'Tom Mooney Hall' condemned. An ILD spokesperson stated in response that it was 'not until the interracial dances were started this winter' that the police began interfering.[50]

The ties between Mary Mooney and the Scottsboro mothers are evident in a letter from Mary Mooney to Viola Montgomery that was printed in the June 1932 issue of the *Labor Defender*. 'With millions of workers us behind us, black and white and all other kinds, ready to fight for my boy and all other victims of the bosses, we will win this fight yet', declared Mary Mooney in the letter's closing lines.[51] Of course, this is not an unmediated source: Mary Mooney was described as illiterate and so the letter was likely dictated. Yet there is no reason to doubt the sincerity of the message. Mary Mooney's belief in her son's innocence and the injustice of what had happened to the sons of the Scottsboro mothers is revealed through the energy she poured into the campaign, even as an older person suffering from health issues. Mary Mooney was a *symbol* of solidarity across the US racial divide rather than a central organiser or original theoretician, but her role was no less important for this fact.

After the tour that spanned across 1932, Mary Mooney continued to join Scottsboro mothers such as Ada Wright and Viola Montgomery on a shared platform. One of the final such occasions took place at the New York City May Day parade in 1934. The parade was led by five of the Scottsboro mothers. Mary Mooney walked with them.[52] It was one of her final public appearances before her death later that summer.

Mary Mooney did not live to see the event that she anticipated: her son's release. She died in September 1934, after a summer of wide-scale labour action in her adopted home of San Francisco. San Quentin authorities did not allow Tom Mooney to attend the ceremony. *Republican Congress*, a leftist periodical in Ireland, printed Tom Mooney's funeral tribute to his mother: 'A wonderful place awaits you in working class history', he wrote, 'and nothing can rob you of that'.[53] Tom was finally released in 1939. He planted a rose bush on his mother's grave on the morning following his release.[54] Tom Mooney died in early 1942, his health undermined by years of incarceration.

Exoneration for the crime he did not commit was delayed for Tom Mooney. Yet justice for the Scottsboro Boys proved even more elusive. In 2013, the last three Scottsboro Boys who had not lived to experience their exoneration were finally pardoned by the Alabama state parole board. The Scottsboro case remains alive in the popular imagination; the questions the story foregrounds about the white supremacist logic underpinning the workings of power in the US retain a burning urgency. Mooney's story, in contrast, is less well known. The 1932 Scottsboro-Mooney campaign, however, deserves to be remembered for the unprecedented coalition it sought to bring into existence. The Mooney case died with Tom Mooney. Scottsboro lived on through its enduring political relevance.

One lasting conversation that emerged during the tour revolves around the sincerity of the ILD in championing the case. Was the Communist International genuinely interested in saving the lives of the condemned or was the case a useful stick with which to beat their political opposition? The politics of solidarity are always worth analysing critically. Yet, even if we were to accept that communist involvement was dictated by an attempt to undermine impressions of the US justice system and elevate the image of a progressive Soviet Union rather than a politics of racial justice with real integrity, we would still need to acknowledge the tangible anti-racist legacies of this moment.

The Scottsboro-Mooney movement was profoundly creative; a moment of political imagination and inter-communal solidarity, with mothers at the forefront of its campaign. In consciously aligning a white Irish American man's destiny with the fate of the Scottsboro accused, the movement sought to upend assumptions regarding innate divides within the working-class United States. African American activists did not lack evidence to suggest that Irish communities regarded them with suspicion at best and violent hatred at worst. Yet such evidence did not prevent this coalition coming into being nor present an insurmountable obstacle to its many tangible successes. In following Mary Mooney's example, we can hold strong to a simple idea her life defiantly symbolised: a commonly experienced injustice can unite communities across the divisions constructed by the powerful to keep those same communities apart.

NOTES

1. *Daily Worker*, 12 September 1934.
2. Peter D. O'Neill, *Famine Irish and the American Racial State* (New York: Routledge, 2017), esp. 5. O'Neill's analysis is among the best works exploring Irish US, race and 'whiteness' in historical context. Besides Noel Ignatiev's influential *How the Irish Became White* (New York: Routledge, 2009 [1995]), other useful contributions to the discussion include: Lauren Onkey, *Blackness and Transatlantic Irish Identity: Celtic Soul Brothers* (London: Routledge, 2010) and Cian T. McMahon, *The Global Dimensions of Irish Identity: Race, Nation and the Popular Press, 1840–1880* (Chapel Hill, NC: University of North Carolina Press, 2015).
3. The goal of the African American Irish Diaspora Network, founded in 2020, is to foster greater awareness of these histories. Examples of studies of shared histories include: Bruce Nelson, *Irish Nationalists and the Making of the Irish Race* (Princeton, NJ: Princeton University Press,

2012); Virginia Ferris, "'Inside of the Family Circle": Irish and African American Interracial Marriage in New York City's Eighth Ward, 1870', *American Journal of Irish Studies* 9 (2012): 151–77; Brian Dooley, *Black and Green: The Fight for Civil Rights in Northern Ireland & Black America* (London: Pluto Press, 1998).

4. As an exception, see Nadja Klopprogge's notes on Mary Mooney in an article on the Scottsboro mothers: Nadja Klopprogge, "'The South Had to Reap What She Sowed" – Scottsboro and the Critique of Motherhood', *Amerikastudien/American Studies* 66, no. 4 (2021): 597–8.

5. Curt Gentry, *Frame-up: The Incredible Case of Tom Mooney and Warren Billings* (New York: Norton, 1967), 34. For Mary Mooney's age at emigration, see *Irish Independent*, 9 December 1932.

6. Gentry, *Frame-up*, 34.

7. Ibid.

8. Ibid., 38.

9. Ibid., 40.

10. Estolv E. Ward, *The Gentle Dynamiter: A Biography of Tom Mooney* (Palo Alto, CA: Ramparts Press, 1983), 170.

11. Rebecca Roiphe, 'Lawyering at the Extremes: The Representation of Tom Mooney, 1916–1939', *Fordham Law Review* 77, no. 4 (2009): 1731.

12. Ward, *Gentle Dynamiter*, 170.

13. Gentry, *Frame-up*, 136.

14. Tom Mooney Molders Defense Committee, *Justice Raped in California: Story of So-called Bomb Trials in San Francisco* (San Francisco, 1918), 24–5.

15. Tom Mooney Molders Defense Committee, *Pardon Tom Mooney He Is Innocent* (San Francisco, 1929).

16. Edward M. Steel, ed., *The Correspondence of Mother Jones* (Pittsburgh, PA: University of Pittsburgh Press, 1985), xxxiv.

17. Ward, *Gentle Dynamiter*, 29.

18. 'A Letter to Tom Mooney', *Soviet Russia Today* 3, no. 12, 18.

19. 'The Peril of Tom Mooney', *The Liberator* 1, no. 1, 29.

20. Ibid.

21. Interview with Mary Gallagher, oral history transcript, interviewer: Willa K Baum, Bancroft Library, University of California, BANC MSS C-D 4011, 87. Available online: https://digitalassets.lib.berkeley.edu/roho/ucb/text/gallagher_mary.pdf (accessed 17 August 2022).

22. My summary of the events preceding the Scottsboro movement is indebted to James Acker's account; see James R. Acker, *Scottsboro and Its Legacy: The Cases That Challenged American Legal and Social Justice* (Westport, CT: Praeger Publishers, 2007), esp. 1–9.

23. For a study of the movement, particularly in its British context, see Susan D. Pennybacker, *From Scottsboro to Munich: Race and Political Culture in 1930s Britain* (Princeton, NJ: Princeton University Press, 2009).

24. 'Alabama Pardons 3 "Scottsboro Boys" after 80 Years', *New York Times*, 21 November 2013, www.nytimes.com/2013/11/22/us/with-last-3-pardons-alabama-hopes-to-put-infamous-scottsboro-boys-case-to-rest.html (accessed 24 August 2022).

25. Sometimes referred to as MOPR, after its Russian title *Mezhdunarodnaia Organazatsia Pomoshi bortsam Revolutsii*.

26. William L. Patterson, 'Judge Lynch Goes to Court', *Labor Defender*, May 1931, 99.

27. Clarence Norris and Sybil D. Washington, *The Last of the Scottsboro Boys* (New York: Putnam, 1979), 60.

28. William L. Patterson, *The Man Who Cried Genocide: An Autobiography* (New York: International Publishers, 1971), 80.

29. Ward, *Gentle Dynamiter*, 177.

30. Tom Mooney to W.E.B. Du Bois, 5 April 1932, University of Massachusetts Amherst Special Collections, W.E.B. Du Bois Papers, Box 191, Folder 19.

31. Ibid.

32. *Waterbury Evening Democrat*, 22 February 1932.

33. *Liverpool Echo*, 27 April 1932.

34. Ibid.

35. *Atlanta World*, 4 March 1932.

36. *Daily Worker*, 25 February 1932.

37. For an account of the Scottsboro mothers touring journeys focusing on Ada Wright, see James A. Miller, Susan D. Pennybacker, and Eve Rosenhaft, 'Mother Ada Wright and the International Campaign to Free the Scottsboro Boys, 1931–1934', *American Historical Review* 106, no. 2 (2001): 387–403.

38. *Daily Worker*, 13 August 1932.

39. Dorothy Parker, quoted in Ward, *Gentle Dynamiter*, 183.

40. Miller, Pennybacker, and Rosenhaft, 'Mother Ada Wright and the International Campaign', 413.

41. Cyril Briggs, 'Whose Supreme Court?', *Labor Defender* 8 no. 11 (November 1932), 206.

42. Ibid., 184.

43. Mary M. Leder, *My Life in Stalinist Russia: An American Woman Looks Back*, ed. Laurie Bernstein (Bloomington, IN: Indiana University Press, 2002), 69.

44. Ibid.

45. Susan Duffy, *The Political Plays of Langston Hughes* (Carbondale, IL: Southern Illinois University Press, 2000), 31.
46. Ibid.
47. *Chicago Defender*, 6 March 1932.
48. Ibid.
49. *Daily Worker*, 22 April 1933; William J. Baker, 'Muscular Marxism and the Counter-Olympics', in S.W. Pope, ed., *The New American Sport History: Recent Approaches and Perspectives* (Urbana, IL: University of Illinois Press, 1997), 293.
50. *Afro-American* (Baltimore), 4 February 1933.
51. 'Voices from Prison', *Labor Defender*, June 1932, 116.
52. *Chicago Defender*, 12 May 1934.
53. *Republican Congress*, 17 November 1934.
54. Gentry, *Frame-up*, 431.

4

TESTIMONY: The Power of Women's International Solidarity with the Palestinian Revolution

Jehan Helou

The two decades between the mid-sixties and mid-eighties witnessed a golden age of solidarity and cooperation between women around the world. It was an age of revolutions and liberation movements against colonialism and neo-colonialism, and it is not an exaggeration to say that the Palestinian women's struggle was at its heart. This was an era when the Cuban, Chinese and Algerian revolutions inspired the world; and when the legendary struggle of the Vietnamese people against the ultra-mighty United States stunned onlookers. The Palestinians were keen to learn about these other revolutionary experiences and reading about them was essential to cadres' education. It was very significant that 'Vietnam Passed the Banner of Victory to Palestine'. The rise of the Palestinian Revolution happened after the June 1967 Arab-Israeli War. It was like a 'genie out of the bottle' after twenty years of dispossession and marginalisation. It was embraced by the Palestinians as well as the Arab people; it became their dream of redemption from colonialism and oppression. Our struggle – against colonialism, Zionism and Arab reactionism – became inspirational; it was the embodiment of a thorny struggle against a remaining outpost of settler colonialism in the world. This era was also the height of a feminist movement in Europe and the United States. These feminists started to listen to our narrative and joined solidarity movements. At the same time, women's movements in the Global South believed that women's liberation was interlinked with national liberation. We read Nawal El Saadawi, Kate Millet, Germaine Greer and others. Ultimately, these movements embraced our struggle and gave surge to our cause. This testimony, based on my memories and the few documents I have remaining, is a brief account of my participation in the Palestinian Revolution and some of our most prominent international solidarity activities.

—Jehan Helou, April 2023, London

I was born in Haifa, Palestine, in 1943. My father was one of the founders of the Arab Trade Union in Haifa. I was four years old when I was uprooted with my family during the Nakba (catastrophe) of 1948, to Lebanon. We lost our home and were dispossessed. Yet, we believed this was temporary, that we would soon return home. In high school in Lebanon, I started to advocate for our right to return to Palestine. When I joined the American University of Beirut, I was elected in the graduation year as the president of the Political Science Society. It was an easy decision for me to join Fatah (the largest of the Palestinian resistance organisations, founded in 1959) immediately after 1967, and I was quickly appointed to the Fatah leadership in Lebanon.

Fatah became the largest party and the leadership of the Palestine Liberation Organisation (PLO) after the 1967 war. I participated in its media section and international relations, but my main work was to organise women in the Fatah movement. The task was not easy. Most Palestinian women in Lebanon were living in a ghetto-like situation imposed by the government on the refugee camps and were oppressed by reactionary social norms.

I held a deep belief in the right of women to struggle for their full liberation. Grassroots struggle was challenging, especially at the start, but amazingly the liberation of the camps and social transformation within them was speedy. The General Union of Palestinian Women (GUPW) was established in Jerusalem in 1965 as a body of the PLO with the goal of social, economic, and political advancement for Palestinian women. I had an important role in the establishment of the GUPW branch in Lebanon (1969–1974), where we aimed to be a grassroot organisation representing all Palestinian women. Serious and extensive struggle resulted in having a leadership committee in most of the seventeen Palestinian refugee camps (by 1982 around half of the Lebanese branch leadership was from the camps).

Unfortunately, soon we had to face the civil war, launched in 1975 by the Lebanese fascists, and continuous Israeli aggressions on Lebanese villages and camps. In this dangerous revolutionary road, many beloved comrades were lost and sacrificed. We fought for the revolution to grow and solidify, all while we were under fire and facing attempts of liquidation. At the same time, there was also the enemy from within. Fatah was an ideologically pluralistic movement and the rift between the rationale of the Left and the right-wing was growing. My early Fatah leader did not like my feminist views and expressed his dismay by asking if I were there to liberate women. I said yes, I want to liberate women and liberate Palestine, you can't liberate Palestine without liberating women. At the time, I was demoted and marginalised, accused as being too left-wing. However, I regained my position after two years.

Amongst the first international activities I was chosen to participate in was the International Conference in Support of the Arab Peoples; initiated by Egyptian president Gamal Abdel Nasser and held in Cairo in January 1969. Here I had the opportunity to meet revolutionaries from around the world, who came together in support of the Palestinian armed struggle. I remember meeting Amílcar Cabral [leader of the liberation movement in Cape Verde and Guinea Bissau] in one of the workshops; we had a very interesting conversation and discussed how both of us anti-imperialists had studied in imperial universities!

After that, I was part of the first Palestinian delegation after the revolution to India in 1969. We were invited by the Organisation of Afro-Asian Peoples' Solidarity (AAPSO). The delegation was formed of two prominent male Fatah cadres and me. It was a very heart-warming and rich visit, lasting around one month. We visited many districts. There were rallies attended by tens of thousands. There were meetings with leaders of civil society, grassroots organisers, the foreign minister, and officials such as the famous political leader Krishna Menon. A large reception was organised by the National Federation of Indian Women in my honour and a long interview with me published on 21 September 1969 in the *Hindustan Times* weekly, quoting:

> *Al Fateh, she says, is not without a philosophy: 'we want to liberate the oppressed Arabs, but we also want to bring back the oppressors to humanity'.*

The Indian people we met wanted to donate for Palestine, even the very poor people. It was so heart-warming. India was liberated from British colonialism in 1947, but they had also experienced the disaster of partition. There was a strong anticolonialist feeling, and the Left was strong, ruling many states. What really inspired me was that I felt no sectarianism despite hundreds of ethnicities. Rather, what angered me were the very poor people and the caste system. India today is very different – although there is still solidarity with Palestine on the grassroots level, a lot has changed.

Throughout the early 1970s I participated in many such international activities. In 1970, Palestinians were invited by the UN World Council of Churches to a conference in New York and to visit a few other states. It was a successful visit in which we met with solidarity groups from the feminist movement, the Black Panthers, and the US Left. I also participated in the conference of the World Peace Council in 1979 in Basel, Switzerland, where I met Romesh Chandra, president of the Council, Emile Habibi and Felicia Langer.

The Second General Union of Palestinian Women (GUPW) Congress was in Beirut in 1974, and it was then that I was elected to the General Secretariat and became International Relations Officer. This 1974 Congress was at the peak of women's global solidarity and coordination. Many women's organisations from around the world attended, including high representatives from the Women's International Democratic Federation (WIDF), the Soviet Women's Committee (SWC), Cuba and Vietnam and some other socialist countries; many delegates from Africa, including a representative of the African National Congress and, from Guinea Bissau, Ana Maria Cabral, the wife of Amílcar Cabral, who had been assassinated in 1973. Western representatives including from West Germany, Italy and France attended. We had a programme for them alongside the Congress: visiting our institutions and meeting with Palestinian women in refugee camps.

This Congress was historic as we were struggling against endorsing the '10 points resolution' proposed by the PLO National Council, to establish a state on a part of historic Palestine. There were splits amongst us as Fatah members, but we allied with other representatives, independents, and those from other Palestinian organisations. Our Union represented a national front, and this was one of its biggest successes. The Vietnamese delegation expressed their admiration of our courage and supported our position against the 10-point programme.

ZIONISM AS RACISM AND THE WOMEN'S DECADE

In 1975, I went to the Soviet Union to attend a preparatory meeting for the UN International Women's Year that was initiated by the Women's International Democratic Federation (WIDF), the largest women's federation in the world, established in 1945 against fascism and colonialism. The WIDF aimed to address issues that hindered the liberation and integration of women in society at equal levels, and it had very substantive results. One year earlier, in 1974, the PLO had been officially recognised as the representative of the Palestinian people by the UN General Assembly and granted observer status. The PLO was then invited to attend the UN Women's Conference in Mexico, to coincide with 1975 International Women's Year.

I was part of that delegation to Mexico, headed by Issam Abdul Hadi, president of the GUPW. The conference became a historic event, where women started the condemnation of Zionism as a racist movement. It was a big achievement – we had the support of the Arabs, the Non-Aligned Movement, and of the socialist countries. Amongst us, it felt natural to condemn Zionism. We decided that when the Israeli delegate, Lea Rabin, gave her speech, we would withdraw from the hall. We and all our allies withdrew, leaving some observers and some Western and pro-Israel states. The Israeli representative almost cried and asked why the hall was empty? There was great interest and questions from the media. We started to explain settler colonialism, the Nakba, everything. This great achievement confirmed that women united can make miracles! Later that year, the UN General Assembly passed resolution 3379, declaring 'Zionism as a form of racism and racial discrimination'.

After the success of the Women's Year, the UN decided to have the Women's Decade. The second conference of the Women's Decade was in Copenhagen, in 1980. Because the US and their allies were furious about the women's condemnation of Zionism, we expected that they would try to revoke the 'Zionism as Racism' resolution, if they could get two thirds of the votes. With Mai Sayegh at the head of our delegation, we prepared ourselves with very serious coordination amongst our friendly delegates. It was successful; the US couldn't overcome our position.

On the conference agenda were two main items: South African women under apartheid and Palestinian women inside the Occupied Territory and in Exile. This was an additional victory. There were discussions about the connections between South Africa and Palestine. I was on one of the committees and an Israeli delegate had spoken in her speech about how the situation of Palestinian women under occupation had improved much more than for Arab women anywhere else – 'now they have washing machines and ovens', she said. I commented: 'that is really good, everyone around the world should dream of having an occupier!' Of course, she was upset. Later that year, the GUPW had its third Congress, with many high international representations in attendance. Its final statement and the delegated interventions acted as a political platform against the US brokered Camp David Accords, agreements between Israel and Egypt, leading to the 1979 peace treaty that was essentially a surrender to Zionism and to imperialist hegemony in the region.

In 1985, I went to Nairobi for the third UN Women's Conference, to attend the NGO Forum, the parallel and non-formal forum to the main conference. The PLO, through a GUPW delegation headed by Salwa Abu Khadra (president of the Union at the time), went to the official conference. What happened there was sad. Many people think that there was a direct or indirect agreement between the PLO and the US to revoke the resolution or not to include it, promising to support the PLO to have a Palestinian state. Arafat – who knew that Israel is an outpost for imperialism and colonialism – accepted this deception thus betraying his legacy of steadfastness during the 1982 siege of Beirut. We were furious. Zionism wasn't mentioned in any conference document. There was no determination to keep the resolution. This was the route to the revocation of resolution 3379 in the United Nations General Assembly in 1991.

However, there was a completely different picture in the NGO Forum. There was a large Palestinian and Arab WIDF members delegation. The WIDF coordination was very effective. We agreed to meet every day and to divide ourselves on all relevant workshops. The Israelis came to the Forum thinking that they would have a workshop with the Egyptian delegation, but the Egyptian delegation were strongly opposed to the Camp David Accords. Many of the arguments being made at the Forum linked Israel to South Africa. Israel's support to the South African apartheid regime to develop their nuclear power is well-documented in history.

The Israeli delegation and right-wing women were trying to hinder the discussion on colonialism, Zionism, and racism by saying 'We are here to talk about women not politics'. But they failed. There was clarity, coordination, and cooperation between women. I believe it had to do with our commitment to justice. I always say it was one of the best conferences I attended because we could really silence all the lies. These factors and spirit were rather missing in the fourth – and last – World Conference on Women of the UN Decade, which I attended in China in 1995.

WIDF AND SOVIET SOLIDARITY

There was another important Women's Conference in East Berlin, organised by the WIDF and hosted by the German Democratic

Republic (GDR), as an auxiliary to the 1975 UN Mexico conference. Rather than attended by state representatives as in Mexico, it was primarily made up of women's organisations and prominent representatives from civil society. The presence of Palestine was strong, with a large delegation. In the conference, there was a struggle over the inclusion of a sentence in the final communique about the need to guarantee the security of Israel. We argued: 'who should guarantee the security of who? They are the occupier and very powerful'. We struggled to remove the sentence in the first WIDF Bureau meetings we attended – arguing that its inclusion had been undemocratic, and we won. We had excellent support from our Cuban friends, especially Vilma Espín, head of the Federation of Cuban Women.

We also attended the WIDF Congress, where we were elected as members of its Bureau and Palestine given the status of WIDF Vice President. Our relations with the WIDF developed positively every year. Nothing was easy because of the Zionist influence, but with our narrative reaching a wide audience, and with the political developments in the policy of the Soviet Union and within the different women's unions, support for Palestine in the WIDF became more radical. WIDF escalated their solidarity with us and with the Arab women's organisations that stood against the Camp David Accords. They visited us in Lebanon twice, and again immediately after the 1982 Israeli invasion. There was very positive solidarity coverage in their magazine *Women of the World* and their external communications.

Our relations with the Soviet Women's Committee in particular developed day by day. Their first visit to Beirut was in 1972 and they participated in all our Congresses. They provided us with university scholarships, reaching 30 scholarships in total. After the attack on Tal al Za'atar refugee camp, they sent us emergency help including a piano for Beit Atfal al Sumoud (house of steadfastness) which was established by GUPW after the massacre in the camp, for the children whose parents or families were killed. Unfortunately, the piano was taken by the fascist Phalangists because they were controlling the harbour.

A GUPW delegation (of myself, Issam Abdul Hadi and Siham Rahal) was invited for a special visit to the USSR in 1981. We visited different institutions and attended many activities reflecting women's role in society. Nihaya Mohammed and I also travelled to Moscow in 1978 to attend the conference on 'Women and Socialism', which was more ideological. I presented a paper expressing the belief that socialism is the best solution for women's liberation. Most of us read the books of Clara Zetkin and Alexandra Kollontai. We believed that socialism and social justice is essential for women's liberation. We also had a similar visit to the GDR and attended many conferences in other socialist countries. As they were strongly against Camp David and US hegemony, they continued to support us, continuing to grant us university scholarships and inviting us to the World Congress of Women in Moscow (1987), with the title 'Toward 2000 – Without Nuclear Weapons: for Peace, Equality, Development'.

VIETNAM AND LATIN AMERICA

The GUPW visit to Vietnam in 1980 was a landmark moment! It was a one-month cadre training activity for ten women activists from the different Palestinian factions. I was the head of the delegation. We were very enthusiastic to learn more about the Vietnamese experience that we highly admired and that inspired us. We viewed the limitless support of Hanoi to South Vietnam as a model that we wished could be practiced by the Arab states surrounding Israel. We highly admired the prominent role of Vietnamese women including in the armed struggle – some even as generals. We wanted to learn from their remarkable experience.

We attended lectures, visited different institutions, and held long conversations about their experience. We always had three delicious meals a day which meant a lot with their difficult economic situation. We witnessed their excellent provisions of support to women, such as childcare when the mothers were in the military bases. They had a motto at the time: 'If you are engaged, you can delay your marriage; if you are married, delay having children'. But they also stressed that life should go on – you can't really suspend everything and expect people to go on struggling. For married people in the military bases, they provided camps for the couples to meet at certain times.

We learned a lot about their trenches, and how they communicated with the Vietnamese soldiers in the South by going to the checkpoints and asking them, with megaphones, 'what are you doing here? You should think of your family, your future'. I think we should do the same today with the security coordination of the current Palestinian Authority (PA). They took us to a house where one of the leaders of the Vietcong was living as an ordinary labourer in the South. This house was a shelter for weapons from North Vietnam to South Vietnam. They had to dismantle the pieces of tanks to reach the South. In the areas where there were heavy bombardments, especially in North Vietnam, the women made it one of their targets to create safe areas for education (like kindergartens). This was part of a campaign to avoid more losses to society and children than those already imposed. Before we left, I asked every delegate to leave some of their pocket money for the children of the martyrs in solidarity. I had all the minutes and notes from lectures and meetings that took place there, but they were destroyed with the majority of GUPW documents in the aftermath of the invasion of Lebanon in 1982.

After 1982 and the siege of Beirut, we received an invitation from three women's unions to visit Nicaragua, Mexico and Cuba, coordinated to take place at the same time. In Nicaragua, it was only a couple of years after the revolution led by the Sandinista National Liberation Front in 1979. The women told me about a massive demonstration in the capital in support of Palestinians with the participation of the president during the Beirut siege. When I was there, there were many attacks by the Contras [right-wing militia groups] from Honduras borders, which were supported by the US and Israel. I was supposed to go to Honduras and see for myself, but they suddenly said that I couldn't visit. I asked why? They said Ariel Sharon (the architect of Israel's invasion of Lebanon) was visiting Honduras on the same day, and it could be very dangerous. The most touching experience of my visit to Nicaragua was when I was invited to meet the mothers of martyrs. There were around twenty women, and I was expressing our solidarity with them, how heroic they are bearing all this loss and suffering. They interrupted me by saying 'no, no, it is nothing in comparison to the Palestinian mothers'. I did not think these ordinary women would know about Palestine.

Then we reached Mexico, where the UN conference had been convened in 1975. The Mexican Women's Union was very keen to express solidarity. It was an opportunity to talk about the Palestinian struggle and the siege on Beirut. Yasser Arafat had become very popular there and was considered a great hero. We visited women's institutions and attended some of their activities, always accompanied with discussions about the Mexican women's struggle and the importance of international women's solidarity and coordination.

Of course, Cuba was very significant because of the relations between the PLO and Fidel Castro, as well as our close relation with Vilma Espín – a great revolutionary, feminist, and outspoken supporter of gender equality. I met Vilma several times in different conferences. The Cuban women's union prepared rich meetings and visits to learn about women's achievements and activities as well as Cuban educational and medical institutions and achievements. They told me about the large demonstrations against the siege of Beirut and how Arafat had become a great symbol of liberation. They said that for the first time, people were angry with Fidel Castro, as they wanted him to send the army to Lebanon to help the Palestinians. I think Castro explained that they couldn't go unless requested by the Lebanese government; their support of the Popular Movement of Liberation of Angola (MPLA), in comparison, was requested by the Angolan government. Cuban intervention in Lebanon without invitation would have started World War 3. Cuba supported the Palestinians in other ways, including with weapons, scholarships and political support. I remember Mai Sayegh, General Secretary of the GUPW, telling us that when she travelled to Cuba for the 1974 Second Congress of Cuban Women, between the long speeches, the conference hall would together sing revolutionary songs. Stories like this remind us that ordinary women felt connected by different revolutionary experiences – it gave us hope.

ARAB AND PALESTINIAN WOMEN'S JOINT STRUGGLE

The long history of joint struggle between Palestinian women and Arab women against Zionism and colonialism is very rich. It is necessary to understand the centrality of the Palestinian Revolution to the Arab world in order to understand the wider international relations of the movement. With the collapse of the Ottoman Empire, the colonialist powers took over and effectively divided the Ottoman provinces outside the Arabian Peninsula into areas of British and French control and influence, in the Sykes–Picot Agreement. These Arab provinces had a long-shared history and culture under the Ottoman Empire and the Islamic Caliphates before it. The Arab people and Arab women realised that the colonialist scheme supported, militarily and politically, the Zionist project to build a settlement in Palestine. Huda Sha'arawi, an Egyptian woman pioneer, started an Arab women's movement that later developed into the All-Arab Women's Federation (AAWF) in 1944.

When the Palestinian Revolution took off, thousands came to join the struggle including many revolutionary women. Women's movements and unions started supportive initiatives. After the revolution moved its base from Jordan to Lebanon in 1970, we had excellent cooperation with the national and progressive Lebanese women's organisations. Many Lebanese women also joined the Palestinian organisations. In reality, it was a joint struggle against common enemies – Israeli occupation and Israeli aggressions alongside the fascist Lebanese forces.

It is necessary to mention an important radical experience of women's cooperation against Egypt's capitulation in the Camp David Accords. As a result of the support of the Egyptian president of the All-Arab Women's Federation for these accords, and the absence of freedom to express opposition to this position, representatives of women's unions from the Arab Resilience and Resistance Front states (Algiers, Syria, Iraq, Libya, Yemen, Iraq and the PLO) opposing Camp David met together and arranged to move the Federation from Cairo to a new location, to be decided on at the following Congress.

Historically, the Federation had only one union from each Arab country, which were each largely representative of their regime. A radical decision was taken in our early meetings to include more than one organisation and to welcome women representing liberation movements rather than states only. This meant that groups from Bahrain, Oman, Eritrea, and Western Sahara joined us, as well as progressive unions and alliances from Lebanon, Syria, and Jordan, and groups in opposition to their regimes like the women of the Egyptian Progressive Women's Union, the Sudanese Women's Union and the Iraqi Women's League.

The General Federation of Iraqi Women had an early departure from the AAWF, when their leadership ambitions were unsuccessful. At the beginning, a few GUPW members opposed their leadership, which was supported by Yasser Arafat who wanted to appease Iraq. However, sticking to its values, the GUPW was united in supporting the progressive developments in the AAWF – for women's rights, and in the struggle against the Camp David Accords, Zionism, colonialism and Arab reactionism. Arafat embraced our success and later offered to support the initiative of a Cultural Journal for the AAWF when we had our first meeting in Beirut in April 1982, but this publication became impossible after the invasion of Lebanon.

In the Tenth Congress of the All-Arab Women's Federation, convened in Damascus in 1981 and attended by many international representatives including the WIDF and the Arab League, elections of the general secretary and different responsibilities took place. I was elected as assistant general secretary of the Culture, Research and Media committee. Our main activities were to campaign for democratic freedoms in the Arab world, emphasising that democratic freedoms cannot be elections only; they are the right to organise and express opinion. This is one of the problems of the Arab world: from the very beginning, Arab reaction was our enemy. We implemented solidarity activities for events in the Arab region, publishing pamphlets and organising our joint work in international conferences, with a vital role in the success of the UN Nairobi conference in 1985. However, most of the Arab regimes and their unions did not support the development of a progressive Federation. Syria imposed a General Secretary who was not up to the job; and Libya, hosting the Federation, did not stand up to its commitment to support the expenses of the committees.

REFLECTIONS

I left the Fatah movement after the 1982 Israeli aggression, because I thought the movement should make reforms to restore its revolutionary status. In Beirut during the siege, I had never seen such high morale and heroism amongst the fighters. But the PLO made an agreement with the US to withdraw its fighters and cadres from Lebanon in 1982 in exchange for the guaranteeing of civilian protection. The deal was based on lies, evidenced in the horrific massacre of Sabra and Shatila that followed with the full cooperation of the Israeli army.

I remained in Lebanon when the PLO withdrew. I had to go underground during the Israeli presence in Beirut. Later we, the few GUPW cadres remaining, had to face the tragedy of Sabra and Shatila, and the grasp of the Lebanese fascist forces on the capital. We worked in urgent relief matters, and on a campaign to identify the names of those detained and to call for their release. By mid-1983 it became too dangerous for me to stay in Beirut, so I left for Damascus to continue grassroots work in the Palestinian camps and to pursue the struggle within the GUPW and with Arab and international women's organisations. I lost my seat in the Palestine National Council that I had held since 1981 because I, with many others, opposed its convening in Amman (1984), seeing it as another appeasement.

With the departure from Beirut, the PLO lost its unified structure and revolutionary positioning, and much of the leadership moved to Tunis. In 1985, the fourth GUPW Congress was convened in Tunis. Those of us who opposed the leadership's policies of appeasement and compromise on Palestinian rights didn't attend. As I felt that the struggle had reached a sort of dead-end, I decided to move to England to pursue doctoral studies. I continued my work in some of our international relations, including the first Palestinian delegation to South Africa, when their apartheid ended in 1994 and a few important international women conferences. In the 1990s, the GUPW became incorporated to the new political reality brought in by the Oslo Accords. Though in the international arena our narrative continues to resonate, the GUPW endorsement of the Palestinian Authority hinders the building of a solid women's solidarity movement across the globe.

While I no longer participated in the struggle through women's organisations due to the new political situation, I chose to document some of the rich experiences of our struggle by giving a voice to women freedom fighters (grassroots and leaders) through oral history testimonies. They were published in Palestine by UNESCO (2009) and later in English by the Bertrand Russell Peace Foundation (2022). My main area of political struggle shifted to children's books and culture. I left for Palestine – the United Nations Development Programme helped by providing my temporary residence visa. There, I became the General Director of Tamer Institute for Community Education (2000–2006) which was established during the First Intifada, when schools were closed and education interrupted. In 2002, we launched a serious struggle to attain Palestine's membership in the International Board on Books for Young People (IBBY) which had been denied for many years because of Zionist influence. This achievement was an act of justice and beautiful solidarity with the support of very enthusiastic personalities involved in children's books, mainly children's writers, librarians, publishers, educators and others. I have been the president of the Palestinian Section of IBBY since its establishment. One of our main activities to this day has been setting up and supporting children's libraries in Gaza through the Children in Crisis programme.

International solidarity with the Palestinian women's struggle was a great practical expression of the importance of unity in the struggle against colonialism and oppression. This is what international solidarity means – good coordination and cooperation. Sympathy is not enough. There is much to learn from this rich history, its achievements, and shortcomings. One thing we learned is the ways in which regimes and the patriarchal system will interfere with women's organisations. Another was that the Palestinian Revolution needed a base – we can't leave our people trapped under occupation.

There are many stories and testimonies that still need to be told about the Palestinian Revolution which cannot be included here. It is hoped that this testimony of our international solidarity work will inspire more learning about the rich experience that was the Palestinian Revolution, as the struggle goes on. Knowing our history is vital, to understand the contemporary conditions of the struggle and to move forward. Oral history needs to come from real experiences – it is of course always subjective, but it must be factual. We cannot go to the Arab states for archives about this past. Telling this history is important mostly today as many people are demoralised. During the 1970s, you would find students leaving university and people leaving their employment to join the revolution – they had confidence and great expectations. Despite the relapse and weakness of progressive movements, the struggle goes on. I am optimistic, the solidarity movement with Palestine is growing extensively around the world and real change will come. We should find the means to face the challenge of reviving the seventies bonds of women's cooperation and solidarity around the world!

Part of Jehan Helou's testimony was recorded in London in 2022–23 with Roba Salibi who transcribed it and translated the Arabic part of the conversation.

5

Shigenobu Fusako: From Japan to Palestine in World Revolution

Jeremy Randall

On 28 May 2022, several dozen leftists gathered outside kokusai-hōgō-senta medical prison in Tokyo, Japan, to welcome the release of Shigenobu Fusako (b. 1945) who had spent over 21 years incarcerated. Shigenobu was the leader and spokesperson for the Japanese Red Army [Nihon Sekigun] (JRA), a Lebanon-based offshoot of the Japanese Red Army Faction [Sekigun-ha] (RAF). The group was infamous for their militant activities in the 1970s and 1980s. Holding banners with the slogan 'We love Fusako', the people patiently waited for the release of a woman who had been simultaneously cast as a revolutionary hero advancing the Palestinian cause as well as a terrorist within the Japanese media.[1] A small contingent of right-wing extremists tried to use noise vans to drown out Shigenobu as she gave a short speech alongside her daughter May Shigenobu (b. 1973). In this speech, Shigenobu upheld her support for Palestinian liberation and apologised for any innocents harmed by the JRA's actions.[2] Her release came just days before the 50th anniversary of the JRA's most famous action: the Deir Yassin Operation, when the JRA attacked Lod Airport in Israel. As the leader of the JRA, Shigenobu was a major figure in Japanese far-leftism during its peak in the early 1970s and represented for many a unique figure due to her desire for revolution and radical change to Japanese society and the world at large.

Before she became leader of the JRA, Shigenobu was a high-ranking member of the RAF in Japan. Unlike the localised RAF, her Lebanon-based small group undertook direct action internationally and gained global notoriety. The JRA's most famous attack, the Lod Airport attack, heralded its entry onto the global stage as one of the leading militant groups supporting Palestinian liberation. Other groups from Latin America and Europe had trained with the Popular Front for the Liberation of Palestine (PFLP) and collaborated on missions, such as the Sandinista Patrick Argüello in the September 1970 Dawson's Field Hijackings, but the Lod Airport attack by the JRA was the most high-profile attack yet.[3] On 30 May 1972, three JRA militants disembarked from an Air France flight from Rome and for three minutes shot randomly into the crowds in the baggage claim area of Lod Airport: 27 people died, dozens were injured, and two of the attackers were killed either by Israeli security or by suicide. Most of the dead were Puerto Rican Christian pilgrims who had arrived on a flight around the same time. Multiple Israelis also died. There was no independent inquiry into the attack, leaving it unclear if the deaths were caused by the JRA or the Israeli forces.

As news of the attack spread, there was global shock that the three attackers were not Palestinians but Japanese. In press releases, the JRA announced that the group committed the operation as part of its alliance with the PFLP, whose members had brought international attention to their liberation cause through hijackings and airport attacks in years prior to this operation.[4] The PFLP celebrated the attack heavily in the pages of *al-Hadaf* (The Target), a weekly Palestinian magazine founded and edited by Palestinian author Ghassan Kanafani in Beirut.[5] Global shock was palpable as Israeli intelligence did not expect violent solidarity actions by a Japanese leftist group and the media expressed further shock that the JRA was led by a young woman, Shigenobu Fusako, when most far-Left groups were led by men. A committed female militant leftist, Shigenobu represented a new type of leftist radical dedicated to implementing theory into praxis.

The historiography of the JRA and the RAF as well as the RAF's successor the United Red Army (URA) are fraught with problematic trends. There is a general focus on treating the JRA as a violent terrorist group without acknowledging how it understood violence as a revolutionary tactic. Generally, the idea dominant in the scholarly work on the group focuses on how violence was irrational and driven by a destructive impulse.[6] Other scholarly works focus on sexualising the JRA due to the leadership of Shigenobu as well as other JRA members', Adachi Masao and Wakamatsu Koji's, work on making pinku films (softcore erotica).[7] This overt sexualisation of the JRA replicates tropes about revolutionary women and the misogyny found within leftist culture and society at large. When discussing Shigenobu and her role as leader of the JRA, it is important to recognise that her being a woman did play a role in interacting and engaging with fellow leftists, but to reduce her womanhood to tired tropes reduces her agency and wherewithal to enact revolution. Rather, Shigenobu, marginalised by capitalism simultaneously through her status as a worker and student as well as by her experiences as a woman, called for revolution to liberate the oppressed. For Shigenobu, revolution would liberate all people, men and women, from capitalist and imperialist exploitation.

SHIGENOBU'S EARLY LIFE

Born in 1945 shortly after the end of the Second World War, Shigenobu grew up in a politically active family. Her father, during the war, was a member of the military police of imperial Japan and maintained his support for Japanese militarism and its defunct empire afterwards.[8] Shigenobu grew up in post-war Japan, as the country oriented away from its violent past as a major imperial power to be a comprador nation under US occupation.[9] Following the Second World War, the fear of a communist insurgency witnessed in China and Korea pushed the US to rebuild the Japanese economy to prevent such a similar outcome in Japan. Japan became newly wealthy after prolonged poverty caused by the war, but Shigenobu's family remained on the economic margins as the post-war Japanese economy initially benefitted elites.[10] As a teenager, Shigenobu became increasingly engaged in politics by arguing with her father who continued to hold right-wing views.

In the late 1950s, Japan experienced the first major post-war leftist movement when the US sought to solidify Japan's role as a bulwark against communist expansion in the Pacific. In 1959, Japan and the US entered negotiations to continue the US military presence within Japan to counter the threat of communist expansion in East Asia and Southeast Asia. Protests against this security treaty, known as the anpo protests, shook the country as a student-led movement expanded to include vast swaths of society protesting US imperialism, the Japanese government's complicity, and socioeconomic problems.[11] The movement demonstrated that the Japanese elite had joined the US imperial machine, but that many Japanese rejected the new order. The protests also brought new life to the student movement and led to an ongoing period of radical politics from universities.

Shigenobu was swept up in the leftist student movement of the 1960s. She started her studies in Meiji University in 1965, while working in an office job in Tokyo that allowed her to study at night and not burden her parents with the cost of tuition. She quickly immersed herself in the vibrant student movement, while chafing at the conservative office culture and its standard anti-feminist orientation at the time. Rejecting the easy access to a solid middle-class lifestyle found in the corporate world, Shigenobu embraced radicalism and feminist politics. Joining the Second Bund, a constellation of leftist student movements, and eventually the RAF, she quickly became a prominent figure in the radical Japanese student movement.

SHIGENOBU IN THE RED ARMY (JAPAN)

Shigenobu joined the RAF when it was founded in 1969 after it broke away from the Second Bund. Formed from the radical student Left and close-knit circles, the RAF initially drew its membership from elite universities in the Kansai region of Japan. The RAF innovated upon the earlier Japanese student movements by advocating for revolutionary violence to bring about communism. The group articulated a theory of simultaneous global revolution that showed how its membership felt that the conditions within Japan could initiate radical change if the necessary push was made.[12] Part of this need for internationalism pushed the RAF to seek connections with other groups operating globally. Most notably, they reached out to the Black Panthers in the United States to give talks in Japan on internationalist solidarity of shared causes.[13]

The RAF embraced violence against the Japanese capitalist state. This was new territory for the Japanese student movement, which had until then been content with distributing pamphlets and organising peaceful protests. The RAF had, at its peak, over 1000 members operating throughout Japan. However, the group operated somewhat autonomously depending on location and had different goals in which different cohorts worked towards revolution through various tactics.[14] The RAF felt that direct confrontation with the state – attacking the police, robbing banks, and learning to use weapons – could provoke the needed clashes to spark revolution. As such, they were heavily surveilled by the Japanese police. During a large rally, the group's leadership attempted to hide their identities with ski masks.[15] Despite such efforts, the police knew the identities of their leadership. When the RAF attempted a more audacious attack on the Japanese Prime Minister, the police quickly arrested hundreds of members. The pressure on the group pushed it to become more clandestine, while also encouraging its members to embrace more ambitious attacks. On 31 March 1970, several members hijacked an airplane and eventually went to North Korea, viewing it as a hub for revolutionary leftism for international movements. However, North Korea rejected the RAF's plan to use North Korea as a base for global revolution as it contravened their understanding of Marxist revolutionary politics.

SHIGENOBU GOES TO LEBANON

With North Korea proving to be an unviable base for the RAF's world revolutionary ambitions, the group searched for other locations where they could receive training and participate in global revolution. With the group in disarray following a wave of arrests,

Shigenobu was aware that the Japanese police would soon arrest her as well. The leadership of the RAF turned its gaze west towards the Middle East and North Africa, and tasked several members with contacting the PFLP which already had a well-established international reputation for its revolutionary struggle since its founding in 1967.[16] As head of the International Relations Bureau of the RAF, Shigenobu was sent to Lebanon alongside Okudaira Tsuyoshi to connect with the Lebanon-based PFLP. To evade Japanese authorities, Shigenobu married Okudaira and took his family name. Traveling as Okudaira Fusako, she departed Japan and began a journey towards Lebanon.

Posing as newlyweds on honeymoon to circumvent questions of a single woman traveling alone, Shigenobu and Okudaira reached Beirut on 28 February 1971.[17] In Lebanon, Shigenobu assumed the role of a foreign exchange student and met with PFLP members at the offices of *al-Hadaf*. While traveling internationally was easier as a married woman, Shigenobu did not abide by traditional gender roles and assumed leadership of the RAF's Lebanon branch without difficulty. Shigenobu organised for around 10 members of the RAF to join their faction at this time in Lebanon, and more would join in later years. RAF members present in Lebanon trained with the PFLP on weapons usage, field training, and guerrilla warfare in Palestinian camps and in Baalbek, northeast of Lebanon. During their training, Shigenobu worked in PFLP offices. The RAF members in Lebanon, led by Shigenobu, distanced themselves from the Japan-based group and deployed a theory of revolution in which the occupation of Palestine was viewed as the culmination of capitalist contradictions and its liberation would ignite global proletarian struggle.

Once firmly established within Lebanon, she assisted in drawing fellow travellers from the Japanese Left to experience the lived revolutionary praxis of the PFLP and the JRA. Two films directors, Wakamatsu Koji and Adachi Masao, came to Lebanon after attending the Cannes Film Festival. In Lebanon, they worked on a newsreel film titled *Red Army/PFLP: Declaration of World War*. This film served as a propaganda vehicle for the JRA and its nascent ideology of global revolution. Within the film, the Palestinian camps were portrayed as sites of revolutionary potential, while Japan was presented as a resolutely capitalist space needing to learn from the international conditions of Palestinians. To push this view forward, the film featured interviews with numerous PFLP and JRA members.

Towards the end of the film, there is an extensive interview with Shigenobu who explicates the reasons for the JRA's presence in Lebanon and its collaboration with the PFLP. Aware that RAF members received criticism for relocating to Lebanon, Shigenobu justified it by explaining that the PFLP engaged in militant struggle and Lebanon served as a staging ground for revolution. For Shigenobu, the conditions within Japan precluded a revolutionary struggle from starting. She argues that, 'I think this points at a problem of the New Japanese Left. When I arrived here and I saw class struggle in Japan, the subjective attempting to enlighten the objective could only be but swept away by the objective current'.[18] According to Shigenobu, Japan – as a resolutely capitalist state – did not have the preconditions needed to enact a successful revolution. Compared to what Shigenobu witnessed in the Palestinian camps, in her eyes, Japan did not meet the conditions for radical change. If revolution could spread beyond Palestine, Shigenobu deemed it possible to change the objective conditions preventing a successful anti-capitalist revolution within Japan.

Even though the RAF leadership encouraged the internationalisation of their group and assisted Shigenobu and others in relocating to Lebanon, some RAF members felt that the relocation of core members to Lebanon diluted the revolutionary strength of the group within Japan as the members abroad focused on causes not immediately applicable to revolution in Japan. Shigenobu remarked that, 'Some say that wanting an international base is idealistic or shows escapist logic, others harshly criticise the Red Army's international base theory'.[19] The diverging goals of the nascent JRA and the established RAF laid the groundwork for a more serious split that would take place the following year. Shigenobu sought to straddle the emerging differences by asserting how her faction still operated within the parameters of the RAF's notion of revolution. For her, the internationalist component was core to revolution. Revolution starting in colonised countries could spread to the metropole; Japan as a metropole country did not have the capacity, in her view, to be an initiator for global revolution.

Shigenobu left Japan when the RAF was still operating with semi-independent groups working towards distinct goals for the wider group. In *Red Army/PFLP: Declaration of World War*, she states that:

> For that reason, I anticipate the emergence of the question of a strategy for world revolution, of how we can defeat world imperialism through military actions in concert with the Black Panthers and Tupamaros [a Marxist-Leninist urban guerrilla group in Uruguay]. Can the problem of 'world party' be discussed fully? In this sense, what we have long talked about … the formation of World Party, World Red Army, World Revolutionary War United Front will be realised only through actual struggle.[20]

The JRA aspired for a World Red Army connecting discrete leftist movements into a singular revolutionary movement. A nationalist outlook towards revolution contravened the ideological goals of Shigenobu. For her, a singular focus on local revolution would not work as it did not sufficiently challenge the capitalist world-system. Rather, a global unified struggle could create the conditions needed for change. Operating in Lebanon, the JRA could help initiate a new site of revolution within Palestine that could be equal to the ongoing one in Vietnam for liberating all peoples. Likewise, the Black Panthers in the US and the Tupamaros in Uruguay represented movements similar, for Shigenobu, to the RAF in advocating for militant revolutionary change. Shigenobu, in her internationalist view of revolution, echoed Che Guevara's famous call for 'two, three, or many Viet-Nams', as a model for global proletarian struggle.[21]

LEADER OF THE JAPANESE RED ARMY

As leader of the RAF members in Lebanon, Shigenobu carved out a distinct path for the group. By late 1971, members were training with the PFLP and in spring 1972, they were preparing for their mission against Lod Airport. The Lebanon-based branch continued to attract members and develop its own ideology distinct from the Japan-based RAF. Due to the distance and intermittent communications, the two groups diverged; the RAF in Japan became the United Red Army and grew intensely antagonistic towards the Lebanon-based group. Shigenobu learned of the Asama Sansō Jiken, a purge of many members of the RAF and hostage standoff that ended the URA as a leftist movement within Japan from late December 1971 to late February 1972, from a phone call she received from Japanese journalist Yamaguchi Yoshiko at the *al-Hadaf* offices.[22] Shortly thereafter, Shigenobu penned a farewell letter to the comrades still in the URA.[23] In this letter, Shigenobu made it clear that the group based in Lebanon was a distinct group from the near defunct Japanese group. While the group based in Lebanon had not yet adopted the moniker Japanese Red Army, it was in effect the JRA.

Several weeks later, Shigenobu became internationally known when the JRA committed the Deir Yassin Operation. Writing communiques and speaking with the media, Shigenobu represented a new form of internationalist leftism. However, Shigenobu, as the head of the JRA, went underground following the Lod Airport Operation to evade being targeted for Israeli reprisals. While in hiding, Shigenobu gave birth to her only child, Shigenobu Mei. The choice of Mei as a first name references both the month of the Lod Airport attack as well as the second kanji used in the Japanese word for revolution 'kakumei'. Even though she was a mother and in hiding, she continued to lead the JRA in its mission for global revolution, drafting political statements and reports on the actions of the JRA.

The next major attack by the JRA was the hijacking of Japan Airlines Flight 404 in 1973 in the Netherlands. Eventually, the hijackers were able to land the plane in Dubai and demanded the release of prisoners held by Japan.[24] The plane went on to Libya where the militants destroyed it after being condemned by the PLO, the PFLP, and the Libyan government.[25] The hijacking was an effort to show that the group persisted and would still target symbols of

Japan. While the attack was much smaller in scope than the one on Lod Airport, the JRA learned that the Japanese government could negotiate with JRA members. As a result, the JRA started to incorporate attacks that would not result in deaths or injuries. Rather, they also undertook hostage-taking missions as a strategy more capable of initiating negotiation with governments.

Moving beyond the Middle East and underscoring the JRA's dedication to global revolution, several militants launched an attack on a Shell Oil facility on Laju Island in Singapore on 30 January 1974.[26] This attack on Shell happened simultaneously with an attack by the PFLP against the Japanese embassy in Kuwait.[27] It was a daring operation that showed that the JRA could fight beyond the confines of the Middle East. It also demonstrated that the JRA remained committed to their idea of global revolution. In communiques related to the attack, they argued that the operation was to undermine US imperialism in Southeast Asia. The Vietnam War still raged and the JRA, in press releases articulating a theory of global revolution, wanted to show that they viewed it as an anti-imperialist war.[28]

In what proved to be a fateful operation, the JRA attacked the French embassy in The Hague, the Netherlands, and took several hostages in September 1974, demonstrating that they could operate on European soil beyond airline hijackings. A witness misidentified one of the assailants as Shigenobu, which resulted in Interpol issuing a warrant for her arrest.[29] This warrant remained in effect, leading to her arrest almost 25 years later in 2000. The next year, in 1975, the JRA also staged a similar hostage operation in Kuala Lumpur in Malaysia. These operations proved costly as they shifted the choice of targets away from ones that the JRA had experience attacking and also saw further international reprisals against the JRA. The last major operation in the 1970s was the hijacking of Japan Airlines Flight 472 that forced the plane to land in Dhaka, Bangladesh, in September 1977.

In subsequent years, the JRA's dwindling membership made it difficult for the group to stage large-scale attacks. Some minor attacks did take place during the later 1970s and 1980s, but these gained little attention. Most importantly, the JRA members still in Lebanon took part in the Palestinian resistance to the Israeli invasion in 1982 of Lebanon.[30] Shigenobu detailed the Israeli invasion of Lebanon and the expulsion of Palestinian fighters from the country following the occupation of Beirut. The monumental shift in the Palestinian leadership's geopolitical position following their expulsion also led to a period of instability for the JRA. Shigenobu and others left Lebanon or went much deeper into hiding. After the expulsion of the Palestinian leadership from Lebanon in 1982, the whereabouts of Shigenobu become murkier as she traversed the globe to sympathetic locations on a false passport. The JRA continued to publish statements showing the movement's reaction to changing geopolitics; it indicated that Shigenobu remained critically engaged with the JRA's history and ideology.

SHIGENOBU'S ARREST AND THE FATE OF THE JRA

In October 2000, Shigenobu was arrested by the police near Osaka. She had entered Japan earlier on a passport with a false name. Interpol's warrant from 1974, when Shigenobu was falsely accused of taking part in a JRA-PFLP operation in The Hague, was the justification used by the Japanese police to arrest her. Notably, the Israeli state never issued an arrest warrant for her as it could not prove that she was connected or in any way responsible for the attack. The trial lasted several months and resulted in a jail sentence of 21 and a half years for Shigenobu.

After her trial, in a statement published on 14 April 2001, Shigenobu took the unprecedented move to dissolve the Japanese Red Army.[31] It marked the closing of a tumultuous period of Japanese leftism. Even though Shigenobu was the head of the JRA, her unilateral decision was met with some backlash from supporters who felt she had exceeded her authority as the group's leader. Regardless of these critiques, the JRA ceased to exist as a formal organisation from that point forward in any real capacity.

Shigenobu's release from prison in May 2022 marked the end of imprisonment of major members of the group and heralded a new reckoning with the JRA and its aftermaths. Minor members remain on the run with their whereabouts unknown. Of the prominent members, only Okamoto Kozo, the sole survivor of the Deir Yassin Operation, remains outside the grasp of Japanese authorities as he resides in Lebanon as a political refugee. Adachi Masao, deported from Lebanon in 2000, continues to talk publicly about his time in the JRA, while Japanese authorities prevent him from leaving Japan. Shigenobu remains active in publishing about her leadership role in the JRA, as well as books of poetry that reflect her views on history and current events ranging from the Nakba to the fiftieth anniversary of the Lod Airport attack to the conflict in Ukraine.[32]

The JRA with Shigenobu leading it represents a unique moment in the history of Japanese leftism and internationalist solidarity with Palestine. She broke the mould of staid Japanese student movements and forged an internationalist path that centred Palestinian liberation as the forefront cause for global liberation and revolution. Aware of the controversies of the movement, she has accepted criticisms of the repercussions for the group's actions in some cases that did not necessarily further their goals and desire for change. Shigenobu's leadership for the JRA also represents a rare moment in leftist internationalism when a Japanese group actively sought radical change abroad and did so for several decades. She broke the confines of the sexism and misogyny rampant across the political spectrum to show how women could lead and theorise a distinct political ideology and praxis in the turbulent 1970s. Even though Shigenobu and the JRA did not directly engage in a feminist revolution, her leadership and the roles accorded to women within the JRA demonstrated that they were equally capable of militant revolution. Her theory of global revolution was a means and vision for the liberation of all oppressed peoples whether Palestinians, women, colonised peoples in Asia or the global proletariat. While the JRA no longer remains a potent force, its actions cast a long shadow on the histories of Japanese leftism and Palestinian internationalism.

NOTES

1. 'Japanese Red Army Founder Fusako Shigenobu Freed from Prison after 20 Years', *Japan Times*, 28 May 2022, www.japantimes.co.jp/news/

2022/05/28/national/crime-legal/fusako-shigenobu-prison-freed/ (accessed 28 May 2022).

2. "'Higai wo ataeta koto wo owabi" Shigenobu Fusako moto saikō kanbu ga shussho-go massaki ni mukatta "shien-sha no shukugakai'", *Daily Shinco*, 31 May 2022, www.dailyshincho.jp/article/2022/05311222/?all=1 (accessed 31 May 2022).

3. Federico Vélez, *Latin American Revolutionaries and the Arab World: From the Suez Canal to the Arab Spring* (London: Routledge, 2017), 105.

4. Francesco Leopardi, *The Palestinian Left and Its Decline: Loyal Opposition* (Singapore: Palgrave Macmillan, 2020), 18.

5. 'Risalat al-nidal al-ʾamimī fī dawr al-fidaʾiyyīn al-yābāniyyīn', *al-Hadaf*, 154, 3 June 1970, 3.

6. William Andrews, *Dissenting Japan: A History of Japanese Radicalism and Counterculture from 1945 to Fukushima* (London: Hurst & Company, 2016); William R. Farrell, *Blood and Rage: The Story of the Japanese Red Army* (Cambridge, MA: Lexington Books, 1990); Patricia G. Steinhoff, 'Portrait of a Terrorist: An Interview with Kozo Okamoto', *Asian Survey* 16, no. 9 (1976): 830–45.

7. Christopher Gerteis, *Mobilizing Japanese Youth: The Cold War and the Making of the Sixties Generation* (Ithaca, NY: Cornell University Press, 2021).

8. Fusako Shigenobu, *Waga ai waga kakumei* (Tokyo: Kōdansha, 1974), 156.

9. The Japanese Left felt that Japan had become a vassal state for the US after the Second World War. Kevin Coogan and Claudia Derichs, *Tracing Japanese Leftist Political Activism (1957–2017): The Boomerang Flying Transnational* (New York: Routledge, 2022), 32.

10. Ibid., 76–7, 191.

11. ANPO comes from anzen hoshō jōyaku [security treaty] by combining the first kanji in anzen and hoshō, respectively. Nick Kapur, *Japan at the Crossroads: Conflict and Compromise after ANPO* (Cambridge, MA: Harvard University Press, 2018), 20–2.

12. Kei Takata, 'Cosmopolitan Publics in Isolation: The Japanese Global Sixties and Its Impact on Social Change' (PhD dissertation, The New School for Social Research, 2015), 142–3.

13. Gerteis, *Mobilizing Japanese Youth*, 51.

14. Patricia G. Steinhoff, 'Hijackers, Bombers, and Bank Robbers: Managerial Style in the Japanese Red Army', *The Journal of Asian Studies* 48, no. 4 (1989): 731.

15. Ibid., 727.

16. Leopardi, *The Palestinian Left*, 15–16.

17. Shigenobu, *Waga ai*, 9–18.
18. Wakamatsu Koji and Adachi Masao, *Sekigun-P.F.L.P: sekai sensō sengen (Red Army /PFLP: Declaration of World War)*, 2009.
19. Ibid.
20. Ibid.
21. Che Guevara, 'Message to the Tricontinental', special supplement, *Tricontinental* (16 April 1967), 24.
22. Fusako Shigenobu, *Kakumei no kisetsu: Paresuchina no senjo kara* (Tokyo: Gentosha, 2012), 72.
23. Nihon Sekigun, *Nihon Sekigun 20-nen no kiseki* (Tokyo: Hanashi no tokushū, 1993), 144.
24. Fusako Shigenobu, *Nihon Sekigun shishi: Paresuchina to tomoni* (Tokyo: Kawade shobō shinsha, 2009), 150.
25. Ibid., 151.
26. Sashō Henshū Iinkai and Sekai Kakumei Sensen Jōhō Sentā, *Taigo o totonoeyo!: Nihon Sekigun sengen* (Tokyo: Sashō shuppan, 1975), 112.
27. Dae H. Chang and Masami Yajima, 'The Japanese Sekigun Terrorists: Red Army Samurai Warriors', *International Journal of Comparative and Applied Criminal Justice* 13, no. 1 (1989): 9–10.
28. Sashō Henshū Iinkai, *Taigo*, 113–14.
29. Mei Shigenobu, 'Fusako Shigenobu, an Open-ended Revolution', *The Funambulist*, 13 April 2022, https://thefunambulist.net/magazine/decentering-the-us/fusako-shigenobu-an-open-ended-revolution (accessed 13 April 2022).
30. Fusako Shigenobu, *Bēiruto 1982 nen-natsu* (Tokyo: Hanashi no Tokushū, 1984).
31. '"4/14 shūkai" meishō to kojinmei de no "kaisan sengen" to nitaisuru gimon', *People's News*, 15 May 2001, 3.
32. Fusako Shigenobu, *Akatsuki no hoshi* (Tokyo: Koseisha, 2022).

6

Marziyeh Ahmadi Osku'i: Guerrilla Poetry between Iran, Afghanistan and India

Marral Shamshiri

On 26 April 1974, a figure dressed in a chador, a full-length woman's veil, ran through the backstreets of Tehran, Iran, closely followed by secret police (SAVAK) agents struggling to keep up. Tapped recordings of the wireless communications between the security agents frantically trying to capture the figure revealed the panic in their voices as they shouted, 'it's a man dressed in women's clothing!'[1] Yet, unbeknown to them, the person they feared was a woman – one of the Iranian communist movement's most important female revolutionaries. In what would be the final moments of her life, Marziyeh Ahmadi Osku'i (1945–1974), a 29-year-old teacher, poet, writer, organiser and guerrilla fighter, courageously pulled out her revolver and engaged in a shoot-out with the secret police. As Marziyeh was eventually outnumbered, she shot at the agents and swallowed a cyanide pill to claim her own life before they shot back and killed her.[2]

Marziyeh was a member of Iran's most prominent Marxist-Leninist organisation in the 1970s, the Organisation of Iranian People's Fada'i Guerrillas (OIPFG), which in 1971 launched an armed movement against the dictatorship of Mohammad Reza Pahlavi, the Shah of Iran. The origins of the armed struggle that she died fighting for lay in June of 1963, when the Pahlavi regime violently crushed massive demonstrations organised by the opposition, shooting thousands of peaceful protestors and killing, wounding and imprisoning hundreds of people. The Iranian Left opposed the Shah's repressive rule and saw him as a 'puppet' of the United States, as a decade prior the CIA-MI6 engineered coup in 1953 had overthrown the democratically elected government of Iran and restored the Shah's power. As a climate of repression strangled the political opposition in the 1960s, a younger generation of leftists including the militant OIPFG were disillusioned with the ineffective traditional political tactics and strategies of the old Left. The OIPFG were among many groups who, influenced by anticolonial revolution in Asia, Africa and Latin America, reached the theoretical conclusion that armed struggle was necessary.

Fada'i guerrilla fighters like Marziyeh operated in clandestine networks and carried cyanide pills on them in case they were captured by the Pahlavi regime's security forces. If caught, it was a courageous and strategic decision to take one's own life rather than risk being arrested and tortured by SAVAK – Iran's notorious secret police force – to give away highly sensitive information about their organisation, comrades and networks. Aged only 29, Marziyeh became one of the many 'martyrs' of the Iranian Left. Marziyeh is remembered and celebrated in leftist circles for being a talented poet and fearless revolutionary. While she became a symbolic figure in the Iranian Left following her martyrdom, she is hardly mentioned in the male-centric historiography of the Iranian Left.[3] In this literature, far less recognition has been granted to the revolutionary lives and political activities of Iranian women in comparison to their male counterparts. As a generation of leftists fought and died in the lead-up to, and in the aftermath of, the Iranian Revolution of 1979, the roles and contributions of women as historical actors within these movements are yet to be fully documented – yet we have much to learn from revolutionary women such as Marziyeh Ahmadi Osku'i, whose legacy has travelled to unexpected places beyond Iran's borders.

MEMOIRS OF A COMRADE

Marziyeh Ahmadi Osku'i was born on 25 March 1945 in Osku, Azerbaijan, in the northwest of Iran, to a lower middle-class family.

There are few sources with which we can reconstruct Marziyeh's revolutionary life – a selection of her writings and poems were published posthumously as *Memoirs of a Comrade* (1974), her martyrdom is recalled in political and revolutionary pamphlets, she left behind some letters, and she is remembered in the recollections of those who knew her, such as Ashraf Dehghani (b. 1949), Iran's most famous Iranian female revolutionary.[4] Given the repressive conditions in which clandestine revolutionaries operated, unable to leave a trace behind as they moved from one location to the next, *Memoirs of a Comrade* is an important surviving document of the Left which presents a rare portrait of a female revolutionary.

In *Memoirs of a Comrade*, we see the fierce, sensitive and inquisitive observations of a young revolutionary reflecting on her experiences. From a young age, Marziyeh became politically aware of the inequalities around her. She agonised over the differences in her life and upbringing in comparison to those less fortunate than herself in her encounters with friends, orphans, poor classmates, child labourers and workers. As a child, Marziyeh befriended an orphaned girl named Nobar. She noticed the differences in how they lived – while her own mother scolded her for playing in the rubbish bins on the street, Nobar did not have a mother to tell her off and spent hours fishing for shiny objects. Marziyeh witnessed the horrific living conditions that Nobar and her only brother lived in: a collapsed roof, broken walls, bare floors and not even a mattress.[5] As she entered the lives of her poor peers, these formative experiences instilled in Marziyeh a strong sense of justice.

While Marziyeh was not aware of it a young age, her early exposure to poverty and inequality, tied with a maturing sense of right and wrong as a curious young girl, formed the early stages of her political and class consciousness. On one occasion, Marziyeh lied to her mother, claiming that her winter coat no longer fit her so that she could give it to Khalil, the son of a blind and disabled beggar in her neighbourhood. Khalil's mother had died of tuberculosis and he and his father's lives had fallen apart. In her later writings in *Memoirs of a Comrade*, Marziyeh would question her motivations for giving the coat away – she had been proud of her act and wanted her friends to know that she had given it away, and she had done so knowing she had a newer coat to wear. She criticised her younger self for giving the shabbier coat away, and extended her analysis to a critique of the societal acceptance of inequality and the very idea of donation or charity – giving away that which one does not want, rather than a fair and equal distribution of what everyone needs.[6] While she was highly critical of her childhood self, Marziyeh's reflections in her memoir revealed her sincere capacity to analyse and learn from her experiences.

It is unclear if Marziyeh's reflections and observations in *Memoirs of a Comrade* were reworked to present the worldview of her political organisation, the OIPFG.[7] We can assume that Marziyeh would have reached the political conclusions she writes about in her memoir, as her critical mindset led her to apply theoretical knowledge acquired through the likes of revolutionary peers Nader Shayegan, Mostafa Sho'a'iyan, and Hamid Ashraf, to the inequality and injustice she witnessed around her.[8] Marziyeh's love for reading led her to texts including Lenin's *State and Revolution*, which she claimed had an impact on her intellectual development, providing her a lens to see the world with. Crucially, she is remembered for increasing her knowledge about society in order to advance the people's struggle for liberation rather than an interest in increasing her own intellectual capabilities.[9] She was drawn to praxis – implementing what could be done – rather than theory alone.

Marziyeh's pursuit of knowledge and education led her to train professionally as a teacher. After finishing secondary school, she studied at the Teachers' Training College in Tabriz and taught in Osku primary schools for three years before enrolling at the University of Tabriz. However, she left the university within a year and entered the Literacy Corps (Sepah-e Danesh), an educational programme which enlisted young men, and later women with high school diplomas in a two-year national service instead of being drafted in the army. The Literacy Corps, largely formed of the urban middle class, were tasked with teaching formally illiterate children and adults in rural villages of Iran as part of the White Revolution, a series of top-down social, political and economic reforms implemented between 1963 and 1979. The reforms were suggested by the US Kennedy administration as a way to subvert the communist 'red' revolution and modernise Iran.[10] An unanticipated consequence of sending young, urban Iranians to the rural parts of the country was that exposure to the extreme poverty, neglect and struggles in villages radicalised many of them.

In this way, Marziyeh heightened her awareness of class struggle through her experiences spending time with poor families, children and workers in villages in Varamin, a city in the southeast of Tehran close to the Literacy Corps' Training College. She used a class assignment as an excuse to visit the village of Khatun Abad, where workers, including child labourers, largely from the minoritised Azerbaijan and Khorasan regions, were known to work in the scorching kilns of the brick-making industry. Marziyeh was critical of the Shah's land reforms that had resulted in wealthy capitalists purchasing the fertile lands of Varamin villages from villagers for little money in order to maximise their profits in the worst labour conditions.[11] Shocked and angry to witness young children from the ages of 8 to 12 forced into work, she saw 15-year-old boys who looked like aged, old men. A believer in political education, Marziyeh set up a library and sent books to schoolchildren in the villages of Varamin.[12] Talking to workers was also a transformative activity which allowed her to understand the material conditions of poverty and their strategies of resistance.[13] She learned about the kiln workers' strikes in 1954 which had been suppressed by regime forces as protestors were shot and even buried alive.[14]

Young Iranian revolutionaries like Marziyeh were not separated from global events. The global 1960s was a period of political upheaval as radicalised and politically conscious people across the world – students, workers, peasants, trade unionists, revolutionaries, activists – took to protest, rebellion and strikes to fight for a radically better world, inspired in part by the decolonising world and the Third Worldist liberation movements that fought for independence. In Tehran, Marziyeh played a key role in organising the student strike of February–March 1971 at the Literacy Corps Training College.[15] The strike was organised after the sudden arrest of two students to protest the creeping climate of repression at the college. In the context of armed struggle which had begun at the same time, arrests of suspected dissidents, particularly students, were widespread, and oppositional political activity was criminalised and labelled as terrorism in the media in an effort to control the situation.

Marziyeh was known to SAVAK but arrested several months later in May–June 1971. Because of her popularity and the unity of the striking students, SAVAK agents waited until the end of the academic term to arrest her when students could no longer organise.[16] During her interrogation, Marziyeh was even compared to Palestinian revolutionary Leila Khaled, and eventually released. She was sent back to Osku as a way to limit her potential political activities. The students' strike was ultimately successful as the two students were released after 20 days and the students gained tactical experience. It coincided with strikes by the Tehran Bus Company and Varamin sugar cube factory and attracted international attention, which contributed to their victory and SAVAK's release of the students.[17]

THE URBAN FEMALE GUERRILLA

Marziyeh's social awareness and strong desire to move to action led her to organisational politics. Her first experience was in Tabriz, close to her hometown, with the People's Democratic Front (PDF) in 1972 where she singlehandedly set up their Tabriz branch. The PDF joined the OIPFG in 1973, and Marziyeh was known for her organisational abilities which made her a brilliant recruiter and the connecting link between the OIPFG and former PDF members.[18] Like other Fada'i guerrilla fighters of her generation, Marziyeh went underground and became what Lenin termed a 'professional revolutionary', in other words, a full-time devotee to revolutionary activity. In the city, the teamhouse became a base for urban guerrilla activities, where revolutionaries navigated not the rural mountains or forests as the Guevaran and Maoist theories of guerrilla warfare proposed, but the streets and corners of the city instead.[19]

Marziyeh was operating from the same teamhouse as Ashraf Dehghani on the tragic day that she died. Like Marziyeh, Ashraf Dehghani was from the northern Azerbaijan region and knew Marziyeh through her brother, Behrouz Dehghani, who also had a relationship with Marziyeh.[20] Women played an important role in the teamhouse as they provided 'cover' in diverting any suspicion or attention, and they also carried out reconnaissance missions with greater invisibility, as well as tasks such as writing and communication work.[21] Dehghani, a fugitive, became a household name when the OIPFG published her prison memoirs *The Epic of Resistance* in 1973 about her escape from the Shah's prisons – a book which was banned under the Shah. In the teamhouse, Marziyeh edited and rewrote parts of Dehghani's prison memoirs which became the most celebrated Fada'i text.[22] In the mid-1970s Marziyeh's own revolutionary writings, *Memoirs of a Comrade*, joined Dehghani's in circulation.

Yet as academic Peyman Vahabzadeh notes, neither the Dehghani nor Osku'i memoirs – iconic texts from the two most well-known Iranian female guerrilla fighters – were celebrated for their views on gender or femininity, but for the ranks that these women held. While there was some evidence of a gendered sensibility in both of these texts, they largely reproduced a de-gendered and androcentric leftist discourse – a main critique of the Iranian guerrilla movement at large which collapsed and eliminated questions of gender and womanhood even as it recruited women.[23] Women's liberation as the question of the oppression of women in relation to men was subsumed under the proletarian revolution which prioritised class oppression and saw the oppression of women only in relation to the economic system. Women's liberation was dismissed as a bourgeois interest that would come after the leftist revolution.[24] Marziyeh would not have identified as a feminist, and while her writings contain instances of feminist curiosity, her main concern was the class-based struggle. For instance, she agonised over the traveller (kowli) girls that she saw in Ahvaz, southern Iran, who as young as nine years old worked in a brothel. Her reading of this distressing reality was that the capitalist system which required these girls to work had failed them, rather than considering the failures of the patriarchal system.[25]

Marziyeh lived in a teamhouse on Shotordaran Alley in Tehran with high-ranking Fada'is Ashraf Dehghani, Shirin Moazzed, and Hamid Ashraf, a leader of the OIPFG.[26] An underground activity in the teamhouse was intercepting SAVAK radio waves to monitor discussions. They took turns to listen and make notes, working out the code words used by SAVAK agents. The tapping of these radio waves was important as it prevented them from showing up to secret meetings if SAVAK had infiltrated a cell.[27] On the April morning of Marziyeh's death, the four teamhouse members tapped into a SAVAK conversation. Shirin was due to head out to a secret appointment with a new recruit. There was tension in the house as they could not decipher the location of a meeting that the agents had discovered, and Shirin hesitated and asked if they were discussing her meeting point. According to Ashraf Dehghani, Hamid Ashraf dismissed her fears by replying 'no!' in a strong tone, so she headed out.[28] Not long after, Dehghani and Ashraf suddenly jumped up as they realised that the agents had indeed been discussing Shirin's secret meeting place. Marziyeh sprinted out of the house to try and warn Shirin to abandon the meeting.[29] It was this act of courage and bravery to stop her comrade from getting caught by SAVAK that ultimately brought Marziyeh's life to a tragic end.

A woman named Behjat Mahbubi, a sympathiser of the OIPFG from Tabriz, was whom Shirin was due to meet that day, known to both herself and Marziyeh.[30] What they didn't know, however, was that Behjat's cell in Tabriz had been infiltrated by SAVAK and she had given away sensitive information under interrogation. They had forced her to take undercover agents to her appointment to identify Shirin. On that day, Shirin trusted her instinct and she did not show up to the appointment after all. However, she was recognised in the area by Behjat and the agents. Shirin Moazzed tried to swallow a cyanide pill but was obstructed, arrested, and later tragically died under torture.[31] Marziyeh, on the other hand, found herself in the middle of a street shoot-out until the security forces led her to her death. Marziyeh's death and Shirin's capture came as a result of disastrous circumstances: the poor error and practice of the organisation – they later concluded that Shirin should have been prevented from attending her appointment that day since the location on the tapped radio communications was unclear; and the betrayal of Behjat Mahbubi who had given into SAVAK's interrogation to give away information.[32] In this deeply unfortunate incident, Marziyeh showed her fierce courage and commitment in protecting her comrade and organisation.

GUERRILLA POETRY

The lifespan of a guerrilla fighter was short, and Marziyeh and Shirin became immortalised figures in their martyrdom. The name of a Fada'i guerrilla fighter was only made public after their death, as the observation of secrecy was no longer necessary for the individual's underground activities. After her death, some of Marziyeh's revolutionary writings and poetry were collated and published by her political organisation in *Memoirs of a Comrade*. Her experiences from the children, families, workers and people she met throughout her life, especially those who were struggling and living in impoverished conditions, formed the basis for most of her revolutionary writings.

Marziyeh's poetry was dedicated to the armed struggle: tributes to martyrs, the path of liberation, the symbolism of forests, mountains and nature, and dedications to her fellow comrades. In 'Dalgha [Mowj]', meaning wave – which was also Marziyeh's nom de guerre – she depicted a narrow stream in the mountains and valleys which sought to join the sea despite the physical obstacles along the way, knowing that still waters die in their stagnation. This could be understood as a metaphor for joining the armed struggle – and the larger life that being part of the movement would give to a guerrilla fighter. The influence of the renowned Iranian writer and poet, Samad Behrangi, is present in this poem, whose legendary children's book *The Little Black Fish* told the story of a fish who took the courageous journey beyond its local stream to embark on bigger adventures in the sea. His book was banned in Iran and considered an allegory for joining the armed movement against the Shah.

The poem that Marziyeh is widely remembered for within the political movement, 'Eftekhar [Pride]', also known as 'I am a Woman', presents a rare example of a gendered lens on capitalism and armed struggle. It is a powerful expression of the labouring woman in mid-twentieth century Iran who is capable of becoming a revolutionary subject. The woman is a 'worker whose hands move the tremendous machines of factories', a peasant who 'together with her lean cow from dawn to dusk' 'has felt the heavy weight of suffering', and a mother who 'gives birth to her child in the mountains and who mourns the loss of her sheep in the fields'. The poem presents the female subject as being capable of radical change, the 'woman whose eyes reflect the red bullets of freedom, and whose hands are moulded for holding a gun!' While it hints at a Marxist-feminist sensibility, the poem considers the woman as a revolutionary subject only in relation to taking up arms. Yet, this poem, celebrated within the Fada'i movement, is incorrectly attributed to Marziyeh Ahmadi Osku'i – it was in fact written by her dear comrade Paridokht (Pari) Ayati (1952–1977).[33]

Pari Ayati, known by her closest people as Ghazal, became a professional revolutionary with the OIPFG in 1975. Prior to this, she had been a supporter of the Fada'is and spent six months in prison in 1973 interrogated and tortured on charges of carrying revolutionary propaganda.[34] Ayati had written poems from her schooldays, gaining her love for poetry from her father who was a literature teacher. She was a talented singer who even in prison impacted her wardmates with her artistic abilities. Despite the most torturous circumstances, she sang well-known songs with her own lyrics, or put on mime performances in her ward.[35] Ashraf Dehghani, the only surviving woman cadre mentioned in this chapter, explained in a 2017 biography of Ayati that when the Fada'i movement became a mass movement in 1978–79, Fada'i texts were circulated and reprinted by supporters. First, Ayati's poetry was published under Marziyeh's name by the student movement in the US – in the Confederation of Iranian Students National Union, and second, when Marziyeh's 1974 memoirs were republished, members did not know or have information about Fada'i female poets other than Marziyeh, so they incorrectly published several of Ayati's poems in the second edition of *Memoirs of a Comrade.*[36]

The clandestine nature of the armed guerrilla movement in Iran partly explains why Ayati's poem was misattributed to another woman, Marziyeh. Due to untraceable underground activities and the steady annihilation of its core cadres, the organisational memory and collective history of the Fada'is was fragmented and became virtually non-existent. A great many women took part in the armed Iranian guerrilla movement, but only the names of Ashraf Dehghani and Marziyeh Osku'i were exceptionally known as their two respective memoirs had been published. To this day, the names of male leaders and martyrs of the movement are more widely known than Fada'i women such as Pari Ayati or Shirin Moazzed, and even Marziyeh Osku'i, the main exception being Ashraf Dehghani. The poem 'Eftekhar [Pride]' or 'I am a Woman', then, must be remembered as written by Pari Ayati. Like many others, she too tragically died in a shoot-out with SAVAK agents in 1977 after devoting her life to the armed struggle, and leaves us with the tender portrait of labouring Iranian women and an implicit critique of capitalism which would cease to exist without women.[37]

A LEGACY ACROSS BORDERS

Marziyeh Ahmadi Osku'i might have died in 1974, but her legacy did not end there. Her internationalist and transnational legacy remains in how her name, imagery and poetry have travelled across borders to places such as Afghanistan and India. Marziyeh became a celebrated figure in the leftist and women's movements in Afghanistan. To this day, the oldest revolutionary social and political organisation fighting for women's liberation in Afghanistan, the Revolutionary Association of the Women of Afghanistan (RAWA), celebrates Marziyeh alongside other fearless revolutionary women such as Clara Zetkin, Rosa Luxemburg, Sakine Cansız, Meena Keshwar Kemal, and others. Meena was a revolutionary Afghan woman and political activist who founded RAWA in 1977 aged 20 at the University of Kabul. From her schooldays, Meena was deeply engaged in social issues and activism. Her history teacher and mentor, Madame Nooria, had given Meena a memoir written by Ashraf Dehghani, *The Epic of Resistance*.[38] Marziyeh's memoirs too would have most likely circled to the revolutionary women's movement in Afghanistan. Meena, like Marziyeh, was assassinated by secret agents and her life was cut short aged 30 in Quetta, Pakistan.

Meena's organisation, RAWA, has remained at the forefront of organising for Afghan women's liberation. RAWA has consistently opposed fundamentalism and condemned local patriarchs such as the Taliban and ISIS for their violence and tyranny against women and girls, as well as international actors such as the US and NATO, who are responsible for aerial bombings and other weapons of war which have devastated Afghanistan since 2001. Today, RAWA contends that 'civil society' and NGO approaches to women's liberation in Afghanistan cannot liberate women. Independence, freedom and liberation for women will not come from 'reactionaries and their foreign imperial masters' but from within.[39] In many of RAWA's publications, posters and events, we see the imagery and in fact incorrectly attributed name of Marziyeh Osku'i raised in relation to the poem 'Eftekhar [Pride/I am a Woman]'. A practical reason why the Afghan movement has claimed Marziyeh as a celebrated martyr is the similarity in Persian language between Farsi, used in Iran, and Dari, used in Afghanistan, which has allowed for a meaningful engagement with her writings and poetry.

Beyond Afghanistan, Marziyeh Ahmadi Osku'i's name has found a permanent home in the prominent cultural sphere of the Indian Left. The iconic Indian street play 'Aurat [Woman]', written in 1979 by Safdar Hashmi and staged by the left-wing people's street theatre group, Jan Natya Manch (Janam), begins with the full cast reading a version of the poem 'Eftekhar [Pride/I am a Woman]' – wrongly but in any case attributed to Marziyeh Osku'i. The poem was translated by the Indian poet Keshav Malik and Safdar Hashmi, the communist playwright and cultural activist who co-founded Janam.[40] Janam was founded in 1973 by young radicals who believed in making amateur theatre accessible to the people, using culture as a way to powerfully engage workers, revolutionaries and activists with political issues on the streets. Unlike Pari Ayati's original, the final lines of the poem which valorised armed struggle were modified in the translation to replace the picking up of a gun with the raising of a red flag. Challenging bourgeois theatre in the same tradition as Berthold Brecht, Hashmi, who was also a member of the Communist Party of India, believed street theatre to be a 'militant political theatre of protest. Its function is to agitate the people and to mobilise them behind fighting organisations'.[41]

Building on Pari Ayati's ideas, Hashmi's play showed that in order to challenge patriarchy, the capitalist structure also had to be dismantled, and used street theatre as an opportunity to share socialist-feminist ideas. Extending the themes in 'Eftekhar [Pride/I am a Woman]', the play critiques bourgeois definitions of womanhood, painting a picture of the everyday woman instead to show the links between gender, class, womanhood and revolution. The woman is a worker in the factory, an animal-rearing peasant working in the fields, and a creator, in producing capitalism's workers. Without women, there would be no reproduction, no labour-power, and thus no capitalism. As a play written and deeply connected to the Indian Left, 'Aurat [Woman]' is unique in its gendered critique of capitalism by articulating the revolutionary subject among the peasant and working classes as the woman.[42]

The play became 'a landmark play of the women's movement in the country' and has been performed more than 2500 times, translated into almost all Indian languages, and has been produced in Pakistan, Bangladesh and Sri Lanka.[43] In bringing issues of women's experiences at home, such as various forms of male violence, dowry deaths and bride burning, to a public audience, the play contributed to and impacted feminist consciousness-raising in India in the 1980s as a large-scale movement against violence against women emerged. Janam's plays continue to be performed in working-class neighbourhoods, villages and factories. While the translated poem continues to be incorrectly attributed to Marziyeh Ahmadi Osku'i, perhaps this matters somewhat less than the fact that the powerful political message raised in Pari Ayati's poem, originating in a specific Iranian context of peasant and working women's experiences, was able to reach and speak to a much wider audience on a universal issue – women and their position and relationship to capitalism. We can guess that Marziyeh would have been moved to know that her comrade Pari Ayati's guerrilla poetry had reached the working classes beyond Iran through a radical form of theatre.

Revisiting Marziyeh's tragically short yet impactful revolutionary life marks her on the map of the 1960s–70s generation of the Iranian Left and the longer history of the Iranian Revolution of 1979. As a teacher, militant, poet, writer and organiser, Marziyeh's political activities and underground contributions to the Iranian armed movement took place within Iran, but her muddled legacy powerfully lives on in the revolutionary and progressive movements of the region. Centring her life shows us both the revolutionary commitment and courage of several Iranian women as well as insights into the material reasons why a generation of Iranians sought to topple the Shah's regime. It shows us how, in fact, the guerrilla poetry of her comrade, Pari Ayati, presented ideas about womanhood that resonated across borders because the experience of working women under capitalism and imperialism was, and is, for the most part universal. At the same time, the male-dominated politics of the Left has contributed to Ayati's erasure in the movement's historical memory. Marziyeh's political activities – in organising, writing, teaching and operating underground – were based on her belief in moving to action, and she leaves us with a lesson to not only notice injustice around us, but to do something about it.

NOTES

1. Ashraf Dehgani, 'Qoqnus-e Sorkh', in *Khaterati az yek rafiq* [Memoirs of a Comrade], by Marziyeh Ahmadi Osku'i, 3rd ed. (Berlin: Iranian People's Fada'i Guerrillas Publications, 2016), 54.
2. Ashraf Dehghani, *Bazrha-ye* (Berlin: Iranian People's Fada'i Guerrillas Publications, 2005), 102–8.

3. For example, Maziar Behrooz, *Rebels with a Cause: The Failure of the Left* (London: I.B. Tauris, 1999); Peyman Vahabzadeh, *A Guerrilla Odyssey: Modernization, Secularism, Democracy, and the Fadai Period of National Liberation in Iran, 1971–1979* (Syracuse, NY: Syracuse University Press, 2010); Ali Rahnema, *Call to Arms: Iran's Marxist Revolutionaries* (London: Oneworld Academic, 2021). Exceptions include Dehghani, *Bazrha-ye*; Naghmeh Sohrabi, 'Writing Revolution as if Women Mattered', *Comparative Studies of South Asia, Africa and the Middle East* 42, no. 2 (2022): 546–50.

4. Marziyeh Ahmadi Osku'i, in *Khaterati az yek rafiq* [Memoirs of a Comrade], by 3rd ed. (Berlin: Iranian People's Fada'i Guerrillas Publications, 2016). It has not been translated into English.

5. Ibid., 74–80.

6. Ibid., 83–92.

7. Vahabzadeh, *Guerrilla Odyssey*, 209; Sohrabi, 'Writing Revolution', 548.

8. Ashraf Dehghani, 'Chehreh-haye Mandegar', *CPI*, n.d., https://cpiran.org/2020/2/maghalat/page7.html (accessed 10 December 2022).

9. Osku'i, *Khaterati*, 63.

10. Farian Sabahi, 'The Literacy Corps in Pahlavi Iran (1963–1979): Political, Social and Literary Implications', *CEMOTI* 31 (2001): 191–220.

11. Osku'i, *Khaterati*, 133.

12. Ibid., 63.

13. Ibid., 133–48.

14. Ibid., 149.

15. Dehghani, 'Qoqnus-e Sorkh', 30.

16. Osku'i, *Khaterati*, 63–4.

17. Ibid., 184–5.

18. Vahabzadeh, *Guerrilla Odyssey*, 209.

19. See Rasmus Elling, '"In a Forest of Humans": The Urban Cartographies of Theory and Action in 1970s Iranian Revolutionary Socialism', in *Global 1979: Geographies and Histories of the Iranian Revolution*, eds. Arang Keshavarzian and Ali Mirsepassi (Cambridge: Cambridge University Press, 2021), 141–77.

20. Dehghani, 'Qoqnus-e Sorkh', 34–5.

21. Vahabzadeh, *Guerrilla Odyssey*, 209, 375; Sohrabi, 'Writing Revolution', 548.

22. Vahabzadeh, *Guerrilla Odyssey*, 210.

23. Ibid.

24. For the literature on the 'woman' question, see Haideh Moghissi, *Populism and Feminism in Iran: Women's Struggle in a Male-De-*

fined Revolutionary Movement (New York: St. Martin's Press, 1994); Hammed Shahidian, 'The Iranian Left and the "Woman Question" in the Revolution of 1978–79', *International Journal of Middle East Studies* 26, no. 2 (1994): 223–47; Parvin Paidar, *Women and the Political Process in Twentieth Century Iran* (Cambridge: Cambridge University Press, 1995); Minoo Moallem, *Between Warrior Brother and Veiled Sister: Islamic Fundamentalism and the Politics of Patriarchy in Iran* (Berkeley, CA: University of California Press, 2005); Manijeh Nasrabadi, '"Women Can Do Anything Men Can Do": Gender and the Affects of Solidarity in the U.S. Iranian Student Movement, 1961–1979', *Women's Studies Quarterly* 42, no. 3/4 (2014): 127–45; Shahrzad Mojab, 'Women and Revolution in the Middle East', in *Handbook on Women in the Middle East*, eds. Suad Joseph and Zeina Zaatari (New York: Routledge, 2023), 197–211.

25. Osku'i, *Khaterati*, 157–63.

26. Dehgani, *Bazrha-ye*, 109; Rahnema, *Call to Arms*, 474. Today, the street is named Martyr Diyani Alley.

27. Dehghani, *Bazrha-ye*, 103.

28. Ibid., 105. Dehghani reflects on the typically male reaction to say 'no' to women, and notes how upset Hamid Ashraf was by the situation as he was partially to blame for sending her out.

29. Dehghani, *Bazrha-ye*, 105.

30. Ali Moradi Maragheie, 'Chegunegi-ye Marg-e Marziyeh', *Yuldashlar*, 5 January 2017, http://solanzh.blogfa.com/post/429#_edn5 (accessed 1 December 2022); ibid., 105.

31. Dehghani, *Bazrha-ye*, 108.

32. Ibid.

33. Ashraf Dehghani, 'Ghazal-e Sorkhe Ma', *Ashraf Dehghani Website* March–April 2017, https://ashrafdehghani.com/pdf/RGhazale-sorkhe-ma.pdf (accessed 1 December 2022), 3.

34. Ibid., 8.

35. Ibid., 10.

36. Ibid., 14–15, 17.

37. Ibid., 19.

38. Melody Ermachild Chavis, *Meena: Heroine of Afghanistan* (New York: St Martin's Griffin, 2004), 19.

39. 'Sisters, Let's Break the Chain of Foreign Domination and Local Despotism with a Resolute Struggle!' *RAWA*, 7 March 2018, www.rawa.org/rawa/2018/03/07/sisters-let-s-break-the-chain-of-foreign-domination-and-local-despotism-with-a-resolute-struggle.phtml (accessed 1 December 2022).

40. Dia Da Costa, *Politicizing Creative Economy: Activism and a Hunger Called Theater* (Champaign, IL: University of Illinois Press, 2016), chapter 4.
41. Safdar Hashmi, 'The Tradition of Street Theatre', in *The Right to Perform: Selected Writings of Safdar Hashmi* (Delhi: Sahmat, 1989), 9.
42. Richa Nagar, 'Women's Theater and the Redefinitions of Public, Private, and Politics in India', *ACME: An International Journal for Critical Geographies* 1, no. 1 (2002): 55–72.
43. 'A Play Called "Woman"', *Google Arts and Culture*, n.d., https://artsand-culture.google.com/story/a-play-called-woman-jana-natya-manch/hQXRwxo8TRcA8A?hl=en (accessed 1 December 2022).

7

Madame Bình and Madame Nhu: The Vietnamese Woman as Icon of Solidarity in Palestine and Iran

Thy Phu, Evyn Lê Espiritu Gandhi and Donya Ziaee

During the Second Indochina War (1955–75), known as the Vietnam War in the United States and the War of National Salvation against the US in Vietnam, communist North Vietnam and republican South Vietnam projected different visions of a revolutionary internationalist woman. In the North, Nguyễn Thị Bình represented a form of modern femininity in her public role as an advocate of the communist-sympathetic Provisional Revolutionary Government–National Liberation Front (PRG-NLF). At the Paris Peace Accords of 1973, she understood the importance of presenting herself in a way that playfully reversed clichés about the so-called Orient. 'After all', she reminisced in her memoir, 'a gentle, petite woman from a land where war raged had stood before them, speaking with reason and feeling. Indeed, our first steps had created sympathy among the press'.[1] Significantly, Madame Bình appeared at the Paris Peace Accords wearing an áo dài, the traditional Vietnamese dress, as a gendered display of nationalism (figure 7.1). Her self-consciously feminine demeanour enabled the PRG-NLF delegates to appear progressive in contrast to the representatives of the southern Republic of Vietnam, who, seated alongside the all-male delegation of US diplomats, projected an old-boys' club cronyism.

While the connection between socialist liberation and female emancipation first emerged in the Soviet and Chinese revolutions, the revered communist Vietnamese leader Hồ Chí Minh also

Figure 7.1   Nguyễn Thị Bình wearing áo dài at the Paris Peace Talks, 1971. Courtesy Getty Images.

expressed his commitment to women in several speeches. At a 1959 Cadres' meeting, he declared that '[w]omen make up half of society. If they are not liberated, half of society is not freed. If women are not emancipated only half of socialism is built'.[2] Madame Bình's presence at the Paris Peace talks seemed to bring to fruition this socialist promise of women's emancipation, which aligned with the Vietnam Women's Union's (VWU) 'three responsibilities' movement, in which women were tasked with recruiting soldiers, labouring at home and in factories, and fighting on battlefields (figures 7.2 and 7.3). The 'three responsibilities' movement was heavily promoted by the socialist state-run Vietnam News Agency, and as such, many images presenting the northern Vietnamese revolutionary woman as militant mothers in battle were circulated.

However, leaders in the North were not the only ones to claim women as allies and to broadcast their vision of the revolutionary Vietnamese woman. In South Vietnam, Madame Nhu (Trần Lệ Xuân) projected a competing version of this figure. In contrast to Madame Bình's modesty, Madame Nhu favoured an elegantly

Figure 7.2   Peasant harvesting crops. Photograph by: Le Minh Truong.

Figure 7.3   Women clearing a road. Photograph by: Le Minh Truong.

immodest style of áo dài, which Saigon-based intellectuals worried bore the taint of foreign influence (figure 7.4). Traditionalists revered the áo dài as a hallmark of a distinct Vietnamese national identity. This dress, however, has evolved over the course of the nineteenth and twentieth centuries to incorporate foreign fashions. In the 1960s, the increased presence of US advisers and soldiers brought urgency to the issue of foreign influence as the injection of billions of US dollars in aid encouraged corruption, created a market for sex work, and stimulated a black market of illicit goods, drugs and services. Signs of this influence are visible in Saigonese fashions, as women adopted elements of risqué Western dress. Accordingly, the hemlines of the áo dài inched higher, while the stiff mandarin collars that hid the neckline disappeared – a style that Madame Nhu favoured and popularised.

As de facto First Lady, Madame Nhu symbolised South Vietnam through her dress. When magazines remarked on her

Figure 7.4 Madame Nhu wearing áo dài. Courtesy Getty Images.

open-necked áo dài, they also speculated on how open she, and by extension the southern Diệm regime, was to US influence. While in the communist North Madame Bình's embodiment of gendered nationhood and revolution was characterised by modest virtue, Madame Nhu crafted an image of grandeur. These competing versions of the revolutionary Vietnamese woman within a divided Vietnam lay bare the contested terms in which women and revolution came into visibility and were cohered into visual icons during the war.

Only one version of the revolutionary Vietnamese woman icon, however, would survive the end of the war and circulate globally, inspiring other revolutionary struggles of Third World liberation. In the wake of Madame Nhu's exile following the 1963 assassination of her brother-in-law, South Vietnamese president, Ngô Đình Diệm, and her husband, Ngô Đình Nhu, the republican interpretation of this icon disappeared. Thus, the northern vision of the revolutionary Vietnamese woman as a symbol of socialism ultimately won out. The example and symbolism of the communist militant Vietnamese woman was significant to many of the national liberation movements across Africa, Asia and Latin America in the 1970s and beyond.

Yet the meaning of this revolutionary woman icon did not remain static or the same, as it gained global resonance and became incorporated into different traditions of revolutionary struggles around the world. In Vietnam, internal contests for moral authority on the question of female liberation and revolution underscored the icon's fluidity. In Palestine, freedom fighters sought to borrow the spotlight focused on the then highly visible war in Vietnam to illuminate their own, relatively overshadowed, struggle. In Iran, feminist activists who strove to advance women's emancipation against the patriarchal influence of religious authoritarianism and leftist freedom fighters took inspiration from the figure of the revolutionary Vietnamese woman. The very malleability and portability of the icon of the revolutionary Vietnamese woman made this image amenable to, if not always successful in, brokering a sense of shared experiences and political objectives between different Third World liberation movements and their struggles for women's emancipation during the global Cold War.

VIETNAM TO PALESTINE: ONE STRUGGLE, MANY FRONTS

The Vietnamese War for independence inspired contemporaneous struggles for national liberation around the world. The Palestinian national liberation movement, for example, praised the war as a 'struggle of a small Third World people against the greatest power of the North'.[3] During the 1960s and 1970s, Vietnam and Palestine were linked in their struggle against US Cold War policies which were driven by an agenda of socialist containment. In the 1950s, the US had intervened in Vietnam to deter the spread of communism, combat Soviet Union influence and defend capitalist interests in Asia. In the mid-1960s, the US perceived the Soviet Union as opening a 'second front' in the Middle East and moved to support Israel against a coalition of Arab states led by Egypt's president, Gamal Abdel Nasser.[4] After the June 1967 Arab-Israeli War, the US president, Lyndon B. Johnson, agreed to sell Phantom jets, which were used in Vietnam, to Israel. This sale marked the start of a sharp increase in US military, economic and political aid to Israel at the expense of Palestinian self-determination.

Despite US foreign policy objectives, connections between northern Vietnamese leaders and Palestinian liberation fighters flourished through independent circuits of solidarity. Flouting a Cold War logic of containment, Palestinian and Vietnamese militants highlighted points of connection between their movements, drawing rhetorical and visual parallels between their goals of anti-imperialist national liberation. The icon of the Vietnamese woman formed an important visual part of this solidarity. Notably, the version of the icon that circulated in Palestine privileged the northern Vietnamese project of national liberation while viewing the southern Vietnamese vision of anti-communist republicanism as aligned with US imperialist interests.

In 1970, Fatah, the largest Palestinian resistance organisation at the helm of the Palestine Liberation Organisation (PLO), circulated a poster drawing parallels between the Palestinian and Vietnamese struggles for national independence by using the icon of the revolutionary Vietnamese woman (figure 7.5).[5] This poster was part of a 'Fateh 5' Series celebrating five years since the official launch of the Palestinian Revolution in 1965.[6]

The poster made a clear visual analogy between the struggles in Palestine and Vietnam. Seeking to capitalise on Vietnam's

Figure 7.5   'Palestine-Vietnam'. Photographer unknown. Published by the Palestinian National Liberation Movement as part of the Fatah 5 Series, 1970. Courtesy Palestine Poster Project Archives (Portfolio 1201-1300).

international visibility, the comparatively overlooked Palestinian liberation movement used the visual iconography of the northern Vietnamese struggle against the US to garner international support for its cause. Black text written in English frames two side-by-side black-and-white photographs of different women resisting male figures of authority. In capital letters, the overhanging text designates the left photograph as 'PALESTINE' and the right one as 'VIETNAM'. The equal height of the two rectangular photographs suggests a parallelism, though not necessarily equivalence: the Palestinian photograph is slightly wider, implying its prominence and making the overall poster asymmetrical. Likewise, the Vietnamese and Palestinian national liberation struggles were not viewed as equivalent. While the two struggles identified common goals and points of solidaritiy, they also attended to historical specificity, such as the different legacies of French and British colonialism, and the role of direct US military intervention in Vietnam versus US support of the Zionist Israeli state.

The poster reflected increasing political connections between the revolutionary movements.[7] By 1968, North Vietnam and the PLO had established diplomatic ties. In March 1970, Yasser Arafat and a delegation of Palestinian liberation fighters visited President Hồ Chí Minh and General Võ Nguyên Giáp in Hanoi. The Palestinian liberation fighters imagined turning the Middle East into a 'Second Vietnam' and one of the surrounding Arab capitals, such as Amman or Beirut, into an 'Arab Hanoi', which would serve as a revolutionary base modelled on the Vietnamese strategy.[8] Three years later, the PLO was invited to take up the 'banner of the global struggle' from communist Vietnamese freedom fighters at the 1973 Tenth World Festival of Youth and Students in East Berlin.[9]

What is surprising, then, is not Fatah's invocation of the Vietnamese liberation struggle but rather the choice to feature the revolutionary Vietnamese *woman* to symbolise that struggle in this poster, since Fatah's own default image of Palestinian resistance consisted of an armed *man* wearing a black-and-white keffiyeh. To invoke the international power of the icon of the revolutionary Vietnamese woman and provide a visual parallel, Fatah substituted its typical masculinist image of Palestinian resistance for a photograph of a Palestinian woman, in a move characteristic of 'tropes of women's militancy' becoming a 'defining characteristic' of the transnational Third World movements for liberation.[10] The icon of the revolutionary Vietnamese woman also inspired many women who joined the Palestinian Revolution. After 1967, a handful of female freedom fighters, many of whom served long sentences in Israeli prison, gained fame, and were upheld as heroic models of Palestinian resistance. Of these, the best-known female armed militant is Leila Khaled.[11]

Khaled captured international attention with her high-profile hijackings of flight TWA 840 on 29 August 1969, and El Al Boeing 707 on 6 September 1970, conducted to bring international attention to the Palestinian cause. This bold act of hijacking, combined with an iconic photograph of Khaled – 'the gun held in fragile hands, the shiny hair wrapped in a keffiah, the delicate Audrey Hepburn face refusing to meet your eye' – solidified her, in the words of the British *Guardian*'s Katharine Viner, as 'the symbol of Palestinian resistance and female power' (figure 7.6).[12] Although her time as an active commando was brief, cut short by her rise to fame and subsequent lack of anonymity (necessary for hijacking missions), Khaled became an emblem of female Palestinian resistance, whose image has subsequently been reproduced in murals, posters and zines, and whose story has served to inspire contemporary Palestinian women continuing to fight for social and national liberation.

Throughout her continued activism, Khaled expressed solidarity with the Vietnamese struggle for national liberation. In her autobiography *My People Shall Live*, published in 1973 when she was just 28 years old, Khaled describes how the Vietnamese revolutionaries were 'a great source of inspiration' for her decision to join the Palestinian armed struggle:

Here was a small nation in black pyjamas fighting the mightiest empire in world history and defeating it. As Johnson intensified his bombing attacks, and as his generals promised him victory if only more tons of bombs were dropped in Vietnam, I became angrier and angrier with myself for not being able to do anything to protest or undermine American savagery.[13]

Determining that the 'Palestinians must learn the secrets of the Vietnamese', she connects Vietnam and Palestine via a larger Third World struggle against US imperialism:

I went to Frankfurt in the full knowledge that we, the Palestinians, the children of despair and now of revolution, were carrying the torch of freedom and human liberation on behalf of humanity: if we failed, America would have succeeded in reversing the tide of the world revolution, with the notable exception of Vietnam.[14]

Figure 7.6 Hijacker holding machine gun, Bettmann, 17 October 1969. Courtesy Getty Images.

Khaled identified with the Vietnam struggle so intimately that when she heard of Hồ Chí Minh's death in 1969, she felt struck by 'lightning', like 'a part of me had died'.[15] Khaled's words underscore the importance of the Vietnamese revolution for Palestinian women fighting for liberation.

IRANIAN IMAGINARIES OF THE REVOLUTIONARY VIETNAMESE WOMAN

During the 1960s and 1970s in Iran, the leftist opposition to the dictatorship under the Shah, Mohammad Reza Pahlavi, drew on the icon of the northern revolutionary Vietnamese woman within its own visual idiom of revolutionary struggle. Visual representations of these women highlighted their role as fearless fighters in armed combat – informed by the Iranian Left's own imaginaries of revolutionary womanhood. Pamphlets produced by two leftist groups demonstrate this remediation and its limitations. Relying on the revolutionary Vietnamese woman – here as an archetype for a desexualised female fighter – whose emancipation was found in anti-imperialist struggle alone, these groups' reinterpretation of this icon reinforced their limited view of women's militancy and liberation. This interpretation further occluded the possibility for a genuine articulation of cross-border solidarity.

The Iranian Left's construction of militant womanhood cannot be understood apart from the geopolitics of the global Cold War. Given its strategic location and oil reserves, Iran was an important source of military, political and economic competition between the two great powers. Beginning with the Azerbaijan crisis of 1946, which concluded with Iran officially in the pro-US camp, the country was the site of several events central to the Cold War, most notably the CIA-MI6-led coup against Prime Minister Mohammad Mosaddegh in 1953. As mass unrest grew in Iran in the 1960s and 1970s in response to increasing political suppression, the Shah introduced a series of pre-emptive reforms from above, which he dubbed the 'White Revolution', in an attempt to prevent a red revolution. These reforms, and US support for the Shah's brutal royal absolutism, only exacerbated popular discontent and a growing cultural and social backlash against the West. Against this backdrop, both the Shah and various oppositional forces instrumentalised gender and womanhood to further their political agendas, and the figure of the revolutionary Vietnamese woman was invoked by the Left in politicised ways.

Some segments of the Iranian Left referenced the revolutionary Vietnamese woman as a potent icon in constructing imaginaries of militant womanhood. Several organisations described, analysed and provided visual representations of Vietnamese women in material they circulated both internally and to the broader public. In 1967, the Revolutionary Organisation of the Tudeh Party of Iran (ROTPI) produced a pamphlet containing three essays on women in Vietnam, including first-hand reports from a delegation to Vietnam in 1965, as well as nine photographic representations of female Vietnamese fighters. The ROTPI was a Maoist offshoot of the Tudeh Party – the most organised and influential communist party in Iran, formed in 1964 when members of the youth section broke off from the leadership. The Organisation of Iranian People's Fada'i Guerrillas (OIPFG) was a Marxist guerrilla group that, by the 1970s, was Iran's most prominent armed organisation. In 1985 an OIPFG women's committee in the province of Sistan-Baluchestan designed a pamphlet on the occasion of International Women's Day and featured an essay on the role of women's struggles in Germany, Bolivia, El Salvador and Vietnam.

Despite political differences between the two organisations, the pamphlets from the ROTPI and OIPFG had some shared understanding of Vietnamese and Iranian women's struggles, including in the dominant imaginary of a militant womanhood. The ROTPI pamphlet's cover page exemplifies the visual representation of Vietnamese women in these documents. It features a photo of armed women fighting shoulder-to-shoulder with their male counterparts on the frontlines of combat, with the words 'Women in Vietnam' in large print at the top. The image visually summarises a prevailing theme in ROTPI and OIPFG writings: praise of Vietnamese women for taking up arms alongside their brothers towards victory. This sentiment is paralleled in an iconic poster by the OIPFG, which features an armed and resolute Iranian woman named Mandana standing triumphantly next to male fighters, with the popular refrain of the period featured at the top: 'No revolutionary victory is possible without the active participation of women' (figure 7.7).[16]

The images in this literature are strikingly devoid of any representation of Vietnamese women outside fields of combat (figure 7.8), echoing much of the official rhetoric in the Vietnamese liberation movement itself about the martial skills, courage and heroism of these 'long-haired warriors', to quote Hồ Chí Minh. The OIPFG report details how the Vietnamese struggle unleashed the military, political and intellectual capacities of women, particularly their tenacity in guerrilla warfare.[17] Similar themes about Vietnamese

Figure 7.7 Poster from the Organisation of Iranian People's Fada'i Guerrillas marking International Women's Day, n.d. The larger text at the top reads: 'No revolutionary victory is possible without the active participation of women'. Ken Lawrence collection, 1940–2010, HCLA 6312, Special Collections Library, University Libraries, Pennsylvania State University.

women's military expertise emerge in an essay from the ROTPI that was written after a visit in 1965 by a delegation from the group to the People's Liberation Armed Forces – communist guerrillas who had infiltrated South Vietnam to oppose the Diệm administration and its US allies. The report remarks on the substantial number of women engaged in direct combat, the command of military units, the maintenance of security in liberated villages, the organisation of the peasantry, and education and training. It also speaks at length about displays of self-sacrifice, revolutionary faith, and emotional and physical strength by Vietnamese women on the frontlines and in prisons.

At first glance, visual representations of Vietnamese women in this literature appear not only to correspond to the image crafted and propagated by the socialist-aligned Vietnamese national liberation struggle itself but also to provide a promising display of internationalist solidarity. Yet, a closer examination reveals their failure to

Figure 7.8   Photograph of woman demonstrating her martial skill. From Women in Vietnam, a pamphlet of essays published in 1967 by the Revolutionary Organisation of the Tudeh Party of Iran. Courtesy Archiv für Forschung und Dokumentation Iran (AFDI).

reflect Vietnamese women's complex subjectivity and multilayered strategies of resistance.

The male-dominated Left in Iran reduced Vietnamese women's quest for liberation to anti-imperialist struggle alone and muted their efforts to organise for women's emancipation. The revolutionary Vietnamese woman served as archetype for a desexualised female revolutionary, whose liberation lay in her undivided dedication to national struggle. This process of remediation reinforced the Iranian Left's tendency to give short shrift to the issue of male domination. Instead, the icon of the revolutionary Vietnamese woman was conjured in ways that bolstered these organisations' overall blindness to women's attempts at addressing the specificity of their gendered experiences as part of the larger revolutionary struggle. It also distorted the image that Vietnamese revolutionaries, at least among the Vietnam Women's Union, held of themselves. This significantly hindered the capacity of the Iranian Left to articulate genuine solidarity with Vietnamese women.

Women's bodies became a site of political contestation for the Left partly in response to top-down gender reforms undertaken by the Shah, which, while allowing for improvements in women's legal status, exacerbated the state's control over women's bodies, labour and sexuality by the late 1970s. Yet, rather than meaningfully expand the question of women's liberation beyond the state's individual rights-based approach, the revolutionary Iranian Left subsumed gender-based concerns under class and national struggles, expressing an overall hostility towards autonomous feminist politics.[18] The Left's crafting of the female revolutionary subject revealed key ideological blind spots relating to gender politics and women's emancipation. The pamphlets produced by the ROTPI and OIPFG highlighted the importance of women's political participation but were discernibly silent on the distinct needs, interests and challenges of women in the Vietnamese liberation struggle.

Iranian women refused to remain passive in the face of this male-defined revolutionary movement. On 8 March 1979, only a few short weeks after the Pahlavi monarchy toppled, they took to the streets of Tehran in unprecedented numbers. Responding to statements made by leader Ayatollah Khomeini about the need for mandatory hejab (veiling) and occupational gender segregation, they poured out in the hundreds of thousands in commemoration of International Women's Day to register their discontent with the fruits of the revolution. While these women were united by their opposition to mandatory veiling, the struggle for many activists went much further. This was a movement not only to protect women's individual rights and freedoms but also to safeguard the revolution's egalitarian spirit and promises of liberation. Unhappy that other political and economic grievances overshadowed their concerns, scores of women took advantage of the brief political opening that emerged with the fall of the Shah to compose and articulate their own demands and to make a case for women's liberation. In their contestations, they created a new and now iconic image of revolutionary womanhood – one that centres women's liberation as a primary site of struggle and resolutely refuses any revolutionary politics that fails to do so.

*   *   *

In Vietnam, Palestine and Iran, the icon of the revolutionary Vietnamese woman highlighted the relationship between national liberation, leftist revolution and women's emancipation. In Vietnam, the North and South vied for political control over the icon of the revolutionary Vietnamese woman, contesting who would wrest moral authority over the question of female liberation and national independence. In Palestine, the icon of the revolutionary Vietnamese woman drew international attention to the relatively overlooked Palestinian national liberation struggle and paralleled Palestinian leaders' attempts to theorise the entanglement of national liberation with women's emancipation. In Iran, the Left remediated the icon of the revolutionary Vietnamese woman as a desexualised guerrilla fighter in service of a male-led revolutionary struggle, erasing gendered demands for liberation. What brought these sites together was not a unified understanding of the meaning of this icon but a variety of interpretations and complex processes through which this icon of the Vietnamese woman was re-envisioned at disparate sites of revolution. Indeed, the 'revolutionary Vietnamese woman' was a multiform category, whose meanings changed as it travelled along asymmetrical circuits of Third World revolution.

NOTES

1. Nguyễn Thị Bình, *Family, Friends, and Country*, trans. Lady Borton (Hanoi: Tri Thức Publishing House, 2013), 154.
2. Bernard B. Fall, ed., *Ho Chi Minh on Revolution: Selected Writings, 1920–66* (London: Pall Mall, 1967), 336.
3. Alain Gresh, 'Reflections on the Meaning of Palestine', *Journal of Palestine Studies* 41, no. 1 (2011): 168.
4. Judith A. Klinghoffer, *Vietnam, Jews and the Middle East: Unintended Consequences* (London: Palgrave Macmillan, 1999); Warren Bass, *Support Any Friend: Kennedy's Middle East and the Making of the US-Israel Alliance* (Oxford: Oxford University Press, 2004); Rashid Khalidi, 'The United States and Palestine', *Cairo Review of Global Affairs* (Spring 2015).
5. Fateh is the Romanised reverse acronym of the Arabic *ḥarakat al-taḥrīr al-waṭanī al-Filasṭīnī*, which means 'Palestinian National Liberation Movement'. Fateh means 'opening', 'conquering' or 'victory'. Sometimes the Anglicised spelling appears as 'Fatah' or 'FATAH'.
6. Palestinian Poster Archive, www.palestineposterproject.org.
7. For more on this history, see Evyn Lê Espiritu Gandhi, *Archipelago of Resettlement: Vietnamese Refugee Settlers and Decolonization across Guam and Israel-Palestine* (Oakland, CA: University of California Press, 2022), 24–34.
8. PFLP, 'Palestine Resistance Rejects Settlement', *Al-Tali'ah* (Kuwait), 30 October 1968, repr. and trans. in *Selected Arab Documents on the Palestinian Fedayeen*, July 1968–February 1969 (Beirut: IPS, 1969). PFLP, *Military Strategy of the P.F.L.P.* (Beirut: Information Department, PFLP, 1970), 65. Both sources quoted in Paul Chamberlin, *The Global Offensive: The United States, the Palestine Liberation Organization, and the Making of the Post-Cold War Order* (Oxford: Oxford University Press, 2012), 26.
9. 'Hadith Sahafi khas Sayyid Yasir Arafat, Rayiss al-Lajanah al-Tanafithiyah al-Munathamah al-Tahir al-Filastiniyah Huwal Qadaya al-Sa'ah', 28 November 1973, *Al-Watha'iq al-Filastiniyyah al-Arabiyah*, 473; Craig R. Whitney, 'East Berlin Festival Week Ends', *New York Times*, 6

August 1973. Both sources quoted in Chamberlin, *The Global Offensive*, 175.

10. Arielle Gordon, 'From Guerrilla Girls to Zainabs: Reassessing the Figure of the "Militant Woman" in the Iranian Revolution', *Journal of Middle East Women's Studies* 17, no. 1 (2021): 67.

11. Hamida Kazi, 'Palestinian Women and the National Liberation Movement: A Social Perspective', in *Women in the Middle East*, ed. Khamsin (London: Zed Books, 1987), 29.

12. Katherine Viner, 'I Made the Ring from a Bullet and the Pin of a Hand Grenade', *The Guardian*, 26 January 2001.

13. Leila Khaled, *My People Shall Live: Autobiography of a Revolutionary as Told to George Hajjar* (London: Hodder & Stoughton, 1973), 88.

14. Ibid., 89, 178.

15. Ibid., 154. For more on how Khaled inspired revolutionary women in Iran in turn, see Gordon, 'From Guerrilla Girls to Zainabs', 67, 77, 84.

16. For more on this image, see ibid., 64–6, 89–90.

17. Organisation of Iranian People's Fada'i Guerrillas (OIPFG), 'Zan-e Baluch'.

18. Hammed Shahidian, *Women in Iran: Gender Politics in the Islamic Republic* (Westport, CT: Greenwood Press, 2002), 129.

8

Sakine Cansız: Women's Liberation and the Kurdistan Freedom Movement

Elif Sarican

On 9 January 2013, nearly ten years to the day of writing this chapter, what is believed to be a Turkish state agent walked into the Kurdistan Information Centre in Paris and assassinated three Kurdish revolutionaries. Among them was Sakine Cansız (1958–2013), nom de guerre Sara, a co-founder of the Kurdistan Workers' Party (PKK) and Kurdish Women's Movement (KWM), prison leader, and an inspiration to millions seeking a better world. As the slogan of the movement she founded – Jin, Jiyan, Azadî (Women, Life, Freedom) – resonates around the world, what can we learn from the life of this extraordinary revolutionary, stalwart warrior for freedom and pioneer of women's liberation?

Despite the status she acquired in the movement and across the globe, Sara was always the epitome of revolutionary humility, the consummate cadre of a movement that emphasises self-reflection and self-criticism. In her stunning memoirs, *My Whole Life Was a Struggle*, published in three volumes, the sheer force of her humanity and will to overcome barriers to revolutionary struggle – and her participation in it – leaps from each page.[1] Fighting the fascism of the Turkish state from without, and patriarchy from within, she established a model of revolutionary struggle that placed women's liberation at the heart of a radical vision of postcolonial freedom.

This is a vision indelibly marked by Sara's singular, uncompromising personality. Her own humility makes her instrumental role in establishing the KWM difficult to detect, but her contribution is recognised by the entire movement. In many ways, therefore, Sara *is* the KWM, embodying its principles, shaping its political perspective, and leading its growth into the mass movement it is today.

THE SHADOW OF GENOCIDE

Sara was both Kurdish and Alevi, a woman, and a revolutionary – all identities suppressed by the Turkish state. Her life was marred by experiences and histories of violence, directed at her because of who she was and what she did. Rather than being defined by this violence, she instead made resistance the decisive feature of her life. Indeed, one of the most beautiful things about Sara's life is her synthesis of these distinct identities, giving coherence and significance to this coming together, an achievement that flew in the face of imperialist attempts to fragment individual identity and subjectivity.

Who Sara was, where she came from, and the political trajectory she took can only be understood in relation to the violence her region of Kurdistan experienced. She was born in 1958, in a village in Dersim, an area in North Kurdistan (in Southeast Turkey). She describes growing up in a Kurdish village of 20 houses at a time when the memories and wounds of the Dersim massacre of 1937 and 1938 were very much alive. The massacre had claimed the lives of up to 30,000 Kurdish Alevis, displaced at least 12,000 more and led to shrinking of the population of most villages due to displacement.[2] Sara was shaped by the omnipotent presence of the Dersim massacre that haunted her childhood through the stories and experiences of those around her; specific tales of what happened in a particular house, on a bridge, by a river – the horrors at the foot of mountains. She was born to a place filled with ghosts.

Dersim is a place of pilgrimage and significance to Alevis as both the site of Düzgün Baba – a legendary tale with many different tellings that is believed to have taken place there – as well as the revered Munzur River. Inhabitants maintained an active and conscious connection to the sun and the fire, the central symbols of Alevi philosophy. Keeping a fire burning in one's home was a long-standing Alevi practice that symbolised the continuity of light and life. As Sara's grandmother explains, in a moving documentary about her life, this ritual practice became a way of representing the insistence on life despite the devastation of the massacre and ongoing oppression.[3]

The massacre, one of the first mass killings after the formation of the Turkish Republic – and many more were to follow – aimed at crushing the Kurdish rebellions occurring in North Kurdistan. The Turkish state killed thousands of Kurdish Alevis, many gassed to death in mountain caves in mass aerial bombardments. Among the pilots of the aerial ambushes was Mustafa Kemal Ataturk's adopted daughter Sabiha Gökçen, the first Turkish female fighter pilot – the Turkish army general command unit would boast about the 'serious damage' she caused with her 50-kilogramme bombs.[4]

The most successful part of the genocide, in the view of the Turkish state, was its long-term political and cultural consequences. Many Kurds of Sara's generation grew up in homes subject to the brutal homogenising project of Turkification under the slogan 'One Nation, One Flag, One Language and One Religion'. Making this fascistic ideology a reality involved an outright ban on the Kurdish language (both in public and, incredibly, in private), attempts at forced religious conversion, destruction of Alevi cultural and faith institutions and the deliberate economic underdevelopment of Kurdish regions. This sped up the assimilation of Kurds as many began fearfully hiding their Kurdish and/or Alevi identities.

As Sara came to understand the impacts of the Dersim genocide more – the fear locals had of 'living those days again' as they implored: 'For heaven's sake, may Düzgün Baba make sure we never live through such days again!'[5] – her politicisation truly began. She was her family's eldest daughter, and forced at a young age into a caring role, raising her brothers, and taking care of the house while her parents were working. Undertaking these household duties as a child, while also attending school forced her to confront the limited societal role allotted to women. She recounts that her first political struggle was for permission to continue her state education beyond primary school.

Such experiences were the norm for women in Kurdistan, but what made Sara extraordinary was her determination to struggle against these roles. Kurdish women could be mothers, daughters, wives, sisters, but not revolutionaries, not politicised people with agency. Sara defied these restrictions early on by insisting on her right to realise all the different parts of herself, her full humanity. This involved a principal struggle against her own mother, the state, the nuclear family, and the men who imposed themselves on her.

Stories of women revolutionaries are often told as though women accidently stumbled upon their political convictions, yet Sara seems to have always intended to live a spectacular, revolutionary life. This is evident in how she describes her discovery of political struggle:

> It was wonderful to arrive, so unconditionally and genuinely, through contradictions and struggles, at an ideal. It was an immense joy, and I will repeat it aloud now: I'm the happiest person in the world because I participate in this struggle.[6]

POLITICAL TURBULENCE AND BUILDING CONNECTIONS

During the 1970s, Turkey was the site of a growing anti-imperialist movement. Leaving Dersim, Sara began to experience life and struggle in Turkey's metropoles. In Izmir, a city in the west of Turkey, she was active in organising workers and mobilising for demonstrations. The inclusive vision of politics is captured in her memoirs, where she recalls that:

> As Kurdistan Revolutionaries, we participate in all anti-colonialist, anti-imperialist, and antifascist actions. We do it out of principle, as our task. This demonstration takes place in Turkey, and through our participation, we support it.[7]

Protests would march against imperialism and chant in solidarity with the people of Eritrea and take inspiration from the revolutionary women of Bulgaria – for Sara, such internationalism and pluralism were natural political instincts.[8] Between Dersim and Izmir, Sara had organised in her school, joined demonstrations and strikes, and had been arrested for political agitation, experiences which connected her with sex workers, Roma women, and many other groups brutalised by the Turkish state. As a child of genocide survivors, she was able to instinctively relate to other oppressed people, invariably extending a curiosity and generosity to those she met.

These traits were even more significant as she encountered the notoriously factional organised Left in Turkey. Sara saw potential in everyone and anyone, insisting on building connections despite other Left organisations' rejection of such 'outcast groups'. She did this in the belief that while these groups may have been outside dogmatic Marxist accounts of political agency (of the proletariat leading a working-class revolution towards a new socialist order), they nevertheless had their own revolutionary capacity. This was impressed upon her when she and her comrades resisted police violence alongside Roma women – a clear reinforcement of her understanding of shared realities under an oppressive state, and of the organic solidarity between people. Afterwards, when having dinner at the house of a Roma woman she reflects:

> The conversation turned to the subject of women and revolution. We talked about what women were able to do when they channelled their hatred of the enemy into organization. We praised the Roma women's courage and assertiveness.[9]

She was inspired by the power and position Roma women had in their families, and their way of life constituted a challenge to the same system she sought to overthrow:

> They lived outside social norms and cared nothing for the existing system. They lived according to their own rules. That was what I so liked about them. My admiration for their 'free' lives derived from my rejection of the social order and the family system, which boxed people in and made them unfree. In this respect I still see the beauty of their way of life.[10]

Her openness, her willingness to learn, established connections and solidarity beyond what most people on the Left at the time imagined possible.

Turkey's geopolitical position made it a huge interest for global powers throughout the twentieth century. To cement support for the United States and NATO in Turkey, the CIA trained and supported fascist militias such as the Grey Wolves from the 1940s onwards.[11] Turkey became an important partner in the Cold War, joining NATO in 1952 and becoming a key nuclear base for the US.

The Turkish state and its NATO allies exploited existing tensions and racist stereotypes by sowing further divisions, brutalising ethnic minorities, and extinguishing the possibility of political opposition in the country. The Dersim Massacre was followed by the 1955 anti-Greek Istanbul pogroms, and later the executions of revolutionary leftists in the 1970s. The deep state in Turkey was working overtime: strategising and planning how to crush left-wing movements and expunge anti-imperialist sentiments from villages, towns and cities.

By the 1970s, facing existential threats from the state and fascist groups, Left alliances were beginning to falter within the borders of Turkey. Sara records the conversations asking: 'where do we look towards? / where is our revolutionary mecca? / where do we get our perspectives from?'[12] The Turkish Left was limited by its inability to connect global revolutionary perspectives from the student movement in Europe or the decolonial struggles in Africa with local and regional realities on the ground.

This was a time of ruptures across Turkey: riots and strikes swept across the country, and the state responded with brutality. Leftist revolutionaries were executed, and the constant threat of a military coup remained throughout the 1970s. After the coup d'état in 1980, huge parts of the already fragmented Left would be destroyed.

THE BIRTH OF THE KURDISH MOVEMENT

What distinguished the Kurdish movement from the broader Turkish Left was its perspective on where revolutionary change would come from. In their analysis they argued that class struggle in Turkey must go hand in hand with self-determination for the Kurdish people and they believed that a class struggle in Turkey was incomplete without a recognition of its colonial relationship to the Kurdish people. Kurdistan was an internal and international colony, and therefore the Kurdish people would need to organise autonomously and create their own anticolonial revolutionary movement.[13] This was met in parts of the Turkish Left by charges of 'national chauvinism' and the division of the working class along national lines.

Yet we can see the salience of this analysis in Sara's own life. Whenever she joined a mobilisation, she felt accepted as a worker but denied as a Kurd, with political 'unity' requiring the marginalisation of her national identity. Sara describes how the Turkish Left's perverse logic:

> equated denial of one's own identity with 'internationalism' and 'fraternity' and conversely considered social chauvinism [i.e. the Turkish workers' class struggle] to be socialist and democratic. This logic had harsh consequences and brought much destruction.[14]

Sara's search led her to the Kurdistan Revolutionaries, a group formed in Ankara University around a young Kurdish student leader named Abdullah Öcalan who later founded the Kurdistan Workers' Party (PKK) and developed the revolutionary ideology referred to as Democratic Confederalism. The Kurdistan Revolutionaries emerged from both the student movement and workers' struggle, which at the time were closely intertwined in their material struggles and political perspectives. For example, universities and factories were managed by men close to the Turkish establishment, who often held very conservative or fascist views.

This overlap provided an organisational space within which the Kurdistan Revolutionaries set about their work. When listing work shifts or calling out names in class, those with Kurdish names were identified and informed of the programme of the emerging group.

Once a critical mass of cadres had been recruited, units were sent to Kurdish cities such as Dersim, Antep and Maraş to scope the political landscape and integrate the movement with Kurdish society.

In 1978, a massacre was committed in Maraş by the state-sponsored fascist movement known as the Grey Wolves (Bozkurtlar in Turkish), murdering hundreds of Alevi Kurds and wounding many thousands. The massacre wasn't a random outpouring of sectarian violence, but a calculated move by the Turkish state to curtail the revolutionary sentiment brewing in Kurdistan. This brutal violence, however, had the opposite effect, with each new atrocity eliciting greater consciousness and determination to expand the movement. This process of constant growth culminated in the establishment of the PKK at a clandestine meeting on 27 November 1978. The meeting was organised in secret to protect the nascent movement, and Sara arrived at the meeting unaware of what was to take place. She had found herself at one of the most important moments in the history of the Kurdish people, recognising its significance as a new era:

> The founding congress opened up a new era for us. We were now PKK members. We had founded a party with a program and bylaws. I continued to be galvanized by this inspiring congress. While it was going on, I'd followed the discussions, but only afterward did I grasp their meaning. I didn't consider myself special for having been there. On the contrary, I was embarrassed by my own low level compared to the others. But more than anything, I felt pride and joy. The problems, the life, and the struggle no longer seemed onerous to me. The life was so beautiful and stimulated me so much that I could not imagine ever being finished with it.[15]

After the formation of the PKK, it quickly grew into a mass movement with active groups all across North Kurdistan (within the borders of Turkey). Two years later, the 1980 Turkish coup d'état took place, leading to a very dark time. It seemed there was very little hope left for any political struggle to genuinely create change in Turkey. Kurdish people, especially those engaged in political activities, were disproportionately targeted in the aftermath of the coup. This created a new battleground in the history of the Kurdish struggle in Turkey – the prisons.

PRISON RESISTANCE

Sara's role in the organised prison resistance propelled her to a central place in the Kurdish movement and she became a well-known figure amongst Kurds, Kurdish women in particular. She spent ten years in prison, during which dozens of her comrades were tortured to death or took their own lives in defiance of the state. The prison resistance, and the astonishing resolve in the face of the horrors inflicted on them in Turkish dungeons, was a ray of hope in the desolate political landscape that followed the coup d'état and inspired Kurdish revolutionaries outside prison to continue and escalate the fight.

In the early 1980s, Turkish prisons were overflowing. The level of incarceration, the sheer numbers of people arrested, almost overwhelmed the new regime. Blinded by their fascist ideals, and determined to destroy any democratic challenge, the regime began a programme of the most unimaginable torture against leftists and revolutionaries. Sara avoids recounting the gruesome details of her own experience in her memoirs, but her brief description of the conditions is a stomach-turning account of what took place in order to secure NATO's Cold War borders.

Particularly infamous was the regime of torture established in Diyarbakir prison by Esat Oktay – a major in the Turkish military – and where Sara was moved to in 1981. In Sara's telling, Turkish Left movements disintegrated when imprisonment and torture of their members destroyed their organisational structures. The PKK meanwhile managed to sustain their operations by the movement of Abdullah Öcalan and other leading cadres outside Turkey and a ferocious struggle waged by Sara and others to maintain organisational coherence of the PKK in the prisons:

> We discussed the need to create a communal feeling and eliminate weak links that the enemy could benefit from. We had so

many internal conflicts. Every single friend had a boatload of problems. The enemy's pressure, the strain of torture, egocentric behavior, moodiness, pessimism, lack of political analysis ... all made it harder for us to adhere to generally accepted principles. But the friends were determined to resolve internal conflicts without the enemy being aware of it.[16]

By all accounts Sara was central to these efforts as both organiser and exemplar, as one contemporary describes:

She never made a sound while enduring torture. She was a tough and committed revolutionary, but she always showed love and softness to other women. She developed relationships with her women comrades and protected them. She showed that you can love your comrades and the world, but also be unwavering in your opposition to the state.[17]

The prison resistance was waged in acts both big and small. Hunger strikes and death fasts took place throughout the 1980s, with Sara herself coming close to death. Equally, mutual education, passing messages to other prisoners, and the illicit reading of political books were important strategies of keeping the struggle going.

Prison resistance plays a major role in many revolutions and political movements, but what is unique about the Kurdish movement is that the experience of imprisonment strengthened the development of women's struggle in particular. Women's collective organisation in defiance of torture in prison showed that beyond women's rightful inclusion in revolutionary struggle, there was an undeniable need for autonomous women's struggle – a women's liberation ideology.

THE DIRTY WAR OF THE 1980s

While Sara and her comrades in prison were waging their own resistance, the PKK – inspired by their example – began their armed struggle against the Turkish state, mobilising large numbers of Kurds. As a response, the Turkish state expanded its model of collective punishment from the prisons to all of Kurdistan in a 'dirty war' of kidnapping, disappearances, false flag operations, attacks on civilians and forced displacement, through brutal tactics and war crimes.[18] State violence and surveillance was normalised in Kurdistan during the latter half of the twentieth century, with an expansion of military and police bases.

This obtrusive presence, oppression and violence boosted support for the PKK. Young people joined newly formed PKK guerrilla units en masse, their departures celebrated in massive occasions in their villages and towns. Certain villages and regions, like Cizre and Botan, became PKK strongholds, only to be destroyed by the military. When 'softer' tactics of education, propaganda and surveillance proved unsuccessful, the state resorted to violent displacement, setting fire to houses, livestock, fields and forests. Kurdistan was turned into an inferno, with thousands of villages burnt to the ground.

THE PKK – A WOMEN'S PARTY

Sara was released from prison in 1991 at the peak of the 'dirty war', by which time her steadfastness had become legendary.[19] She travelled to the PKK's Mahsum Korkmaz Academy in Bekaa Valley in Lebanon to meet with Abdullah Öcalan who was leading the political education work and military training of cadres. She would see en route the scorched Kurdish landscape, but through her revolutionary eyes, also the possibility of something new. There she was received by an admiring Öcalan who credited the PKK's shift towards centring the question of women's liberation in large part to her organisation and mobilisation of Kurdish women. This included a process of transferring experiences of state violence and patriarchy within the state and Kurdish society to autonomous organising.

Thus, the PKK was becoming a women's party – when Öcalan declared, 'Society cannot be free without women's liberation' he marked a step in uniting the fight against colonialism, patriarchy and capitalism against the Turkish state and these tendencies within Kurdish society.

Throughout the PKK's history of resistance, many women became legends for the Kurdish people, and women in particular.

Zilan (Zeynep Kınacı), 'who walked into a Turkish military parade in Dersim and ignited a bomb on her body', was the first woman to do so – and she acted completely independently.[20] Beritan (Gülnaz Karataş), surrounded by enemy fighters in the mountains of Kurdistan, refused to surrender, instead jumping to her death.[21] Their sacrifices catalysed a new phase in women's organisation, with the aim of increasing women's autonomy within the PKK. The PKK's first autonomous women's armed force was created in the early 1990s, indicating that women were engaged in the armed struggle for a free Kurdistan on their own terms.

Throughout the 1990s, women in the PKK were involved in thinking critically about the state, and in emphasising the struggle against patriarchy. Although women's liberation featured in the analyses and practices of other anticolonial movements, the PKK sought to take it still further by creating autonomous structures that kept the fight against patriarchy at the centre of the struggle for self-determination. As a result, the Kurdistan Women's Freedom Party, PAJK, a sister party to the PKK, was created in 1999. The shift was a starting point to rethinking what a free Kurdistan would look like, with a focus on the struggle against patriarchy, and developing alternative concepts for liberation. As a recent book on the Kurdish women's movement, *The Kurdish Women's Movement: History, Theory, Practice* by Dilar Dirik explains, 'for the first time without men's mediation of thought and action, women started to build trust in themselves and each other by way of theorizing, living, building, and fighting together'.[22] This struggle and resistance of women within the PKK was a basis for Öcalan's later work.

Women's active engagement in political struggle, therefore, was instrumental to how the PKK operated and saw its future objectives. For Sara this was a way of life, arguing that 'In a free Kurdistan the struggle will never end, the struggle will be glorious'.

THE TWENTY-FIRST CENTURY WILL BE THE CENTURY OF WOMEN'S LIBERATION

In 1999 Abdullah Öcalan was abducted from the Greek embassy in Kenya in a coordinated effort by the US, Israeli, and Turkish intelligence services (amongst others) while en route to South Africa upon the invitation of Nelson Mandela, in what the Kurdish movement refers to as the *international conspiracy*.[23] The intention was to annihilate the PKK, with the idea that a leaderless PKK would disintegrate into many factions, and ultimately lose influence and strength.

The trajectory from prison resistance to armed struggle, to the development of women's struggle led to this biggest turning point: after Abdullah Öcalan was imprisoned, it was the women who kept the PKK together and defended its revolutionary ideology.

As he had done before prison, Öcalan insisted that 'the twenty-first century will be the century of women's liberation', forming this into a paradigm known as Democratic Confederalism – a form of 'non-state political administration, or democracy without a state' based on strong autonomous women's structures and the equal inclusion for women on all levels of society through mechanisms such as a co-chair system of equal representation and women's quotas within organisations.[24] This ideology influenced the development of the broader Kurdish Freedom Movement, with a range of civil society organisations, grassroots groups and political parties adopting these principles and pursuing the aims of women's liberation, radical democracy and ecology.

Subsequently, the first Kurdish people's assemblies and autonomous women's assemblies were formed across Kurdistan and Europe. In Rojava, North and East Syria, these principles were implemented on the level of local organisation – laying the groundwork for the revolution that began in 2012. In North Kurdistan, within the borders of Turkey, local organisation for grassroots democracy led to significant political shifts, most notably the rise of the HDP, the People's Democratic Party.

THE GLORIOUS STRUGGLE CONTINUES

Sara was assassinated in Paris by a man linked to the Turkish intelligence service (MIT), notorious for its targeted killings of political dissidents. The French authorities have never made public the full investigation into the assassination and her assassin died in a French prison in murky circumstances.

Sara, Fidan and Leyla represented different organising structures of the Kurdish movement, together building a durable and powerful form of women's organisation. Sara was one of the main leaders and organisers of the KWM, Fidan was an internationalist and a rising diplomatic voice, and Leyla was a youth organiser, particularly of young women. Perhaps the state was avenging the success of the new paradigm and its appeal and resonance with people and movements across Kurdistan and the world. In the middle of Paris, the flame of the women's movement was momentarily dimmed. But the assassinations inspired global rage, grief and renewed conviction to keep fighting. In the aftermath of the assassinations, hundreds of thousands marched through Paris declaring their steadfast commitment to their martyrs, and every year they march to ensure the heinous act is never forgotten.

The legacy of Sakine Cansız is woven into the past, present and future of the Kurdish Women's Movement. Sara lives in the resistance of women in Yezidi mountains of Şengal and across Rojava. She lives in the resistance of all revolutionary women across the world. Fittingly, her name is commemorated by the autonomous women's structures and popular festivals named after her, and hundreds of murals of her in community centres and universities across the world, wherever her revolutionary spirit lives on in contemporary struggles. Some of her last political meetings were with Yazidi women – and her legacy can be seen in the Yekîneyên Parastina Jin ê Şengalê (Şengal Women's Protection Units) and former ISIS captives fighting for their lands in Şengal.

Every element of the movement that the Turkish state tried to annihilate through the assassinations of these three women has since blossomed – the young women's movements, the growth of internationalism, the flourishing of the science of women, Jineolojî – are all elements of her legacy.

Sara's extraordinary life offers invaluable lessons for women and revolutionaries worldwide. Her unwavering commitment to her philosophy of struggle, her belief in the power of women's autonomy, and her treatment of others with love, firmness and encouragement make her an inspiring exemplar. She was committed to self-reflection and constant learning. Though she was one of the founders of a mass freedom movement, one cannot detect complacency in her revolutionary methods. As such, Sara always maintained her hope in the transformational ability in people – that would simultaneously change the world. She believed revolution to be inevitable, created in every moment.

Sara is a Şehîd (martyr) of the Kurdistan freedom movement, and of the women's freedom struggle in Kurdistan and the world. The PKK remembers those fallen in struggle in the belief that martyrs become immortal through continued struggle. When a militant is killed, whether in combat or in Sara's case assassinated in the heart of Europe, the movement responds through increasing mobilisation.[25] New recruits will take the names of Şehîds and pledge to live up to their struggle, while Kurdish families will name their children after martyrs. As Sara and other militants remind us – it is our connection to the people that makes our struggle undefeatable.

NOTES

1. Sakine Cansız, *Sara: My Whole Life Was a Struggle*, Vol. 1 (London: Pluto Press, 2018); *Sara: Prison Memoir of a Kurdish Revolutionary*, Vol. 2 (London: Pluto Press, 2019).
2. Martin van Bruinessen, 'Genocide in Kurdistan? The Suppression of the Dersim Rebellion in Turkey (1937–38) and the Chemical War against the Iraqi Kurds (1988)', in *Genocide: Conceptual and Historical Dimensions*, ed. George J. Andreopoulos (Philadelphia: University of Pennsylvania Press, 1994), 141–70.
3. 'SARA – *My Whole Life Was a Struggle*', YouTube, 2019, www.youtube.com/watch?v=YA49qeTScu8&t=22s (accessed 1 December 2022).
4. Reşat Hallı, *Türkiye Cumhuriyetinde Ayaklanmalar (1924–1938)* (Ankara: T. C. Genelkurmay Başkanlığı Harp Tarihi Dairesi, 1972), 382.
5. Cansız, *Sara: My Whole Life*, 24.
6. Ibid., 83.
7. Ibid., 173.
8. Ibid., 179.

9. Ibid., 97.
10. Ibid., 98.
11. T.J. Coles, 'How the CIA Helped to Crush Turkey's Post-War Left', *CounterPunch*, 16 May 2021.
12. Cansız, *Sara: My Whole Life*, 1, 92.
13. Ismail Beşikçi, *International Colony Kurdistan* (London: Parvana, 2004).
14. Cansız, *Sara: My Whole Life*, 117.
15. Cansız, *Sara: Prison Memoir*, 287–8.
16. Ibid., 139.
17. '*SARA – My Whole Life*'.
18. Gareth Jenkins, 'Susurluk and the Legacy of Turkey's Dirty War', *Terrorism Monitor* 6, no. 9 (May 2008).
19. Sakine Cansız and Janet Biehl, 'Translator-Editor's Preface', in *Sara: My Whole Life*, 1.
20. 'A "Goddess" of the Kurdish Freedom Struggle: A Tribute to Zeynep Kınacı', *Medya News*, 30 June 2021, https://medyanews.net/a-goddess-of-the-kurdish-freedom-struggle-a-tribute-to-zeynep-kinaci/ (accessed 1 December 2022).
21. 'Beritan, a Symbol of the PKK's Resistance', *ANF News*, 26 October 2017, https://anfenglishmobile.com/women/beritan-a-symbol-of-the-pkk-s-resistance-22901 (accessed 1 December 2022).
22. Dilar Dirik, *The Kurdish Women's Movement: History, Theory, Practice* (London: Pluto Press, 2022), 46.
23. Ibid., 50.
24. Abdullah Öcalan, *The Political Thought of Abdullah Öcalan: Kurdistan, Women's Revolution and Democratic Confederalism* (London: Pluto Press, 2017).
25. Partiya Karkerên Kurdistan (PKK), *Kürdistanda Daragaçlart, Kisla Kültürü ve Devrimci intikam Üzerine* [Concerning Gallows, Military Culture and Revolutionary Revenge in Kurdistan] (Cologne: Wesanên Servebün, 1985).

9

Lindiwe Mabuza: Culture as a Weapon of Resistance in South Africa

Kebotlhale Motseothata

Born in 1934 in the small mining town of Newcastle, Kwa-Zulu Natal, at the height of colonial oppression in South Africa, Lindiwe Mabuza (1934–2021) was the daughter of Elsie Mthuthukile Msibi and McCullum Elijah Kambule. Like many marginalised Black girls who grew up in racially oppressed South Africa, young Mabuza was familiar with the pain of struggle and poverty. Elsie, her mother, was a domestic worker and her father, McCullum, was a truck driver. Being born into class and racial oppression meant that her parents were always away working and as a result, she was placed under the care of her grandmother. The strain of scarcity robbed her from certain privileges and denied her the experience of simple things like a change of clothes and different meal options. Eating meat was once viewed as a luxury in Black African households and Lindiwe only ate it once a month. In an interview with Elaine Maria Upton, she recalls:

> I remember having no shoes sometimes and not thinking too much about it until I saw somebody else with shoes. Maybe having only one Sunday dress and then one everyday dress, and not worrying about it until I saw other people changing more often than I did ...[1]

Even so, her family's impoverishment did not stop Lindiwe's grandmother from igniting a love of learning in Mabuza's young mind. The smells in her home remained vivid in her memory as she remembered how her grandmother's love for education laid the foundation for other young girls in her community to learn how to read and write. With no electricity in her home, she would watch her grandmother teach hungry children to read under candlelight and kerosene lamps. Girls who wanted to go to school but couldn't found warmth and learning in their home. Lindiwe's experience of adversity propelled her to find a voice in storytelling.

Her grandmother instilled in her a love of the isiZulu language and English philosophy. She was mostly familiar with isiZulu authors as she was passionate about isiZulu poetry and epic tradition. But her love for literature was solidified in high school. Her exposure to European literature included authors such as Jane Austen and George Eliot – the pen name of a woman, Mary Ann Evans, who used a male name to gain acceptance in the writing community. Mabuza drew further inspiration from Irish writers, such as James Joyce, who used literature and culture as a weapon of resistance:

> This helped me to say, well if the Irish were upset with the status quo, with the arrangements in their society ... why can't I be angry about things that are happening in my society?[2]

After high school, she pursued a Bachelor of Arts degree in Roma College, Lesotho, in 1955. Mabuza then moved to Swaziland where she became a teacher of English and isiZulu. Her initial interest in writing rekindled during her time in Swaziland when she met the renowned short story writer Can Themba, who encouraged her to write and to title her story 'Women do not only menstruate'. The title of the piece suggested by Themba was intended as an acknowledgement that women were intelligent, rather than sexual objects.

Following her work as a teacher in Swaziland, she left on a Fulbright Scholarship to Stanford University in California in 1964 where she pursued her first Master's degree in English Literature. Mabuza's writing career took shape during her time in the US, where her engagement with African writers also heightened. She pursued her second Master's degree in American Studies at the University of Minnesota, where she went on to lecture in Sociology in 1968. At that time, it was uncommon for a Black African woman to pursue a university degree, let alone in a prestigious institution in the US. Her pursuit of two Master's degrees in the Global North at the height of racial oppression is an example of her resourcefulness in imagining a new world for herself as a marginalised and racialised subject from the Global South.

Her grandmother's legacy of keeping children off the streets by encouraging a culture of learning and imagination emanated in Mabuza's work. She started an outreach project, The Way Community Project, where she introduced South African and American literature to the young people in Minneapolis. Inspired by the youth culture of the 1960s, Mabuza encouraged these children to write their own literature by telling their stories. A commitment to writing as a way to elevate and liberate communities continued during her time in California, where she wrote and staged a play – the title of which remains unknown – which sought to show how US Americans, particularly African Americans, could support the anti-apartheid struggle in South Africa, while building awareness around global racial oppression. At the same time, Mabuza was a combatant in Umkhonto we Sizwe (MK, the military wing of the African National Congress (ANC)), which brought her love for literature and culture to her revolutionary activities in the anti-apartheid struggle, an extraordinary example of the contributions of Black women to the South African liberation movement.

MALIBONGWE: POETRY AS WEAPON

On 21 March 1960, 69 people were killed and 180 injured in the Sharpeville Massacre, when the South African police opened fire on a crowd of anti-apartheid protesters demonstrating against pass laws – a demeaning and racist segregationist policy designed to control and police the movement of Black South Africans by requiring them to carry pass books. The massacre was a catalyst for the shift from civil resistance to armed resistance by the ANC and the Pan-African Congress (PAC), which were both banned by the apartheid government. The ANC's rival PAC formed its military wing Poqo while the armed military wing of the ANC, MK, was formed on 16 December 1960. Janet Cherry recalls that the ANC manifesto declared this turn as an emergency in which 'the time comes in the life of any nation when there remain only two choices: submit or fight. That time has now come to South Africa'.[3]

The ANC needed to raise funds for its militant political activities. It garnered international recognition and saw the initial training of 250 soldiers in countries like China, Algeria and the Soviet Union. By 1965, the number of recruited soldiers had risen to 500 and camps were situated in Tanzania and Zambia. Following a combative apprenticeship in Tanzania and with five training camps run by the ANC in Angola, newly recruited soldiers received training in 1977 and a select few of Umkhonto soldiers received advanced training in the Soviet Union and the German Democratic Republic.[4] In addition to military training for armed struggle, a militant cultural production gained speed. This included the poetry, music, magazines and visual narratives, particularly posters which were intended to radicalise combatants and mobilise the international community to join the fight against apartheid. However, in the 1970s, the ANC had not yet established a culture which accommodated writing that conveyed the experiences of women. Anthologies existed which were written by men such as those by Keorapetse Kgositsile and Mongane Wally Serote, while the voices of the women remained subjugated. Mabuza made the significant contribution of organising an edited collection of poems by women. She called on ANC women in camps and in exile to come together under the harsh conditions of apartheid to find a united voice which represented the struggles of women. The collection was published in 1981 under her nom de guerre Sono Molefe. Shortly after its publication, it was banned by the apartheid government.

The title of the anthology, *Malibongwe*, means 'Let's thank them. Let's praise them', and was inspired by the anti-pass campaign, on 9 August 1956, when 20,000 women marched for the abolition of the apartheid pass laws. Mabuza recalls that this title, *Malibongwe*, was derived by the men of the 1950s as a tribute to the women who had organised the mass demonstration. The phrase '*malibongwe igama lamakhosikazi*' which loosely translates to 'let's thank the women' was used by these men to describe the resilient nature of the women at the time and hence the title of the anthology. In reflecting on the power of poetry as a weapon of struggle, Mabuza said:

> Poetry is part of the struggle. You use the armed struggle; you use political agitation methods; you use the underground international mobilisation. And so, the poetry is part of a culture, part of a whole arsenal of weaponry to be used against apartheid. You recite a poem. It's better than a three-hour speech. It gets to the heart of the matter. It moves people. They can identify with it because it touches them. It has a certain immediacy of communication because it is compressed.[5]

The original *Malibongwe* anthology was significant in illuminating the lives and struggles of Black women in the South African liberation movement. The 2020 resuscitated version of the anthology, by Uhuru Phalafala, sought to significantly reverse the subsequent erasure of Black women's contributions to the cultural movement against apartheid. The historical archive contains iconographies and contributions of men such as Thami Mnyele, Wally Serote, Keorapetse Kgositsile and many others whose works continue to dominate the conversation on the role of culture in the liberation movement. At the same time, women's contributions remain unnamed and unmapped in the broader historiography of liberation politics and narratives. In the introduction of *Malibongwe* (2020), Makhosazana Xaba introduces Mabuza and the women in the anthology as comrade-cum-poets whose multiple identities 'span from being activists to ambassadors (chief representatives as we called them pre-1999) as well as combatants, feminists, guerrillas, mothers, public intellectuals, scholars, sisters, wives, writers, and more'.[6]

In retrospect, *Malibongwe* is a vital component of the cultural struggle against apartheid and portrays the ways in which Black women were active agents in the transformative anticolonial and socialist projects of the twentieth century. The anthology showed the ways in which Black women in MK camps chronicled their experiences through poetry. Athambile Masola mentions that 'these poems are not only part of the feminist intellectual history and archive but are also part of the imaginative worlds of women who dreamt about the future we now experience'.[7] *Malibongwe* names the otherwise nameless and voices the otherwise voiceless.

Mabuza's use of culture to advocate for the rights of women in a time where gender debates were pushed to the periphery signifies her rebellion in centring women's voices in the anti-apartheid struggle. Recognising culture as a tool against oppression illuminates the ways in which the fight against apartheid was a multi-faceted war which included the use of poetry, music and visual culture as arsenals against the violence of racial subjugation. In this way, it is evident that the cultural front was just as effective as the military front in the overthrowing of the apartheid government.

There are many women exiles who are unaccounted for, unnameable, and unknowable in the history of the anti-apartheid struggle.[8] While we may never know all the names of the women who fought for the liberation of South Africa, the echoes of their voices and the blood of their sacrifices have traces in their use of culture as a weapon of struggle. Mabuza's anthology highlights the impact of protest poetry and provides a view of Black women combatants' ideologies, feelings, histories and radical resistance against oppression. Mabuza's anthology, showcasing the experiences of Black women in exile, provides a window into the harsh realities of life as cultural workers and combatants who were faced with the fight of both the racial oppression of apartheid and the gendered oppression of patriarchy and misogyny. For instance, in the South African context, women exiles were sometimes forced to focus on childcare and other domestic responsibilities at the expense of their cultural work.

These poems serve as an archive of women's individual and collective thinking about their role in the liberation struggle. Their erasure is reversed by listing the names of these comrade-cum-poets, impelling us to position them in the South African literary and historical archive.[9] Therefore, in *Malibongwe* Lindiwe Mabuza wrote under her pseudonym Sono Molefe, Baleka Mbete wrote as Baleka Kgositsile,

Belinda Martins as Gloria Mntungwa, Sankie Mthembi-Mahanyele
as Rebecca Matlou, Yvonne Modiagotle as Jumaimah Mutaung,
S'bongile Mvubelo as Lerato Kumalo, Phumza Dyanti as Alice
Tsongo, Mpho Msimang as Mpho Maruping, Ribbon Mosholi as
Susan Lamu and Thuli Kubeka as Duduzile Ndelu.[10] These names
are a reminder of women's contribution to the cultural struggle
against apartheid. By saying their names, we are not only reminis-
cent of the role played by their poetry in the resistance movement
but are also cognisant of their lives outside of the liberation struggle.
We are reminded that they were autonomous people with histories,
feelings, dreams, desires and families.

Denouncing the notion of being referred to as 'woman writers',
these comrade-cum-poets preferred their writing to be acknowl-
edged as 'resistance literature'. By being linked to the 9 August 1956
anti-pass law campaign, the poems were intended to raise consciousness of the past as a task of national liberation. In this way, the 1981
anthology commemorates historical moments in the anti-apartheid
struggle and contains an implicit narrative which Mabuza defines as
the liberation of South Africa by the ANC.[11] Propagandist by nature,
the poems in *Malibongwe* are a symbol of resistance as they adopt
an Africanist mode of expression and resist the 'the codes associated
with traditional western aesthetic norms and practices'.[12] The poem
'Exile Blues' by Baleka Kgositsile Mbete highlights the sadness of
life in exile:

let them roll
let the blues roll out but 'this load is heavy it requires men'
it has nothing to do with baritone or beard
it is a word of warning wisdom
when the uncontrollable miles
between you and home
the beautiful land
you vowed to liberate
become unbearable
and you ask yourself
if it was worth your leaving the loved ones ...

With this poem, Kgositsile (Mbete) makes visible the loneliness and pain that comes with being alienated from loved ones while in pursuit of national liberation. It engages the trope of loss, longing and unbelonging. Kgositsile (Mbete)'s sentiments echo the experiences of the women of the *Malibongwe* anthology. More than this, the anthology reminds us that these women were real people with lives shaped by multitude concerns and experiences. Life in exile was tumultuous in many ways and it was often the women who suffered the most as they were faced with a triple form of oppression, as Black women subjugated on the basis of race, class and gender. Not only were these women faced with fighting against a patriarchal and misogynist climate of combat, but they were also robbed from experiencing the simple pleasures of daily life. This is evident in the lines:

when having been rejected
like vomit from a stomach
you try to examine
if it's the food that is stale
or the stomach that is sick …

Access to food was scarce in the camps, harmful contraceptives were forced into their bodies, and women had to use torn t-shirts during their menstrual cycles as sanitary towels were scarce. Moreover, they were faced with the challenge of balancing marriage, childbirth and childcare in harsh spaces of combat. The poem 'Exile Blues' highlights the hardships faced by Black women in exile, reminding us of the lived experience and sacrifice of revolutionary women beyond tropes of heroic combatants. The poem touches on the self-destructive habits which combatants adopted such as excessive drinking which they used to numb their ailing mental health during their time in exile. This is relayed in the lines:

… when the demon trinity
inferiority complex
self-assertion
sadism

have become your masters
that you put the stamp
on your own death certificate
as you try to destroy
when you drink yourself insensible ...

Kgositsile (Mbete) further mentions the ways in which women were tasked with fighting against their erasure in the historicisation of the liberation struggle. The lines 'when the song goes "this load is heavy it requires men" it has nothing to do with baritone or beard' suggest that the war against apartheid had women as equal, active and autonomous participants of the revolution.

LINDIWE MABUZA'S CULTURAL POLITICS

Central to Mabuza's politics was her belief in the emancipation of women. Her 1977 role as editor of the ANC publication *Voice of Women* (VOW) created another space for the articulation of Black women's experiences in exile. As a publication, VOW was established in Lusaka, Zambia, with the aim of creating awareness on the triple oppression faced by African women and children under the threat of apartheid. VOW's promotion of these women's voices eventually led to the publication of *Malibongwe*. In many ways, as a true voice of the revolution, Mabuza wrote and published poetry in ways which mirrored the experiences of African women en masse. She wrote with, for and about the soldier, the activist, the mother, the sister, the queer and the marginalised. In instances where combatants needed a platform of expression, her initiative as a journalist saw her adoption of poetry as a tool of propaganda which she broadcast on Radio Freedom in Lusaka.

As an icon who was in community with the then exiled jazz singer Letta Mbulu, Mabuza published a collection of poetry titled *Letter to Let-ta* (1991) as a tribute to their friendship. In addition, her success as a published poet includes publications such as *Africa to Me* (1999), *One Never Knows: An Anthology of Black South African Women Writers in Exile* (1989), *Voices That Lead: Poems, 1976–1996*

(1998) and *Footprints and Fingerprints* (2008). While she has published poetry which depicts the voices of her comrades, Mabuza's own published poetry requires further exploration. For instance, her poem for the legendary musician Quincy Jones highlights the value of their friendship as well as the power of their network as twentieth century international activists of the Black Arts Movement. Mabuza's poem, which starts with a mention of the ancestors, is an ode to Quincy Jones and shows the unity which existed between Black cultural workers of the 1960s and 1970s. In the poem 'For Quincy', Mabuza writes:

Ancestors danced
Waves upon waves of liquid joy
The mountains caught laughter
All streams bubbled back
To the forests and our secret gorges
Echoes of majestic chorals
When every heart tightens
The other's clasps
On the day of your return
In Soweto
Alexandra
Those hearts
This heart
Unleashing unheard melodies
As each now surges forward
Just to touch you
Just to say
One flesh
One blood
There ... by my side ...

Not only was Mabuza an academic, playwright, poet, editor and cultural activist, but she was also a diplomat whose political activities led to important internationalist ties. After joining the ANC as a full-time comrade in 1975, she was appointed as the ANC chief representative in Scandinavian countries in 1979. Mabuza organised for the establishment of the Solomon Mahlangu Freedom College (SOMAFCO) which provided education for children of exiles in Mazimbu, Tanzania, and, in her ideas for the expansion and political education of young children, mobilised the Swedish community's support in establishing a teacher's block and a laboratory in SOMAFCO. Mabuza wanted Black children to learn science as well as for them to know the history of the people of South Africa as taught from a revolutionary African perspective. Her passion for promoting the voices of children is further reflective in her publication of letters titled *Conversations with Uncle O. R. Tambo: Childhood Memories in Exile Paperback* (2019) which chronicle the lives, as well as the curiosity, of exiled children who yearn for the return of revolutionary and national chairperson of the ANC, Oliver Kaizana Reginald Tambo.

Mabuza nurtured the voices of children and highlighted the plight of youth as central to the emancipation agenda. In an interview, Mabuza recalls that 'children have had such horrendous experiences; exile was not such a wonderful place. They witnessed the killings, the deaths of comrades, of aunties and uncles, of friends'.[13]

Lindiwe Mabuza's excellence in mobilising for culture and solidarity is evident in her organising of two tours for the Amandla Cultural Ensemble in Sweden. She was also instrumental in the organisation of the Medu Art Ensemble's Culture and Resistance Festival in Gaborone, in 1982. These two exiled cultural groups were founded in the 1970s and championed the use of culture as a weapon of struggle until the 1980s. Fellow comrade Sankie Mthembi-Mahanyele recalls the value of culture as a bullet against an unjust war that was more than just a military armed struggle, claiming, 'not everyone was a soldier. Being a soldier is a specialised form of training and experience. We need to expose people to the different activities that we were engaged in as members of the liberation movement'.[14] Even so, the cultural group Amandla was associated with the military and was built from the ANC's base in Angola.

Mabuza used her diplomatic position to convince the Nordic countries to bring Amandla to Scandinavia, accounting her reasons for conceptualising the group:

> When we built that group, we said: 'where do we find the people who are sufficiently disciplined and organised? We went to the military camps, where the culture of South Africa continued to thrive. The culture of liberation. The soldiers were writing liberation songs and liberation poems, motivating their military perspective through culture'.[15]

Mabuza's influence ensured the success of Amandla's tours in the four Nordic countries, the Netherlands and Germany. Through this initiative, the anti-apartheid revolution gained momentum and illuminated the horrors of the regime to international societies. However, even with this ensemble's success, there exists an erasure of women who participated in the group. While we may name male members such as Jonas Gwangwa and others who formed part of the 40-member group of musicians, dancers and actors, there exists a list of unnamed women participants. Not only do we have a vague picture of these women's experiences as militants from the Angola base, but we do not know their personal experiences as well as their roles as cultural workers. Moreover, we arguably do not have a clear picture of their cultural and political contributions. In many ways, Mabuza's legacy allows for a broader investigation into the erasure of the women of Amandla and calls on us to position them in the history of the liberation struggle of South Africa. Amandla toured Europe under Lindiwe Mabuza's leadership as chief representative of Sweden and the Nordic countries. These relations were possible because the Nordic countries took an anti-apartheid and pro-sanctions position, with Sweden as the only Western country to give official support to the anti-apartheid movement in South Africa during the early 1970s, a legacy recognised by then president of the ANC, Oliver Tambo.[16]

While in Sweden, Lindiwe worked alongside Swedish politicians like Lena Johansson and developed strategies which widened the

ANC's cultural reach in the international anti-apartheid community. Mabuza's alliances in Nordic countries were strong and impactful. For instance, her leadership garnered support by strengthening affiliations with all levels of leadership in Nordic countries. In 1986 her connections with the US ushered a wave of sanctions against the apartheid regime which initiated boycotts by large corporations. This cultural boycott was initiated by her strong networks with the likes of Quincy Jones, Danny Glover, Harry Belafonte, Reverend Jesse Jackson and Randall Robinson, among others, who used their power and influence to mobilise for the movement against apartheid in South Africa. Additionally, her mobilisation for support from US institutions of higher learning enforced sanctions against the apartheid government from companies such as Coca-Cola which withdrew investments from South Africa. Mabuza was also a Black Panther, an aspect of her political life which is little known, who won the Yari Yari award from New York University in 1993, to honour her contribution to literature and the fight for freedom.

Following a life in exile, Lindiwe Mabuza served in the first parliament of South Africa under Mandela in 1994 and continued her cultural and diplomatic work as ambassador to Germany and later in posts in the United Kingdom, Malaysia and the Philippines. While this chapter has not covered the full range of her political activities and accomplishments, it serves as a tribute to her influence and immense contributions to the armed struggle for liberation in the field of culture. Using her education, her talents and her diplomacy, Mabuza is an example to young Black women of both historical and contemporary South Africa. Her love of her community inspires Black people, especially girls, to carry each other through adversity and to pursue their personal freedoms despite the odds. Through her publication of *Malibongwe* and *Conversations with Uncle O. R. Tambo*, we are reminded of the value of the voices of Black women and children who endured the horrors of trauma in exile.

When we remember the likes of Nelson Mandela, O.R. Tambo and Keorapetse Kgositsile, may we recall women like Lindiwe Mabuza, Baleka Kgositsile (Mbete), Sankie Mthembi-Mahanyele and many others who sacrificed their lives for the liberation movement and whose names we may never know. Through these women's painful experiences in exile such as their alienation from loved ones, the trauma of war and the violence of patriarchy, may we remember the lives of the nameless Black women who married the comrades and combatants of MK, women who left their homes in Tanzania, Zambia, Angola, Botswana, and many other countries to join their husbands in the fight against apartheid. May we remember their children, who endured trauma and may never know what it means to live normal lives. May we remember their struggles, their aches, their losses, and their need for belonging in South Africa's democracy. May we remember that while MK was disbanded at the dawn of South Africa's democracy in 1994, there are women who wrote and continue to write poetry as revolutionaries. Culture was a weapon of struggle, and its role was shaped by Lindiwe Mabuza who imagined a South Africa without apartheid, and without gendered, racialised and classed oppression. Her legacy is the challenge for Black women of the present and future to continue in this path.

NOTES

1. Elaine Maria Upton and Lindiwe Mabuza, 'Born to the Struggle, Learning to Write: An Interview with Lindiwe Mabuza, Poet and Chief Representative of the African National Congress (of South Africa) in the United States', *Feminist Studies* 21, no. 3 (Autumn 1995): 616.
2. Ibid., 618.
3. Janet Cherry, *Umkhonto we Sizwe* (Johannesburg: Jacana Media, 2011), 15.
4. Tom Lodge, 'State of Exile: The African National Congress of South Africa, 1976–86', *Third World Quarterly* 9, no. 1 (1987): 6.
5. Upton and Mabuza, 'Born to the Struggle', 622.
6. Makhosazana Xaba, 'Introduction', in *Malibongwe: Poems from the Struggle by ANC Women*, eds. Sono Molefe and Uhuru Phalafala (Durban: uHlanga Press, 2020).
7. Athambile Masola, *Malibongwe*, 182.
8. In the 2021 colloquium, 'Women, and 60 years of the Armed Struggle in South Africa', Makhosazana Xaba noted this erasure by flagging the existence of women in exile.
9. Uhuru Phalafala, 'Preface', in *Malibongwe*.

10. Ibid.

11. Lynda Gilfillan, 'Black Women Poets in Exile: The Weapon of Words', *Tulsa Studies in Women's Literature* 11, no. 1 (Spring 1992): 80.

12. Ibid., 79.

13. Lindiwe Mabuza, 'Conversations with Uncle OR – Childhood Memoirs in Exile', YouTube, 2018, www.youtube.com/watch?v=7TxYj63A_N8& ab_channel=PolitySA (accessed 1 June 2022).

14. Sankie Mthembi-Mahanyele (aka 'Rebecca Matlou') in interview with Tor Sellstrom, 7 September 1995, 'Interviews from South Africa', The Nordic Africa Institute, 170.

15. Lindiwe Mabuza in interview with Tor Sellstrom, 'Interviews from South Africa', 140.

16. Ibid., 134.

10

Where Are the Revolutionary Women of West Asia and North Africa?

Kanwal Hameed and Sara Salem

Arwa Salih (1953–1997) was a leader of Egypt's student movement of the 1970s and led sit-ins at Cairo University where she had once been a student of English Literature. She was the author of various books on and translations of Marxist literature and was a member of the Central Committee of the Egyptian Workers Communist Party (EWCP) in the 1970s. Salih wrote expansively about the failures of the Left of the 1950s and 1960s, which had left her disillusioned with Marxists more broadly. She ended her life in self-exile in Seville, Spain, struggling with mental illness and the harshly negative responses to her memoir from former comrades.[1] This tragic end to her life speaks to the struggles women revolutionaries faced throughout their lives, and indeed Salih reflects on these – for instance, the sexism she faced from her comrades – in her memoir and other writings.

Her memoir, *The Stillborn*, is an important text that speaks to these struggles, as well as the aftermath of Nasserism in Egypt and the fate of the 1970s student movement. The Nasserist project was led by Gamal Abdel Nasser, Egypt's post-independence leader. Nasserism was broadly characterised by a commitment to Third Worldism, social welfare and state control of the economy. The end of this political project came with Egypt's resounding defeat to Israel in the 1967 June Arab-Israeli War. Following Nasser's death, Anwar Sadat became president, heralding a new political project based on free market principles, a geopolitical orientation to the US, and, controversially, peace with the settler colonial Israeli state. The generation of Egyptian students to which Salih belonged were animated by the defeat Egypt suffered against Israel in 1967, and the need to hold the government to account. As historian Hanan Hammad notes, the 1970s student movement was an incredibly powerful one that gained the support of the broader Egyptian public. Salih similarly recalls that these students were 'born leaders and became the first generation of leftists whom the entire Egyptian people greeted'.[2]

However, the students were unable to maintain this widespread popular support for class-based social justice. This support dissipated after Sadat was seen as winning concessions from Israel in 1973. The 1973 war between Egypt and Israel was settled through the Camp David Accords, during which Sinai – which has been annexed by Israel during the 1967 war – was returned to Egypt. Salih calls the student leaders *al mubtasirun*, or premature, a generation of dreamers. Samah Selim, who translated Salih's memoir into English, describes the 1970s student movement as a 'secret history', fragmented because it was underground and because of the scarcity of material we have about it. Arwa Salih's memoir is one of the few sources we have of this movement, and Salih herself emerges as a key theorist of anticolonialism and its aftermath in Egypt and beyond, a communist and feminist intellectual, activist and writer whose writing expands the contours of how we theorise revolution.

In Arwa Salih's writing there is a blurring of the boundaries between theory, the political and the self. In this chapter, we read Salih's memoir alongside a documentary film by Egyptian film-maker Tahani Rached entitled *Four Women of Egypt* (1997),[3] which follows the lives of four of Egypt's prominent women who were active in the women's movement during and after the Nasser years: Widad Mitri (1927–2007, Cairo, Egypt), a journalist and unionist; Safinaz Qassem (b. 1938, Alexandria, Egypt), a journalist and author; Amina Rachid (1938–2001, Cairo, Egypt), a university professor; and Shahenda Maqlad (1938–2016, place of birth unknown), an activist with peasant communities around Egypt who ran for parliament several times.

The four women were involved in various ways in anticolonial struggle in Egypt, despite their different ideological positionings that traversed socialism, feminism, Islamism and secularism. For instance, Shahenda Maqlad was known as the 'mother of farmers' and, along with her husband Salah Hussein, led an uprising against a feudal landlord family in the village of Kamshish in the Nile Delta. Her husband was assassinated by one of the landlords in an event that was to galvanise peasants across the country in pushing for land reform, which eventually became a partial reality under Nasser's limited land re-distribution project. The four women revisit these events that they were part of, recounting the excitement that animated the Egyptian revolution of 1952. The film was produced in 1994, in the aftermath of both Nasser and Sadat, and like Salih's memoir, it takes feminist memory and the powerful ties of friendship seriously.[4]

Both Salih's memoir and the *Four Women of Egypt* are significant because they attempt to make sense of the Egyptian Left in the aftermath of Nasserism, the defeat of 1967, and the failure of the student movement to become a national movement. This sense-making is also affective; throughout the memoir, for instance, Salih writes about haunting, ghosts, defeat and hope, tracing a political lifeworld through affective registers. Emotion is almost never brought up as an individual experience, although in private correspondence listed as an appendix, she notes that she wrote the book to make sense of her feelings. Instead, emotion is collectivised, made to speak for her comrades and the entire student movement. This approach produces a kind of affective history of that moment, tinged with nostalgia, bitterness, tragedy and failure.

For Salih, haunting is intimately and irrevocably tied to the national struggle, which is almost present as a character in the text. Salih returns again and again to the question: what happened to the national liberation project?[5] Nationalism was the 'language through which we chose to read our world, our historical consciousness', she writes.[6] Throughout the text she refers to 'ghosts of the nation', and juxtaposes this to the weaker power held by class consciousness; here we see a critique of a Left that claimed to be speaking for 'the people' and yet that was more invested in a nationalist project that was ultimately violent. The tension between nationalism – which she admits was impossible to escape from, as a frame of resistance – and class politics animates much of the memoir. For Salih, it is precisely this tension that haunts the Egyptian Left, a tension we see return in the memoir again and again.

This tension also emerges in the *Four Women of Egypt*, through the lens of class positionality and feminism. At the start of the film, Amina Rachid speaks about her wealthy family and growing up in a villa, recalling the memory of a girl throwing stones at her because her grandfather, Egyptian prime minister Ismail Sidqi, had signed a treaty with the British. Reflecting on this incident, she says that the shock came from being attacked by someone and realising that the attacker was right: 'The big house, the poor neighbours. So, this political drama was for me a shock and an awakening. In our big house we spoke French, and Arabic only with the servants. The bitter truth of being the ruling class. Outside the gate, a traitor'. Here the affective nature of her memories adds an important layer to Salih's probing of class and nation, and points to the tension resulting from the fact that figures within the Left were often members of Egypt's economically privileged classes.

Another ghost that appears in the film and the text is Nasser. In the memoir, Nasser is not a hero; when Salih refers to him, it is often to forcefully criticise him and his political actions. Yet these references allow Salih to touch on the nostalgia many on the Left felt for Nasser, even while he imprisoned many of them and repressed leftist forces throughout his time in power.[7] Nostalgia is described as a coping mechanism in the text, a way of making sense of the 'dark times' that came after the defeat of 1967, a time when none of their revolutionary prophecies became reality. Salih's thoughtful exploration of nostalgia opens a discussion around leftist support for anticolonial leaders such as Nasser, in spite of their repression of the Left and betrayal of socialist goals.

For the four women in the film, Nasser similarly emerges as a symbolic figure. Safinaz Qassem notes the power of Nasser's projects, such as the Aswan Dam, stating that they thought the Dam would 'work marvels', and unpacking her own confusion when this did not happen. Despite this, Qassem makes it clear that she supported the revolution and that it represented a moment in which a different Egypt became possible, in which 'our dreams would be fulfilled', pointing out that Nasser was a big part of the dreams of her generation. She states that at Nasser's funeral, 'we sang the same song, felt the same pain, the pain of having lost him, and of what he made us suffer'. Here we see an echo of the tense contradictions in how Salih represents Nasser too, though less viscerally fraught.

The memoir and film both speak to the attachment to Marxism that these women felt. Salih's writing dispels any easy assessments of the role of Marxism in anticolonial liberation struggles:

I'm still not one of those so-called 'disillusioned' Marxists. I despise those people from the bottom of my heart. They never felt it or tried to live the truth of it. For them – those dogmatic friends with whom we wasted the most important years of our lives – Marxism was just an easy key to conquest. I still believe deeply in the truth of Marxism.[8]

A reading of Marxism as more than just textual truths appears in the *Four Women of Egypt* too, particularly in relation to the friendship between the four women. This friendship is what opens up a space for political discussions around the struggle – framed by Maqlad as being in defence of 'peasants and Palestine'. In the film, Marxism emerges through these conversations – full of what Julietta Singh would call 'loving critique' as well as through their affective attachments to the past and to one another.[9] Marxism is something to be felt and lived; understanding it theoretically, textually or abstractly is not enough. Salih's memoir and Rached's film bring to light histories of anticolonialism that are not always present in state or academic narratives of revolution, suggesting that they are of particular value in projects of recuperating lost histories.

'AHKI YA TAIR (TELL YOUR TALE LITTLE BIRD)'

The documentary film '*Ahki Ya Tair (Tell Your Tale Little Bird)*, released in 2007, explores a number of themes: the layers of struggle for national liberation and social transformation that revolutionary women were engaged in; the spatialisation of sites of revolt (how it was produced at schools, in homes, social clubs and prison); the register of Third World internationalism in the Palestinian liberation struggle; and affective relationships of and in revolutionary struggle. The film director, Arab Loutfi, an Egyptian-Lebanese filmmaker who grew up in Saida, South Lebanon, began in 1993 to film conversations with Palestinian militant women who had been active in the Palestinian Revolution. Arab Loutfi, along with Arwa Salih and the protagonists of *Four Women of Egypt*, is moved by the dreams of a generation of women, saying, 'the specialty of my film is that it is a confident, unapologetic, in fact proud, feminist narrative. A narrative that talks about a history which shaped the dream of the seventies generation …'[10]

These themes are explored through the lives, as narrated themselves, of Palestinian revolutionaries Aisha Odeh (b. 1944, Deir Jreir), Amina Dahbour (b. 1945, Kufr Ana), Leila Khaled (b. 1944, Haifa), Rashida Obeida (date of birth unknown, al-Quds), Rasmiyyeh Odeh (b. 1947/8, Lifta), Therese Halassa (b. 1948, Akka – d. 2020, Amman) and Wedad Qamari (date of birth unknown, al-Quds). All seven women were militant *munadilat* (strugglers) and liberation activists in the late 1960s and early 1970s and involved in popular political movements of the time: communist, Ba'athist, Arab nationalist and leftist. Most remained committed to the struggles for Palestinian liberation and for social transformation throughout their lives. These struggles were shaped by the material conditions of their lives, which included imprisonment and exile, which shaped their work to challenge and change unequal gender relations. Wedad Qamari, one of the founding members of the General Union of Palestinian Women (GUPW), writes that the violent dispersal of Palestinian communities meant that the revolutionary base 'was not settled in one place and did not allow for strong foundations that might enhance women's situation'.[11]

Aisha Odeh was a secondary school teacher who became part of the Movement of Arab Nationalists (MAN) while she was in secondary school. As well as teaching, she was part of social initiatives offering literacy programmes to women. After the 1967 war, she joined the PFLP (Popular Front for the Liberation of Palestine) and was given two life sentences by the Israeli colonial authorities for her alleged involvement in the 1969 bombing of a Jerusalem supermarket. She was exiled to Jordan after her release in a prisoner exchange in 1979, before returning to Ramallah in 1994, where she remained politically active for most of her life.[12] Therese Halassa, born in Akka, was a participant in the hijacking of the Sabena Belgian airline in 1972, during which she was wounded and captured, and subsequently sentenced to 210 years in jail. She spent 11 years imprisoned by the Israeli colonial authorities, during which she has described undergoing mental and physical abuse, before being released in an exchange deal. She was exiled from Palestine, and spent the rest of her life in Jordan, where she continued her activism.

Amina Dahbour is known for her role in the 1969 PFLP hijacking of the Israeli El-Al aircraft before its take-off from Kloten Airport, Zurich – after which she was sentenced along with the three surviving hijackers to 12 years in prison by a Swiss court. Amina was taken to Cairo aboard a British military plane in 1970, along with another high-profile PFLP member, Leila Khaled. Born in Haifa, Leila Khaled's family were made refugees by the Nakba, and ended up in Lebanon, where she followed her older brother in joining the MAN, before moving into the PFLP as a schoolteacher in Kuwait. She took part in two aeroplane hijackings in 1969 and 1970 before being detained in London and released the same year along with Amina Dahbour through a prisoner exchange deal. She remains a political figure, based now in Jordan.

Rashida Obeida was part of a militant operation to blow up Super Sol market in occupied Jerusalem in 1968. Her 16-year-old sister and father were jailed, for almost two years and for three months, respectively, under administrative detention to pressure Rashida to surrender but she was never captured. Rasmiyyeh Odeh, born in Lifta and made a refugee as a young child during the 1948 Nakba, joined the Palestinian resistance during the 1960s. She became a member of the PFLP and was jailed for ten years by the Israeli colonial authorities for her alleged involvement in the 1969 bombing of a Jerusalem supermarket. She has described the torture and ill-treatment she experienced in prison, as well as the work she took part in with other inmates to build networks of education and resistance in prison. She lived in the US for most of her life after being released in a prisoner exchange in 1980, where she continued to work as an activist.[13]

The film 'Ahki Ya Tair shows what Rosemary Sayigh describes in 1998 as: 'women's centrality to nation and state formation'. Focusing on their presence in the national struggle highlights 'their absence from written history, [and] the inappropriateness of conventional research methods for discovering women "in history"'.[14] We can think, with Omnia Shakry, of these film and memoirs as an archive, while centring what Mezna Qato calls the 'social scale'.[15] The film-maker herself plays with the concept of archive, at times using a split screen to show archive footage of major historical moments at the same time as one of the film's protagonists speaks about it:

And there's no way that anyone can impose anything on me. I have this revolutionary logic not only in my national work but also in my personal life. *Of course they are linked.*[16]

As Nadera Shalhoub Kevorkian has intricately conveyed, there is a particular consciousness through which work on women in the SWANA (South West and North Africa) region must be carried out: it rejects both the external, Orientalising, culturalising and dram-atising of women's exclusion and oppression and the dismissal of 'women's issues' as a secondary concern of struggles within their own locations.[17] The layer of the struggle in which all others are enmeshed is the national liberation struggle that the participants in the film have engaged in. In most of the militants' conversations we see how, as Rosemary Sayigh describes, 'through resistance group membership, women learned the language of national politics, with its elision of class, gender, and local differences'. Yet as Sayigh herself notes, gender difference (inequality) does not ever fully elide so as to disappear into a large continuum of national revolt – in fact it is again and again being re-negotiated and struggled against within the same field, with reverberations that carry a lineage beyond spaces and moments of revolt.

In the film 'Ahki Ya Tair, both Rasmiyyeh Odeh and Therese Halassa highlight, as numerous scholars have since, that gender is weaponised by colonial powers through the capture and torture of female captives. Therese Halassa recalls that her interrogators 'kept harping on the fact that I was in prison, which meant that I was dishonoured according to Arab traditions'. The women also discuss how their actions and experiences challenged traditional familial and social gender dynamics, at times in alliance with male members of their communities and political groups. The historical moment explored in the film, where women's liberation is explicitly part of the struggle for revolution and social transformation, is also part of a longer historical trajectory of women's participation in national revolt in Palestine which pre-dates the Nakba.[18]

> All the family were resisting ... There was no sense that I am an individual resisting the occupation, but a whole people resisting the occupation. Among them, the old woman, my mother, my sister-in-law, my sister, and my brother, all of them.[19]

As suggested by Aisha Odeh above, these women's conversations encourage us to reconceptualise revolt and resistance by looking beyond visible temporal manifestations and confrontations. They also discuss the practices of revolt before and after critical mobilisations. In the film, Wedad Qamari describes the role of women in hiding militants, including herself, when she was wanted by the Israeli colonial authorities. Rasmiyyeh Odeh describes raising national consciousness through staging plays, performing nationalist songs, and teaching during her time in prison. They show that lines of revolt run through schools, homes, at movement meetings, in refugee camps, on the frontlines of militant struggle, in prison.[20] They also stretch across time: the prominent Palestinian academic, advocate and political prisoner Khalida Jarrar, released from Israeli prison in 2021, writes of the contemporary period that 'prison became a place of action' through actions carried out by women inside, and through the continuity of links with the outside, partly through the ongoing capture and release of prisoners.

Through the protagonists of the film we see references to local, regional and global networks of anticolonial struggle, as well as how they operated. Therese Halassa describes crossing with comrades into Lebanon to join the revolution, arriving at Marj 'Ayoun in South Lebanon, and asking to join a Fatah (the largest Palestinian resistance group) patrol.[21] Leila Khaled describes her PFLP cell in Kuwait carrying out a public fundraiser on Eid to raise donations for the movement, saying, 'The women joined the vanguard. The masses filled our coffers'.[22] Khaled also later took part in a tour of the Gulf and Iraq along with Rashida Obeida and others, with the intention to 'spread revolutionary propaganda as well as collect funds for the Front'.[23] These reflections raise questions about the Palestinian liberation movement and revolutionary struggle in the region at the time, such as: where are the edges of revolt; what are the borders of struggle; and how do they manifest across national borders?

Through the women's accounts we can see that what partially sustained the Palestinian liberation cause was both the work to elucidate it as well as the work to build through its entanglements with movements elsewhere in the region, which upheld Palestinian liberation as a cause connected to their own liberation struggles. For this generation, the Palestinian Revolution was part of an era of global revolt, when anti-imperialist ideology circulated alongside travelling militants engaged in practices and questions of armed struggle and social transformation. As part of this Third World rising (the anticolonial liberatory impetus linking formerly colonised peoples from Africa, Asia and Latin America) both the filmmaker Arab Loutfi and Leila Khaled recall demonstrations in the Southern Lebanese city of Saida, mourning the assassination of Congolese revolutionary Patrice Lumumba at the hands of Belgian colonial authorities.

The film opens with an instrumental version of the folkloric Palestinian song, 'Yumma Mwayel al-Hawa', and includes a reading from 'Barqooq al-Nissan', an unfinished story by Ghassan Kanafani, which Wedad Qamari reveals was written about her and her female comrades.[24] The story is set entirely around the journey of an elderly man who picks a bouquet of flowers for the mysterious Souad, 'a student' volunteer at the UNRWA school, who arrives at her house to find three enemy soldiers holding local captives in her house. The scene sets out an understanding of resistance and mobilisation that weaves together ways of knowing and secrecy, of intergenerational connections, longevity and temporality. Through Kanafani's writing we see the female fighter through the eyes of her community, in a safe house of comrades, neighbours, food, flowers. The dreamy haze of the Nablus morning masks the underlying hum of resistance, although its calm exterior is repeatedly punctured by violence: 'the body of the earth was like the body of a man pierced with bullets, ablaze with plum blossoms'. The red flowers in the story are a gift for Souad, the markers of late spring, a metaphor for the female militant rising from the sites of colonial violence marking the land.

This understanding of collective resistance is echoed throughout 'Ahki Ya Tair', where tales of operations are often told in the presence of family members. Rashida Obeida describes letters from her husband as influencing her decision to join armed struggle: 'Sobhi sent me a letter – we were in love with each other then … he said to me … our role in history is not to watch events as they happen, we should be making the events happen'. From this film, we also gain a sense of the interpersonal and intergenerational nature of struggle, in which the children of these women are present throughout the film discussing their mother's actions. Scenes are filmed in homes and offices, in cars and scenes of landscape, while drinking tea, and talking about birds. Humour and tenderness are a feature of conversations that are memorialising, analysing, and at times fraught.

* * *

Feminist films and memoirs are sites of anticolonial theorising and engaging with them highlights revolutionary women in an expansive anticolonial archive. Exploring the films as affective readings of how the past haunts the present, we see how felt theorising animates the anticolonial moment and its aftermath. Filmmakers and writers provide crucial analysis of revolutionary change, and the work of female revolutionaries can expand our understanding of revolt and how it is produced. Smaller collectives may be formed through friendship and struggle within the broader context of contestational movements and national liberation struggles. All of this shows, as Mezna Qato writes, that:

> methods of collective oral historical retrieval in particular can be fruitful, a purposeful yet lightly managed gathering of organisers and others together in socialities of intergenerational communion, and a positing of some measure of authorial agency, opening up memories of hurt but also of joie de vivre, hope, play and humour, love often expressed in poetry, literature, and song. These memories should be recorded – they are the affective scaffolding under which blows of pain were withstood.[25]

We began this piece from a troubling contradiction: on the one hand, we know that women's participation was central to these struggles. On the other hand, we constantly encounter their absence in discussions, texts and archives. How can we think through this presence/absence, and how might this open up other sites through which we can witness the revolutionary lives of these women? Partly, this is an exercise in felt theorising. Dian Million, who writes on Canadian First Nations women, describes this as privileging forms of history-telling that are 'rich with emotional knowledges, of what pain and grief and hope meant or mean now in our pasts and futures'. Retelling affective histories allows us to tie together Million's notion of felt theory – or feelings as theory – with a focus on expanding what counts as history.

The feminist memoir and films here are crucial sites of knowledge production and theorising, not least because they centre affective attachments. Through focusing on these films and memoir, produced by and about revolutionary women, we have highlighted forms of theorising anticolonialism and revolution that are attentive to the question of feminist struggle. They have much to tell us about the defeat of the Left and nostalgia for socialist struggle of the past as well as the spectres that continue to haunt Egyptian, Middle Eastern and Northern African politics today.

NOTES

1. For more, see Hannah El Sisi, 'Arwa Salih and the Lost Generation of Egyptian Communism', *Jacobin*, 28 September 2020.
2. Hanan Hammad, 'Arwa Salih's "The Premature": Gendering the History of the Egyptian Left', *The Arab Studies Journal* 24, no. 1 (2016): 124.
3. Tahani Rached, *Quatre femmes d'Egypte*. DVD. Directed by Tahani Rached (Canada: Office national du film du Canada, 1997).
4. For more, see Sara Salem, 'Four Women of Egypt: Memory, Geopolitics, and the Egyptian Women's Movement during the Nasser and Sadat Eras', *Hypatia* 32, no. 3 (2017): 593–608.
5. Arwa Salih, *The Stillborn: Notebooks of a Woman from the Student-Movement Generation in Egypt* (Calcutta: Seagull Books, 2018).
6. Ibid., 4.
7. Ibid., 3.
8. Ibid., 137.
9. Julietta Singh, *Unthinking Mastery: Dehumanism and Decolonial Entanglements* (Durham, NC: Duke University Press, 2017).
10. Mohammed Hudaib, 'Ahki Ya 'Asfura … fi Ghiyab al-Fida'iyya Therese Halassa', *AlAraby*, 2 April 2020.
11. Wedad Qamari in *Making Palestine's History: Women's Testimonies*, ed. Jehan Helou (Nottingham: Spokesman Books, 2022).
12. 'CV Aisha Odeh', *Ibn-Rushd.org* (27 November 2015), https://ibn-rushd.org/wp/en/2015/11/27/award-2015-cv-aisha-odeh/ (accessed 2 November 2022).
13. Nahla Abdo, 'Criminalising the Victim: The Life Story of Rasmea Odeh', *Pluto Press Blog*, n.d.
14. Rosemary Sayigh, 'Palestinian Camp Women as Tellers of History', *Journal of Palestine Studies* 27, no. 2 (1998): 42–58.

15. Mezna Qato, 'Forms of Retrieval: Social Scale, Citation, and the Archive on the Palestinian Left', *International Journal of Middle East Studies* 51, no. 2 (2019): 312–15.
16. Sayigh, 'Palestinian Camp Women', emphasis in original.
17. Nadera Shalhoub-Kevorkian, *Militarization and Violence against Women in Conflict Zones in the Middle East: A Palestinian Case-Study*, Cambridge Studies in Law and Society (Cambridge: Cambridge University Press, 2009), 45.
18. Faiha Abdulhadi, *The Political Role of Palestinian Women in the 1930s, Women's Oral Narratives*, trans. Nitham Said (Al Bireh Palestinian Women's Research & Documentation Center, UNESCO, 2015).
19. Aisha Odeh in *'Ahki Ya Tair (Tell Your Tale Little Bird)* directed by Arab Loutfi (2007; Independent Production).
20. Aya Kutmah, 'Khalida Jarrar on Female Prisoners, Resistance through Education, and Liberation', *Institute for Palestine Studies Blog*, 22 May 2022.
21. 'Therese Halassa: Crossing the Border from 1948 Palestine to Lebanon and Joining the Revolution', YouTube, Karma Nabulsi and Abed al-Razzaq Takriti, 'Learn the Revolution', *The Palestinian Revolution*, 2016.
22. Leila Khaled and George Hajjar, *My People Shall Live* (Chapel Hill, NC: University of North Carolina Press, 1975), 53.
23. Ibid., 86.
24. Nada Abdelsamad, 'Turath Ghana'iy Jamed am Qabil lil-Ta'dil (Musical Legacy: Static or Open to Change?)', *BBC Arabic*, 16 November 2017, www.bbc.com/arabic/tv-and-radio-42011119.amp (accessed 2 November 2022).
25. Qato, 'Forms of Retrieval', 313–14.

11

Delia Aguilar: Dissident Friendship and Filipino Feminist Thought

Karen Buenavista Hanna

Delia D. Aguilar was born in Capiz in the Philippines in 1938 and moved to the United States in 1960. Originally politicised by the various US and international social movements of the revolutionary 1960s and 1970s, her engagement in the women's movements in the Philippines and the US began in the 1970s. Aguilar's intellectual works have been breakthroughs in the development of Third World feminism from a Filipino perspective. Her numerous essays and books have contributed to the development of intellectual thought, merging analyses of class, gender and Filipino national liberation.

Filipina American Robyn Rodriguez discusses her own work in the academy as structured through the concept of kasamahal. Kasamahal combines the words 'kasama' and 'mahal'.[1] About the term kasama, Rodriguez writes:

> Being called 'kasama' and calling those with whom I work side by side in the liberation of the Philippines, and thus the liberation of the Filipinx people, connotes a deep sense of trust and commitment ... connection ... maintained over time and space because of a shared sense of love for an alternative future for our people and the planet.[2]

She goes on to describe the word mahal, or love:

> a love that is expansive, a love that emerges from and feeds into community or kasamahan, a love that is revolutionary for

the world-changing transformations it aims toward; love that is rooted in our collective history. It is a love, therefore, that is radical – *radical* meaning 'from the roots;' a radical love that attempts to root out the structures that attempt to annihilate humanity, annihilate all life; a love that roots out the structures of heteropatriarchal, white supremacist global capitalism and empire.[3]

When combined, kasamahal goes beyond simply a sense of love and commitment to one another, but is deeply rooted in an expansive and shared interest in change to the hegemonic order for the betterment of humanity.

Rodriguez likens kasamahal to 'dissident friendships based on revolutionary love'.[4] Transnational feminists name dissident friendships as historically important for anticolonial movements. In their edited collection, *Dissident Friendships: Feminism, Imperialism, and Transnational Solidarity*, Elora Chowdury and Liz Philipose cite Leela Gandhi for her articulations on 'dissident friendship', or 'all those affective gestures that refuse alignment'.[5] Chowdury and Philipose argue that 'regardless of the social and material conditions' and 'irremediable leaky boundaries of imperialism' that frame the 'border-crossing' friendships in their collection, such as those across race, class and caste, 'deep relationships of attachment and belonging' emerge.[6] They show a history of 'resistance to the divisive and fragmenting lies of structural power; the seeds of global compassion, generosity, empathy and love; and the foundation of a world that works on behalf of life … potentially transformative, personally and socially transformative, and in many cases, subversive'.[7]

Indeed, dissident friendships have been necessary for the development of revolutionary anti-imperialist and socialist imaginings. In both the US and the Philippines, Delia Aguilar cultivated dissident friendships and kasamahal locally and transnationally. Her work and writing over time reflects a multi-directional flow of theory-building and development of Filipino nationalist feminism, rooted within pockets of dissident friendship among women within larger political formations on both sides of the Pacific.

GERMINATING FEMINISMS BEFORE AND DURING
MARTIAL LAW: INTRODUCING DELIA AGUILAR

The Cold War is identified as a window into the allied relationship between the Philippine and US governments against communism. Yet these political conditions produced another type of relationship between activists in both countries that contrasted that of their governments: one of anti-imperialism, nationalist solidarity and communist visions. Delia Aguilar's political activities fall into this second camp. Her anti-imperialist collaborations are a direct affront to the legacies of US colonialism in the Philippines.

On 21 September 1972, the president of the Philippines, Ferdinand Marcos, signed Proclamation 1081, otherwise known as martial law. Leading up to his declaration were decades of rising mass discontent. Students, teachers, religious clergy, nuns, factory and office workers, and peasants protested Marcos's corruption and role in the nation's economic crisis. As Anne Lacsamana puts it, hastening this movement were 'iniquitous trade agreements [that benefitted the US] such as the Bell Trade Act, the Laurel-Langley Agreement, and the Dodds Report, coupled with structural adjustment programs mandated by the International Monetary Fund and the World Bank'.[8] These neo-colonial structures built on political and economic arrangements instigated by the US prior to its formally granting the Philippines independence in 1946. Marcos claimed that martial law was his last defence against a growing communist threat and the alleged ambush of his minister of defence, Juan Ponce Enrile, two points that were called into question in later years. The framing rendered invisible the material basis for the demonstrations opposing his administration. In reality, martial law allowed Marcos to maintain power beyond his second four-year term as president, a limit stipulated under the 1935 Philippine Constitution. With a total population of about 42 and 48 million between 1975 and 1980, scholars estimate that Marcos's 14-year dictatorship led to over 3000 extrajudicial killings, 35,000 torture victims, 70,000 incarcerated, and at least 737 activists who have not yet been found.[9]

Aguilar and her husband, Epifanio San Juan, Jr, moved to the US in 1960 where San Juan, Jr pursued his PhD at Harvard University and Aguilar completed a Master's degree at Boston College.[10] In 1966, they returned to the Philippines and witnessed the rising nationalist and anti-imperialist tide and early stages of a militant anti-Marcos movement. When they moved back to the US in 1968 for work, they settled in their new home in Connecticut. Protests against the Vietnam War and for civil rights were frequent, as a revolutionary movement emerged in the US and globally. Some activists and scholars refer to the Marcos era as an 'awakening' of Filipino consciousness. Michael Tan reflects, 'More than Marcos and Martial Law, it was a nation coming of age, awakening and grappling with identity and history'.[11] By the 1972 declaration of martial law, a number of national democratic (ND) groups and individuals in the US were concerned about the Marcos administration's role in the Philippines' worsening conditions.[12]

The couple engaged with numerous groups including the Friends of the Filipino People, dedicated to exposing Marcos's human rights violations and the US government's support of his regime via economic and military aid.[13] The groups organised educational discussions, conferences and campaigns, among other initiatives. They arranged speaking engagements for people from the Philippines who shared their first-hand accounts of martial law, leafletted information about Marcos's atrocities to passers-by at New York City's Port Authority, the United Nations, and other places frequented by Filipina/os and others interested in the ongoing political situation in the Philippines. They collected donations for Filipina/o political prisoners from local homes while singing holiday songs. After becoming professors, Aguilar and her husband became prolific writers and educators in support of Philippine national liberation. These included a campaign to release her younger sister Mila D. Aguilar, who the Philippine military arrested for her participation in the communist underground from 1984 to 1986.

DEBATES ON THE WOMAN QUESTION

From the North American side of the movement, Delia Aguilar has played a significant role in the development of intellectual thought, bringing together theories of gender and Filipino national liberation. During the 1970s and 1980s especially, many of Aguilar's male and female comrades did not value her intellectual labour at these inter-sections. Their underestimation was a reflection of the enduring impacts of patriarchy across race and political perspectives. Not exclusive to the Filipino movement, male Marxists generally con-sidered the 'woman question', as the gender debate has been named, a 'diversion' and even a 'threat' to the movement. In her introduc-tion to *Filipino Housewives Speak*, Aguilar sums up the theoretical debate between traditional Marxists and Marxist feminists:

The subject of debate is the economic base/superstructure metaphor in orthodox interpretations of Marxism which uphold the absolute priority of class struggle and in which a change in the former, being determinant, is believed to lead to change in the latter, being its mere reflex. In the Third World where, indeed, class antagonisms are indisputably acute, revolutionary move-ments of necessity pose strategies for action where economic issues assume ascendancy and are given the corresponding label 'primary' while other struggles, the 'superstructural' ones under which rubric women's oppression, the family, ideology, and social relations are subsumed, acquire a 'secondary' character.[14]

Aguilar's dialogue with her daughter, Karin, in the 2005 anthology *Pinay Power*, elucidates the contradictions inherent in this designa-tion, which she observed within the Filipino progressive movement:

It was in the process of organizing – at rallies, picket lines, house meetings, and, more crucially, in closed meetings where the 'political line' was set forth and discussed – that I was struck by the incongruity of it all. Here we were, talking about fighting for a more humane society, one in which class differences would even-tually be eliminated and where women would gain equality with men. However, I saw that the way we were conducting ourselves contrasted sharply with these stated goals. Without question, men consistently took leadership positions in the most important activities (those requiring the use of the mind), while women were relegated to traditional support roles.[15]

And yet, many of Aguilar's comrades, male and female, did not agree with what she observed or refused to admit it:

I was told in not so many words that women in the Philippines were already liberated because they controlled the purse strings in the family, because they were respected members of society, and because they were strong. Weren't women guerrilla fighters proof of this? That's what I received in response to my mailed queries to the Philippines – underground photos of red women fighters! And aren't women, by merely joining the movement, already beginning to cast off old norms that require them to stay home? I remember addressing an audience of mostly women in the Philippines in the early 1980s, where one very articulate woman stood up and told me exactly that, using this very language.[16]

Adding to their denial was the suggestion that Aguilar's years in the US were 'exacerbated by affliction with the individualist character of bourgeois feminism', resulting in 'estrangement from one's native culture'.[17] Aguilar found the suggestion 'personally annoying' as well as theoretically incorrect. While it was true that revolutionary women in the Philippines, including Gabriela Silang, the Ilocana rebel general who led an uprising against Spain in the eighteenth century and more contemporary women like Lorena Barros who founded MAKIBAKA (Malayang Kilusan ng Bagong Kababaihan, the Free Movement of New Women)[18] in 1970 had long participated in the movement for national liberation from foreign occupation, the 'instrumentalist' assumption dismissed what Aguilar referred to as 'the systematic character of gender relations'.[19] Aguilar fervently argued that 'conventional gender relations' would not change with women's participation in the movement alone, and it was time to 'call attention to the ideological constructs that both reflect and intensify the concrete conditions of women's subjugation' and create alternative theories.[20]

Like many Marxist feminists of her day, Aguilar fought the limitations of this traditional Marxist framework through academic work.
She pursued a doctorate in Women's Studies at Union College and
conducted research to prove her theories. She recalls:

> Those were extremely frustrating times for me, so frustrating that
> I decided to turn to academic work to find empirical support for
> my stand. I set to work on an examination of the gender division
> of household labor in the Philippines, an issue I considered vital
> to my argument, by conducting interviews with women across
> class (women who were mothers) and letting them speak for
> themselves.[21]

The women's narratives 'revealed unmistakeable male dominion
over household arrangements, the daily conduct and management
of which wives supposedly held exclusive responsibility'.[22] Aguilar's research showed that patriarchal domination persisted across
class lines, showing up clearly in the family, and would not be overthrown through a revolution that did not pay heed to gender.

DISSIDENT FRIENDSHIP AS GROUNDING FOR
THIRD WORLD FEMINIST THEORISATIONS

Study groups have historically been important sites for revolutionary
work. The goal is for participants to work through theoretical ideas
with one another and apply these ideas to their political engagements. While friendships are not necessary for a study group to
function or be successful, they can be productive.

One group that Aguilar participated in was a US New England
study group devoted to studying Marxist feminism at the onset of
the 1980s.[23] In her reflections on her participation, Aguilar does not
describe the frequency of their meeting or the number of women
who participated, but study groups were common in these days
and typically occurred rigorously and frequently, often on a weekly
basis. Aguilar describes being one of a handful of women of colour
participants whose political commitments were 'defined by and

bound to the goal of national liberation of [their] respective countries – Puerto Rico, Bangla Desh [sic], Iran, and the Philippines'.
Although nominally dedicated to Marxist feminism, the group's
practice, dominated by 'white professional women', puzzled Aguilar
and the other women of colour in the group:

> As heterogeneous as our experiences were, our discomfiture with
> a vocabulary thick with allusions to patriarchy and gender antag-
> onism, but utterly deficient in the language to which we were
> more attuned (capitalism, imperialism, national democracy, rev-
> olution, etc.) ineluctably drew us together to puzzle out among
> ourselves and question what, indeed, was Marxist about this par-
> ticular group.[24]

Tensions within the group led some of the women of colour to
leave:

> In light of our pronounced alienation, only the compulsion to
> communicate the urgency of our distinct struggles, along with
> sheer bullheadedness, made it possible for a few of us to remain
> in the study group. We talked about the status of women, but
> whether the narration was of women's lives in Puerto Rico,
> Iran, or the Philippines, the recurrent and pervasive motif was
> the determining force of US imperialism. Its effect was, as one
> might well expect, an oversimplified, unidimensional rendition of
> women's subordination, but one that was necessary in the face of
> an abysmal ignorance of 'the Third World perspective' and its cor-
> ollary, cultural chauvinism ... Within the study group itself, the
> attempt to construct a theoretical position – or, as it were, to pre-
> suppose a unity among women – meant, in practice, the glossing
> over of neo-colonialism and the assertion of the lived experience
> of white professional women as universal.[25]

As Aguilar makes clear, the white women failed to see the racist
neo-colonialism implicit in questions they raised in the group.

One academic's question, 'Should US Marxist-feminists [in
other words, this group] support national liberation struggles that

are patriarchal?', felt particularly 'callous' for the women of colour present. At this time in 1981, the political situation in the Philippines was urgent. Even though Marcos ended martial law during this year, the ending was only nominal. The Marcos administration's continued suspension of habeas corpus allowed authorities to arrest and detain people for 'crimes against security' without due process. Strikes continued to be banned and military arrests of suspected rebels were authorised in Mindanao, while Marcos's rewriting of the Constitution granted him immunity from lawsuits during his tenure.[26] The academic's query and the line of thinking it represented 'presuppose[d] a unity among women ... [and] glossing over of neocolonialism'.[27] It also proved convenient for the continued US imperial presence abroad for capital and military gain.

The tensions and struggle within the study group created conditions for the women of colour to observe recurring themes among their stories. To deepen their thinking further, they began to meet separately 'in the safety of a smaller group':

> Our experiences as women, previously flattened by an exclusive focus on imperialism, now began to flesh out and acquire the rich textures of our diverse life histories. In our exchanges – enthusiastic, vigorous, and always impassioned – we accepted the necessity for a philosophical framework that could analyse gender while rejecting the chauvinist impulses that had accompanied the endorsement of Marxist feminism in the study group.[28]

This smaller collective helped them better understand and theorise what we might call today, Third World feminism. The group was dissident in its politics against the implicit racism and cultural chauvinism of the Western feminism of their larger group members and in the fact that the collective had united despite the particularities that distinguished each of their movements. While Aguilar did not use the word 'friend' in her writings on her Third World women's study group, I suggest that they did indeed bond in friendship, sown in shared frustration within their larger group.

This bond, or dare I say dissident friendship, became grounding for their development of Third World feminist understandings.

DISSIDENT FRIENDSHIPS AND TRANSNATIONAL FEMINISM ACROSS THE PACIFIC OCEAN

As Aguilar was struggling with men and women in Filipino movement groups in the US, women in the aforementioned New England study group, and building theory with women in her Third World feminist subgroup, she began conversing with women leaders in the Philippines grappling with similar thoughts:

I was put in touch with a group of women in the Philippines who themselves no longer satisfied with the old line on women, were starting to hold forums about organizing an autonomous women's movement. Many of them had earned their place in the movement as cultural workers; several had undergone incarceration as political prisoners. I am certain that it was their immersion in the movement that gave them the confidence to express dissent without feeling vulnerable to the facile charge of 'divisiveness'.[29]

Aguilar recognised the women with whom she communicated as dedicated movement leaders and suggests an evolution through praxis in their dissatisfaction with the 'old line', rather than a lack of commitment or 'unsharpened' thinking. Her assessment applies the Marxist theory of dialectical materialism in its analysis that political and historical events result from the conflict of social forces and their series of contradictions and solutions. It is also a compliment to the movement for providing the conditions for the women's assertiveness and critical thinking. Aguilar continues:

While these activists called upon me to provide the theoretical frame within which their discomfiture as women could be articulated, the now-gendered stories that they shared with me gave me the foundation, in practice, upon which to base my critique. I was also much encouraged and energized in knowing that there were several such aggrupations of women, not just the one I was meeting with.[30]

Like in her US study groups, the women's stories – based on their experiences in the Philippines – provided the basis for Aguilar's critique. Aguilar's reflection illustrates the transnational multi-directionality of feminist ideas exchanged. It disrupts notions that a feminist analytic in the Philippines was narrowly imported from the US. By noting that her group was only one of several, she is conscious that 'feminist stirrings' in the Philippines were not occurring *because of her*. Rather, the exchanges were synergistic, occurring during a particular historical moment in time that provoked their thinking and encouraged their discussions.

The repressive political climate under martial law and worsening economic crisis disproportionately impacted women in the Philippines: increased militarism and human rights violations, the controversy on the sex-tourism industry, Filipina brides-for-sale ads, sexual harassment of Filipina migrant workers, graft and corruption in government, lack of consumer protection and other issues opened new avenues through which organised women were able to express their concern for women's conditions and general rights and welfare issues.[31]

Further establishing a more unified feminist consciousness in the Philippines was the assassination of Benigno 'Ninoy' Aquino on the tarmac of the Manila Airport in 1983. Aquino had been a long-time political opponent and critic of Marcos.[32] Scholars argue that Aquino's assassination was the catalyst that galvanised the middle class to join the radical Left in both the US and in the Philippines, leading to a surge in protest, articulated through the creation of new organisations, including those devoted to women's issues. According to Leonora Angeles, 'While these groups were not clearly feminist in their orientation and vision, such an understanding could provide brighter potentials in articulating women's issues and possibilities of forming coalitions with other similar-minded women's groups.'[33]

Groups like PILIPINA and KALAYAAN (Katipunan ng Kababaihan Para sa Kalayaan, Organisation of Women For Freedom), formed in the Philippines in 1981 and 1983, respectively, were among the first groups in the nation to apply an explicitly feminist analytic to their activism and were instrumental in leading women to share and analyse their conditions with one another.[34] Leaders of these groups and others founded the umbrella group GABRIELA (General Assembly Binding Women for Reforms, Integrity, Equality, Leadership and Action) in March 1984, which served to coordinate the newly formed women's organisations.[35]

The influence that leaders of these organisations may have had on Aguilar and her study group is found in a letter I found in Aguilar's personal archives.[36] Dated 18 June 1984, it references Aguilar's upcoming visit to the Philippines that summer. Indeed, the preface of *Filipino Housewives Speak* (1991) tells us that Aguilar conducted interviews for the book in the summer of 1984.

The letter, addressed to Aguilar and signed by a member of KALAYAAN named Fe, explained the letter's enclosed contents: an article by Aida Maranan (Santos) expanding on a KALAYAAN paper written by Estrella Consolacion for the group's launching the previous December; writing on 'gender asymmetry' taken from the Latin American women's experience during the last decade; and a hand-out by PILIPINA, explaining 'how clearly they have defined their objectives and activities as a leading feminist group, years before KALAYAAN'. The first piece reflected KALAYAAN's thinking at the time, through Maranan's interpretation, which Fe wrote was both informed by collective research and study sessions and the feminist thinking of PILIPINA. It is interesting to observe that KALAYAAN's feminist study sessions were happening alongside Aguliar's sessions, but on different sides of the world. The letter and contents illustrate a flow of feminist information from the Philippines to the US through Aguilar and provide a partial geographic and temporal map to KALAYAAN's feminist developments.

In discussing these materials, Fe wrote, 'This is not the first time that the woman question has been raised in the Phil. movement'. She referenced Dee Feria who had 'pioneered on the subject with her essays on feminism and the Philippines Left' and Marra P. Lanot, who 'too has written a great deal on Filipino women in cinema, literature, etc.' These lines suggest she was replying to Aguilar about feminist conversations in the Philippines, refuting the idea that feminism was a purely Western concept.

Fe continued with a brief overview of KALAYAAN's status in debates around the woman question:

> Kalayaan ... is still in the midst of a debate whether or not the Woman Question is a major or minor contradiction within the national struggle. Along with our male allies within and without the Movement, we have been trying to come out with a formulation that will not sound divisive, petty bourgeois and (female) chauvinistic. So far, no luck. The word, feminist, is still a dirty [sic] word both to the left and the right. Yet, we won't settle for anything less. We are determined to liberate the term and situate it within the context of the present national struggle.

The word 'feminist' at this time was stigmatised in Marxist circles around the world for its association with Western feminism. This passage revealed that Filipina women in the Philippines were identifying with the word on their own terms, despite common misconception that feminist ideas are uncritically appropriated outside of the US and Europe. I imagine learning about these exchanges was affirming to Aguilar, who had been struggling with little support from other comrades in the US. Fe's letter continued:

> Because it is such a controversial concept, we've asked permission from the people in the Movement to let us work out the idea by ourselves first before identifying ourselves as M/F [Marxist Feminist] within the Movement. *Wala naman silang objection* [They don't really have an objection].

KALAYAAN's actions were not only strategic but crafted rigorously and intellectually in the interests of the movement, carefully navigating class, racial, gender and imperialist hierarchies due to feminism's historic association with the 'West' and the US. The women of KALAYAAN knew the movement was in an advantageous position with new support from the middle classes, so they were careful not to jeopardise such gains by their 'coming out' as feminists and/or making the larger movement appear fractured. Fe's next words gestured towards a sense of dissident friendship: 'When you come this July, you'll see, hindi ka na nag-iisa [You are no longer alone]'. Fe was aware of Aguilar's conflict with her male comrades in the US, as implied in her statement, 'Hindi ka na nag-iisa' (you are *no longer* alone) rather than 'you are not alone'. Such words were a further invite to Aguilar to join KALAYAAN in the shared fight. Fe ended the letter thanking Aguilar and her husband for books they sent to Fe's child. The personal information Fe shared and her warm regards ending the letter suggested that Aguilar and Fe did not yet know one another well and that they were building an emerging friendship with one another.

This friendship continued to grow, as shown in the words of Aguilar:

> Without the energetic interaction I had with numerous feminist friends in Metro Manila, my stay from 1987 to 1988 would simply not have been as inspiring or meaningful. It is their wonderful vitality and resolve that sustained me and enabled me to confront ideas that were unthinkable prior to my visit. I thank them deeply for their openness, warm friendship, and generous support. I want to make special mention of the women in my feminist study group – Tess Vistro, Carol Anonuevo, Sylvia de la Paz, Princess Nemenzo, La Rainne Sarmiento, Guy Claudio, Irene Donato, Fe Mangahas, Miyen Versoza, Fe Arriola, and Nora [Leonora] Angeles. Meeting weekly with them was terribly important to me in ways that they may not have realized.

Not only did the listed Philippines-based women play an important role in Aguilar's life and intellectual development, but Aguilar's contributions to the study group also proved impactful for the women. In 2022, during her recollections about the Philippine feminist movement on a panel commemorating the 50th anniversary of Marcos's declaration of martial law, Leonora Angeles, now a professor at the University of British Columbia, recognised Aguilar for sharing feminist readings with their group many decades ago.[37]

* * *

The dissident friendships and kasamahal shared between Aguilar and the feminist revolutionaries in the Philippines are inspiring and instructive for all interested in transnational movement building. With revolutionary intentions, their dissident friendships were forthright in the collective attempt to dismantle patriarchy and imperialism, showing how the woman question was strategically negotiated, theorised and experienced by Filipino Marxist feminists from both sides of the Pacific Ocean. Aguilar continues to be engaged in conversations about feminism and national liberation. Since the feminist engagements in this chapter, she has published numerous essays and taught at various educational institutions over the past 50 years. These include tenured appointments in the women's and ethnic studies department of Bowling Green State University and Washington State University, the role of Irwin Chair of Women's Studies at Hamilton College, and a fellowship at the Bunting Institute of Radcliffe College. In 2004, she co-edited the anthology, *Women and Globalization* with Anne Lacsamana.

NOTES

1. Robyn Rodriguez, 'Kasamahal: Revolutionary Love, Dissident Friendships, and Pinay Scholar-Activist Praxis in the Ivory Tower', in *Closer to Liberation: Pin[a/x]y Activism in Theory and Practice*, eds. Amanda Solomon and D.J. Kuttin Kandi (San Diego, CA: Cognella, 2023), 369.
2. Ibid., 343.
3. Ibid.
4. Ibid., 346.
5. Elora Chowdury and Liz Philipose, eds., *Dissident Friendships: Feminism, Imperialism, and Transnational Solidarity* (Champaign, IL: University of Illinois Press, 2016), 3; Leela Gandhi, *Affective Communities: Anticolonial Thought, Fin-de-Siecle Radicalism, and the Politics of Friendship* (Durham, NC: Duke University Press, 2006), 10.

6. Chowdury and Philipose, *Dissident Friendship*, 3. Gandhi, *Affective Communities*, 2.

7. Chowdury and Philipose, *Dissident Friendship*, 3.

8. Anne Lacsamana, *Revolutionizing Feminism: The Philippine Women's Movement in the Age of Terror* (Boulder, CO: Paradigm, 2012), 41.

9. Alfred McCoy, *Closer Than Brothers: Manhood at the Philippine Military Academy* (New Haven, CT: Yale University Press, 1999), 193, 206.

10. Interview with the author, Storrs, CT, 6 July 2015.

11. Ferdinand C. Llanes, *Tibak Rising: Activism in the Days of Martial Law* (Mandaluyong City: Anvil, 2012), vii.

12. Barbara Gaerlan, 'The Movement in the United States to Oppose Martial Law in the Philippines, 1972–1991: An Overview', Unpublished paper (2003).

13. Ibid. See also Raymond Bonner, *Waltzing with a Dictator: The Marcoses and the Making of American Policy* (New York: Times Books, 1987).

14. Delia D. Aguilar. *Filipino Housewives Speak* (Manila: Institute of Women's Studies, 1991), 5.

15. Karin Aguilar-San Juan and Delia D. Aguilar, 'Feminism across Our Generations', in *Pinay Power: Peminist Critical Theory: Theorizing the Filipina/American Experience*, ed. Melinda de Jesus (New York: Routledge, 2005), 171.

16. Ibid., 172.

17. Delia D. Aguilar, 'Third World Revolution and First World Feminism: Toward a Dialogue', in *The Feminist Challenge* (Manila: Asian Social Institute, 1988), 19.

18. Aida F. Santos, 'Marxism and the Philippine Women's Movement: Reflections on Praxis', in *Marxism in the Philippines: Continuing Engagements*, eds. T. Encarnacion Tadem and L. Samson (Manila: Anvil), 114.

19. Aguilar, 'Third World Revolution', 19.

20. Aguilar-San Juan and Aguilar, 'Feminism across', 173.

21. Ibid., 172.

22. Aguilar, 'Third World Revolution', 20. Aguilar later published her findings in the book *Filipino Housewives Speak*.

23. Aguilar, 'Third World Revolution', 17.

24. Ibid., 17–18.

25. Ibid., 18.

26. A.B. Tan, 'Marcos Ends Martial Law, Keeps Tight Grip', *Washington Post* (18 January 1981).

27. Aguilar, 'Third World Revolution', 18.

28. Ibid., 19.

29. Aguilar-San Juan and Aguilar, 'Feminism across', 173.
30. Ibid.
31. Leonora Angeles, 'Getting the Right Mix of Feminism and Nationalism: The Discourse on the Woman Question and Politics of the Women's Movement in the Philippines', (MA Dissertation, University of the Philippines, 1989), 172–3.
32. After Marcos declared martial law, Aquino was arrested and imprisoned on charges of subversion, which many believed were trumped up charges due to his vocal criticisms of Marcos. After three years of exile in the US, he returned to the Philippines knowing he was risking his life. He was murdered while being escorted from the plane on national television. Though debated, many people believed at the time that Marcos was the person who ordered the assassination.
33. Ibid., 178. For more about these groups, see Angeles, 'Getting the Right Mix', 173–8.
34. Angeles, 'Getting the Right Mix', 183–5.
35. GABRIELA, *GABRIELA Convention Proceedings* (Quezon City: Mt. Carmel Community Center, 1985).
36. Fe, 'Dear Delia', 18 June 1984, Personal archives of Delia D. Aguilar and E. San Juan, Jr. While there are two people named Fe on this list, I surmise that the sender of the letter is Fe Mangahas, as she has been cited elsewhere as being a KALAYAAN member. See Aguilar, *The Feminist Challenge*, x.
37. Leonora Angeles, 'Diasporic Refusals and the Marcos Restoration Panel', University of British Columbia, Zoom, September 2022.

12

Sister Cities: Salvadoran Refugees and US-Salvadoran Solidarity in the Americas

Molly Todd

From the rural village of Arcatao, in northern El Salvador, community leader Domitila Ayala Mejía wrote a letter to 'Compañera Prudencia [Prudence Barber] and other compañeros' of the Madison-Arcatao Sister City Project in Madison, Wisconsin, United States.[1] 'I send you a million greetings', Ayala's 7 August 1998 letter began, 'hoping that you are well in health and in your work in support of communities in need'. The purpose of the letter, she continued, was to introduce herself as the new member of Arcatao's junta directiva (grassroots town council) in charge of sistering relationships.

'Sistering' began in the mid-1980s as a new form of transnational human rights and social justice activism. At the time, El Salvador was enmeshed in a violent civil conflict. The government of El Salvador – backed by the government of the US – was intent on quashing a coalition of armed insurgents, the Farabundo Martí National Liberation Front (FMLN). Much of the FMLN's support base was in the countryside, where campesinxs (roughly translated, peasants) like Ayala had gained significant experience with agricultural cooperatives, peasant unions and federations, Christian base communities, and other forms of communalism over the previous decade.[2] As opposition to the Salvadoran military-oligarchic regime grew, state forces retaliated; by 1986, their scorched-earth operations' massive, deliberately destructive campaigns of bombing, burning and murder had left more than 60,370 civilians dead; 90,000 houses destroyed;

a half million people internally displaced; and more than a million refugees in other countries.[3] As a grassroots practice, sistering linked war-displaced Salvadorans with US-based groups, and together the Salvadoran and US activists denounced violations of human rights, called for an end to the war, promoted civil and human rights, and modelled alternative structures and relations. Breaking from exclusionary and hierarchical patterns, sistering promoted horizontal relations of engagement, mutual empowerment, dignity and justice.

Although Salvadoran activists engaged with people from all over the world, they paid special attention to the US given repeated US interventions in Latin America during the nineteenth and twentieth centuries. El Salvador felt the full weight of the 'Colossus of the North' in the 1980s and early 1990s as the administrations of Ronald Reagan and George Bush turned the tiny Central American nation into the largest imperial state-building project since Vietnam.[4] Six billion dollars of US military and economic aid propped up the Salvadoran regime during the 1980s alone, and the US cold war-inspired national security doctrine turned all who did not support that regime into an enemy of the state, exacerbating and lengthening El Salvador's bloody conflict.[5]

Ayala knew this history well. Born around 1958 into a campesinx family in Chalatenango department in northwestern El Salvador, at 19 years old she began working clandestinely with the Popular Liberation Forces, one of the largest and most influential of the five armed groups that ultimately formed the FMLN and fought to topple the military-oligarchic complex that had ruled El Salvador for nearly a century. As she rose through the ranks of the Popular Liberation Forces, Ayala formed part of the urban militia in San Salvador, spent two years in Nicaragua learning with the new revolutionary Sandinista government, and then returned to Chalatenango to help organise the civilian population. She served as the president of one of the region's Local Popular Governments. She helped initiate classes for children. And '[w]hen there were military operations', Ayala later wrote to her Madison audience, 'I was responsible for leaving with civilian groups that is to flee sometimes without knowing the terrain we were heading towards.'

The stakes were high. Ayala's father, two brothers and life partner were killed by state forces during the war (late 1970s–1992), leaving her three small children fatherless. She herself sustained injuries from shrapnel. 'The war left me with sorrows', she conceded.

But this was also a time of great hope. In the wake of successful anticolonial movements in the Global South and the neighbouring Cuban and Nicaraguan Revolutions, there was a real sense that a New El Salvador – and a new world – was under construction. In this new society, all people would have access to a life of dignity and justice. And so, even in the midst of violence, opportunities arose as people worked towards this brighter future. 'I learned many things in war', Ayala explained, not least of which were 'using a typewriter' and 'speaking without fear before public audiences'.

In this context of terror and hope, Domitila Ayala's letter to the Sister City committee in Madison, Wisconsin, is significant. It points to her role as a combatant with the FMLN, a defender of civilian groups, an elected member of grassroots governments, a mother, a student, a communications expert, a diplomat. On a broader level, it speaks to the roles that Salvadoran campesinas played on national and international levels, their belief that a better world was possible, and their commitment to take action to bring that world into being.

*   *   *

In the late 1970s, María Mirtala López and her family became active in rural organising efforts in their village of Los Amates, Chalatenango department. Salvadoran leaders perceived such actions as subversive, closely aligned with or even directed by the armed insurgent groups that were then beginning to wage war on the Salvadoran regime. State forces thus responded with brutal repression: first, the selective abduction, torture and assassination of community leaders, followed by massacres and scorched-earth operations that left little more than the charred remains of cornfields, farm animals, houses and humans. After surviving such a campaign, López found refuge in a church-sponsored camp in the capital, San Salvador, where, at 15 years old, she co-founded the Christian Committee for the Displaced of El Salvador (CRIPDES).[6] This organisation, aligned with the Popular Liberation Forces, was 'an organization of popular struggle and human development' with multiple objectives, including organising war-affected people, particularly the internally displaced and refugees; ending state violence; and supporting short-term emergency survival and longer-term development projects. Through these actions, CRIPDES sought to 'contribute to the search for solutions to the causes of the conflict we are living; and to create an economic model of self-management ... so that little by little, we can escape the system of dependence'.[7]

CRIPDES helped the displaced people to form committees and other structures in order to defend their rights: the right to organise, the right to participate in political processes, the right to return to and remain in their places of origin, the right to life as civilians in conflicted zones of El Salvador, the 'right to have access to land and to work, and to build a lasting peace'.[8] CRIPDES's early efforts gave rise to a national rural repopulation movement. Between 1986 and early 1991, tens of thousands of displaced people repopulated more than one hundred villages in eight of El Salvador's 14 departments.[9] In the repopulations, CRIPDES 'carr[ied] out programs in the social, economic, and political sphere', including free healthcare and education, clothing and shoe workshops, small community stores, and public works projects like the construction of homes, roads and bridges.[10]

The rural repopulation movement in many ways upended historical patterns of inequality. Repopulated villages came to stand as 'a model for social, economic and political development' not only for Salvadorans, but also for their international allies. As US-El Salvador Sister Cities National Center staffer Juliana Barnard wrote in early 1992, the repopulations 'have been a source of inspiration for all of us with profound concerns for social justice'.[11]

Barnard would know. She and the US-El Salvador Sister Cities network had been accompanying Salvadoran repopulators since 1986. CRIPDES spurred transnational solidarity connections like this as a tool to ensure the viability of the repopulation movement. As refugees returned to and rebuilt rural villages, groups of concerned citizens in US cities like Madison, Wisconsin, and Cambridge, Massachusetts, 'adopted' those villages, providing moral and material assistance. By the late 1980s, nearly a dozen of these pairings existed and, in early 1990, the US committees joined forces to establish the National Center for US-El Salvador Sister Cities.[12] At the height of the grassroots sistering movement in the mid-1990s, National Center staff coordinated some 50 US-based committees.

Sister Cities committees collaborated with CRIPDES 'to provide sorely-needed financial and moral support to the people' in the repopulations, and 'to maintain ongoing vigilance and pressure upon the Salvadoran government' regarding respect for the human and civil rights of repopulators. This transnational solidarity helped Salvadorans carve out space – in the midst of war – where alternative structures could develop and even flourish. The Sister Cities-CRIPDES collaboration represented an alternative structure in and of itself. They set out 'to succeed in establishing bonds of friendship and cooperation', and modelled a form of international relations based on horizontalism rather than hierarchy.[13] Many of the US American activists applied the lessons they learned from their Salvadoran partners to their own lives, by participating in co-housing communities, community radio and purchasing cooperatives, for example.

Salvadoran women sustained these Sister Cities relationships. Before the internet and mobile phones, they relied heavily on letters sent by post, telex and fax. Two women in particular, Isabel Hernández and Lorena Martínez, sent many letters to US committees during the late 1980s and early 1990s. The two served in various capacities on the governing boards of CRIPDES and affiliated organisations like the National Repopulation Committee. Their letters often encouraged the growth and strengthening of the network in the US in order to strengthen collaboration with Salvadorans. In the first days of 1991, for example, they wrote to US Sister Cities,

> We hope that the activities you have planned for this year will unite us more strongly to create new fruits that benefit our communities – the communities where daily efforts are put in to

remaining in their homes, in struggling for a more dignified life, where human rights are respected and the longed for peace with social justice that all Salvadorans desire reigns.[14]

Many El Salvador-based CRIPDES affiliates also travelled to the US on speaking tours. An important task of the US Sistering committees was 'to build public awareness' in the US about the situation in El Salvador.[15] Tours were a critical tool for such consciousness-raising. While on tour, Salvadorans gave presentations to audiences at churches, schools and community groups addressing the local and global factors that caused the Salvadoran conflict, the role of the US government in perpetuating the conflict, and the unique experiments in collective life that were underway in repopulated communities: popular education and health systems, grassroots governments, revolving community loan funds, cooperative farm and animal husbandry projects, and more.

Salvadoran women also built and sustained transnational relations from sites of long-term or permanent exile. An estimated one million Central Americans arrived to the US in the 1970s and 1980s, seeking refuge from the wars at home. As refugees, many Salvadorans engaged with pre-existing organisations such as churches, cultural centres, schools and human rights groups. They established their own community organisations, such as the Comité de Salvadoreños Progresistas, Casa El Salvador, and the Central American Resource Center to build a sense of community among Salvadorans while also providing support for new arrivals.

Salvadorans also helped to establish and guide many new solidarity groups that took shape in the US, including the Sanctuary movement, a network of individuals and faith houses across the country that provided refuge to people who had fled the Central American wars. The US refused asylum to the vast majority of Salvadorans, Guatemalans and Nicaraguans during the 1980s, claiming that they were economic migrants rather than refugees with a well-founded fear of persecution. Many US citizens argued that this official response was designed to elide the US government's own culpability in creating the mass migration. After all, US government agents advised the region's conservative leadership, trained their soldiers and counter-revolutionaries, and provided aircraft, bombs, bullets and other tools of war that were then turned against not only the armed revolutionary forces like the FMLN, but also unarmed civilians. To save their lives, millions of Central Americans fled north where many encountered US citizens who were concerned about human rights and angry with their own government's complicity in the violence. This set the stage for the development of Sanctuary's 'underground railroad', which provided transportation, safe houses, and legal support to the refugees.

Many Salvadoran Sanctuary refugees remained publicly unnamed and unidentifiable due to security concerns, yet they regularly spoke out before the press and other audiences, and engaged in solidarity work in clandestine or behind-the-scenes ways. Others took on very public leadership roles. Esther del Carmen Chávez Mancia was among these prominent leaders. Chávez had been involved in Christian base community organising in El Salvador during the 1970s. Inspired by those experiences and with a desire to address a need in her family's village, in 1980, she, her brother and a friend established a day care centre. Such activities put Chávez and her family on the Salvadoran regime's 'subversive' watchlist. After state forces abducted her father, Chávez went into hiding. She fled the country, eventually making it to the US where she continued her activism through several different organisations. She worked for years with the American Friends Service Committee, first as a community organiser and later as director of their refugee centre.[16] She co-founded the New Jersey-Los Amates Sister Cities Project, and was pivotal in the formalisation of the national network of US-El Salvador Sister Cities. Chávez also served as one of the first paid staff people in the newly established National Center of the US-El Salvador Sister Cities. Through these positions, Chávez helped to inspire and motivate US citizens into solidary actions with El Salvador.

Also providing inspiration and direction to US organisations were the tens of thousands of Salvadorans residing in refugee camps in Honduras and, after 1986, those who had repopulated rural villages in El Salvador. At the refugee camps, Lorena Martínez and other displaced people explained, 'they succeeded in maintaining and developing a broad organizational structure under the direction of a Camp Committee, democratically elected by the refugee population to defend their interests'.[17] Among the work groups that existed in the camps were committees for 'information and propaganda' or 'social communications', which established and maintained contact with a range of international audiences – with special attention to solidarity groups. When refugees returned to El Salvador to repopulate rural villages, they brought these grassroots governance and communications systems with them.

Women often outnumbered men in the refugee camps and repopulations and, so, they carried significant responsibilities in these systems. Communications committee members gathered and presented information about the lived reality in the camps and repopulations, the everyday struggles of Salvadorans in the context of extreme repression, and ongoing organising efforts. Their communications offered an alternative to mainstream officialist news media, which labelled all Salvadoran citizens working for change as 'terrorists'. Refugees and repopulators flipped that script, calling out state forces as the true 'terrorists'.[18]

Such communications happened on multiple levels. Representatives served as spokespeople when visitors requested interviews. They produced and distributed calendars of abuses and news magazines such as *Patria Nueva* (Honduran camps) and *La Esperanza* (Ciudad Segundo Montes, Morazán). They organised meetings and protests, complete with banners condemning abuses, demanding rights, and calling for international solidarity. They composed and performed poetry and songs that carried important messages. As María, a refugee at the Mesa Grande camp, sang, 'Sowing any seeds / for later harvest; / ... together, working, / we will make society'.[19]

Even young girls contributed to international communications efforts. One of the most prominent ways they did so was through their drawings. During the 1980s, children produced thousands of drawings for international solidarity groups. They depicted their homes before displacement, life in the camps and repopulations, and their hopes for the future. Many explicitly called out the governments of El Salvador, Honduras and the United States as perpetrators of human rights violations. Lorena Ramos, for example, illustrated Honduran and Salvadoran soldiers massacring civilians at the Lempa River as they tried to flee a government bombing campaign. Marina Otero explained the events depicted in her drawing: 'The soldiers came and killed our families in El Salvador'.[20] Alongside a drawing of her house in El Salvador, María Aguilar wrote: 'My right leg was amputated by a bomb from the planes that the USA has sent to the government of El Salvador'.[21]

These young artists also portrayed the dignity and value of rural lifeways and the promise of new communal experiments taking shape in the revolutionary context of the time. In their drawings of their families' small farms, Juana, Alejandrina Reyes and others included domestic animals, heavily laden fruit trees, women tending to clusters of hens and chicks.[22] Rosa Aristide highlighted the day care centre, an important collective project.[23] Others drew collective farms, community kitchens and warehouses, and tailoring and shoe-making workshops. Still others, like Elvira Petronila Mendoza Mázar, celebrated international relations of horizontalism. Her drawing features a group of people near a banner proclaiming 'Long live international solidarity', their left fists raised high.[24]

These drawings had wide impact. Visitors to the refugee camps and repopulations collected the drawings and activated them on the international stage. A common practice was to include children's drawings and photographs, along with personalised stories from Central America, in slide show presentations for church groups, community organisations and elected officials. Patricia Goudvis, a US-based filmmaker, produced the documentary, *If the Mango Tree Could Speak*, featuring children's drawings.[25] Others produced books like William Vornberger's *Fire from the Sky*, and exhibits including 'War through the Eyes of Children' at the Los Angeles Children's Museum in 1986 and 'Exhibition of Children's Art Work from El Salvador' at the Multicultural Arts Center in Cambridge, Massachusetts, in 1991.[26] Such events often included educational kits and guided tours and discussions for school and community groups.

In the repopulated villages in El Salvador, women continued fomenting transnational relations through positions on local and regional grassroots governing councils. Communications representatives continued producing and disseminating reports and other resources about human rights abuses, reconstruction projects and alternative development programmes.

The governing councils in the repopulations also included Sistering Representatives like Domitila Ayala, who wrote the 1998 letter to Madison that opened this chapter. One of the primary duties of Sistering Representatives was to maintain communications with Sister City committees in the US and elsewhere. Ayala and Sistering Representatives from other repopulated communities were, in effect, citizen diplomats; they bypassed official government communications networks and forged their own grassroots channels of information exchange. Like their counterparts in the refugee camps, these representatives relied mostly on letters sent through visitors or postal carriers. They also scheduled periodic telephone conversations and, in emergencies, they sent updates by telex or fax.

Women who served in community and regional leadership roles travelled to the US for speaking tours. In 1992, for example, Marta Cerna Alfaro participated in a one month-long tour coordinated by Sister Cities and other US-based solidarity organisations. Cerna, who served on the board of a regional organisation, the Union of Solidary Communities and Repopulations of Northern La Libertad and San Salvador, spoke to a variety of US audiences about 'the crisis of peace' in El Salvador. Her point was that although the government and insurgent forces had signed a peace accord in early 1992, the struggle for justice was far from over. Cerna provided evidence of the ongoing exclusion of campesinxs from political decision-making in El Salvador, dignified housing, and public services like potable water, electricity, roads and transportation, healthcare and education. She also discussed the damaging effects of continued US military aid to the Salvadoran government. Internal records from hosting organisations indicate that tours by Cerna and her compatriots were often 'very successful in terms of outreach, public education and fundraising'.[27]

Salvadoran women also coordinated delegations from the US. Usually consisting of 3–15 US citizens and lasting up to 10 days, delegations addressed the general situation in El Salvador as well as specific themes like education, healthcare, women's rights and organic farming. Many delegations responded to human rights emergencies, such as when state forces raided the CRIPDES headquarters in the capital of San Salvador in 1989 and imprisoned and tortured six leaders. Delegates met with campesinx leaders at local, regional and national levels, as well as Salvadoran politicians and religious figures, US embassy officials and non-governmental groups. After returning home to the United States, delegates held press conferences, gave talks to community groups, and lobbied their elected officials. Like the Salvadorans who participated in tours, these delegates functioned as citizen diplomats, modelling an alternative diplomacy built on respect and fraternity rather than hierarchy and exploitation.

* * *

State violence displaced tens of thousands of Salvadorans between the late 1970s and early 1990s. Yet, as Inés Alvarenga, a woman who found refuge at the Mesa Grande camp in the early 1980s, wrote, 'Just because we are refuged / doesn't mean we will forget / all of the suffering / that there is in El Salvador'.[28] In sites of refuge within El Salvador as well as in Honduras, the United States, and beyond, Salvadoran women – the vast majority of them from poor rural backgrounds – organised and mobilised for change. They co-founded organisations like the Christian Committee for the Displaced and Sister Cities, demanded that states and international entities respect their rights, repopulated once-razed villages and rebuilt them from the ground up, and modelled viable alternative development initiatives and international relations.

Women learned a lot from the war, but they also gave a lot, as Domitila Ayala explained in her letter to her friends in Madison. But, Ayala wrote, both the losses and the lessons of war inspired her to continue her activism well after the war: '[A]lways, I am fighting

for my community and always alongside my children'.[29] This echoes
a popular saying in El Salvador: la lucha sigue, the struggle continues. If women were pivotal in the formation of transnational
solidarity networks during the cold war era, so too have they maintained those networks to the present. Women across El Salvador
continue to engage their Sister Cities compañerxs and other groups
in working towards liberty, justice and equality for all.

NOTES

1. Compañero and compañera are terms used by Salvadoran revolutionaries and allies, and activists on the political Left. It may be translated
   as comrade or friend/companion, depending on the context. All translations from the Spanish are my own unless otherwise noted. This and
   the following quotes are from Domitila Ayala, letter to Compañera
   Prudencia et al., 7 August 1998, Records of Madison-Arcatao Sister
   City Project (hereafter MASCP Records), US-El Salvador Sister City
   Archive, private archive (hereafter USESSC Archive).
2. Campesinxs are rural inhabitants who have traditionally survived
   through a combination of strategies, including subsistence farming and
   seasonal wage labour on large plantations. Some also engage in sales of
   excess crops, eggs, homemade cheeses or breads, or 'convenience store'
   items. In Spanish, campo means countryside and campesinos means
   people of the countryside. Following traditional Spanish noun gendering, campesina refers to a woman, and campesino to a man. The plural
   form, campesinos, subsumes women into the male-gendered ending.
   This gendered language contributes to the invisibility of women in the
   historical archive. In this chapter, I use the more gender inclusive -x
   ending for this and other nouns. I also intentionally do not italicise
   Spanish-language terms in order to integrate them more fully into the
   narrative. Italicising terms emphasises 'foreignness', and these words
   are anything but foreign to the Salvadorans who use them.
3. Patricia Marín, *Infancia y guerra* (Guatemala City: UNICEF, 1988), 4;
   María Cristina García, *Seeking Refuge: Central American Migration to
   Mexico, the United States, and Canada* (Berkeley, CA: University of
   California Press, 2006), 26.
4. George Wheeler Hinman Jr, 'The Colossus of the North', *North
   American Review* 226, no. 3 (September 1928): 273–80. For a diver-
   sity of studies on US intervention and Latin American responses,
   consider Fred Rosen, ed., *Empire and Dissent: The United States and*

Latin America (Durham, NC: Duke University Press, 2008). On US intervention and state-building, see Greg Grandin, *Empire's Workshop: Latin America, the United States, and the Rise of the New Imperialism* (New York: Metropolitan Books, 2006).

5. García, *Seeking Refuge*, 25–6. Here, 'cold war' is intentionally not capitalised as it sets it apart as a distinct 'event' – one dominated by the US-USSR conflict. The cold war era was made up of multiple experiences and perspectives – not just those revolving around 'the victors' or 'the empires' of the Soviet Union and the United States.

6. Mirtala López Biography, File 1990s-1991 Mirtala López Case, MASCP Records, USESSC Archive.

7. CRIPDES-CNR, 'Programa Global 1992-1993', file 'CRIPDES Global Prjt', Box 6, Papers of Pat Arvidson (New Jersey), USESSC Archive.

8. 'Sister City Project for the City of Arcatao', 1986, file Arcatao Projects 1986-1989, MASCP Records, USESSC Archive.

9. For more on repopulation and grassroots sistering, see Molly Todd, *Long Journey to Justice: El Salvador, the United States, and Struggles against Empire* (Madison, WI: University of Wisconsin Press, 2021). For details on the repopulation movement and campesinx organising in general, see Molly Todd, *Beyond Displacement: Campesinos, Refugees, and Citizen Action in the Salvadoran Civil War* (Madison, WI: University of Wisconsin Press, 2010).

10. 'Sister City Project for the City of Arcatao'.

11. Juliana Barnard to Friends, 27 February 1992, file National Meetings & Encuentros-1992-03 Summit UES, MASCP Records, USESSC Archive.

12. 'Born in Times of War: How US-El Salvador Sister Cities Began', 22 January 1993, file National Meetings & Encuentros-1993-01 NYC, MASCP Records, USESSC Archive.

13. 'Sister City Project for the City of Arcatao'.

14. Isabel Hernández and Lorena Martínez to Brothers and Sisters of the Sister Cities, 17 January 1991, file 1988-1994 National Office, MASCP Records, USESSC Archive.

15. Madison Common Council, Resolution 42,209 establishing a Sister City with Arcatao, El Salvador, March 7, 1986, MASCP Records, USESSC Archive.

16. Summary of testimony of Esther Chávez and Walter Guerra, 17 August 2004, Center for Justice and Accountability, 3 September 2004, www.derechos.org/nizkor/salvador/doc/chavez.html (accessed 29 November 2022).

17. Repatriados y Desplazados de El Salvador Concertación de Refugiados, 'Documento hacia la Conferencia sobre refugiados centroamericanos

(CIREFCA), Ciudad de Nueva York, 23 a 26 junio de 1990', June 1990, Instituto Interamericano de Derechos Humanos (San José, Costa Rica), 12.

18. In this their work overlapped closely with the insurgent communications structures of the FMLN. See Eudald Cortina Orero, 'Disursos en (r)evolución: Lucha ideológica y captación de solidaridad en el movimiento revolutionario salvadoreño', *Naveg@Merica* 17 (2016): n.p.

19. 'Mesa Grande: Rescate cultural', collection of writings of Salvadoran refugees at Mesa Grande (1982–84), compiled by Gisela Ursula Heinrich, 1999, private collection, 119.

20. Papers of Denise Maultsaid, object numbers 2811/60 and 811/13, Museum of Anthropology, University of British Columbia (hereafter MOA).

21. María Aguilar, drawing, c. 1988, file 1980s-1980s-92 communications, MASCP Records, USESSC Archive.

22. Juana, drawing, n.d., Papers of Linda Dale, private collection; Alejandrina Reyes, drawing, n.d., object number 2811/6, MOA.

23. Rosa Aristide, drawing, n.d., Papers of Linda Dale, private collection.

24. Elvira Petronila Mendoza Mázar, drawing, n.d., object number 2811/144, MOA.

25. Patricia Goudvis, *If the Mango Tree Could Speak* (New Day Films, 1994). See also Patricia Goudvis, *When We Were Young There Was a War*, www.centralamericanstories.com/the-project/ (accessed 4 December 2022).

26. William Vornberger, ed., *Fire from the Sky: Salvadoran Children's Drawings* (New York: Writers and Readers Publishing Cooperative, 1986); Ann Japenga, 'A Coloring Book of Catastrophe: Drawings at Children's Museum by Young Refugees from El Salvador and Guatemala Depict the Horrors of War', *Los Angeles Times*, 24 December 1986, View Section, 5; Exhibit of Children's Art, flier, File Sister City-1991, Box 2, Papers of Judith Somberg (Cambridge, MA), USESSC Archive.

27. 'El Salvador: Crisis of Peace', flier for evening with Marta Cerna Alfaro, n.d., file 13-Regional Reports: January–March 1992; and 'UCRES Regional Report April–June 1992', 30 June 1992, file 12-Regional Reports: April–June 1992. Both in Box 6, Arvidson papers, USESSC Archive.

28. 'Mesa Grande', 71.

29. Domitila Ayala, letter to Compañera Prudencia et al., 7 August 1998, MASCP Records, USESSC Archive.

13

INTERVIEW: Building Socialist Feminism on Southern Ground: The Women Democratic Front on the History and Politics of the Left in Pakistan

Mahvish Ahmad, Marvi Latifi, Ismat Shahjahan and Tooba Syed of the Women Democratic Front in Pakistan

On 8 March 2018, long-time political workers with the organised Left – especially the Awami Workers Party (AWP) – established the Women Democratic Front (WDF), an autonomous socialist-feminist political organisation of women in Pakistan. WDF's manifesto commits its members to anti-capitalist and anti-feudal politics and sees its struggle as intimately linked with movements resisting the centralisation of power through the oppression of Pakistan's marginalised nations, broader anti-imperialist and anti-war battles, the fight against religious orthodoxy, and feminist, anti-patriarchal struggles. The formation of the WDF came in the heels of a multi-year debate on the importance of creating an autonomous space for socialist women, one that could openly discuss and critique patriarchy without undermining anti-capitalist politics, and one that could provide an alternative to liberal feminism without sabotaging the struggle against patriarchal formations.

As a member of the WDF based in London, I reached out in 2022 to my comrades to discuss the possibilities and challenges of building socialist feminism in Pakistan. The idea was to interview three members engaged in grounded organising in the country, including Ismat Shahjahan (federal president) and Tooba Syed (federal secretary, Information and Publishing) based in Islamabad and Marvi Latifi (president, Sindh National Unit) based in Hyderabad. Yet, getting my comrades onto one call proved to be a challenge that ironically mirrored the difficulties of building socialist feminism on southern ground.

Our initial plan to speak was postponed because of apocalyptic floods; Marvi's house was destroyed and Tooba got involved in using the skeletal network of WDF chapters to distribute flood relief in the absence of a functioning humanitarian state apparatus. Ismat was constantly travelling for political work, running socialist-feminist political schools or holding branch meetings. When the final edits for this chapter were due, Ismat's dear comrade and mentor, the progressive lawyer Latif Lala, was shot eight times inside the Peshawar High Court. She could not miss his funeral, and she could not fail to pay her respects. An economy on the brink of collapse, and the everyday struggles of making sure the home held together under the weight of skyrocketing inflation and a country at the edge of sovereign default, puttered along in the background for all those who took part in this interview. Insecurity caused by economic downturn, ecological devastation, militarisation and militarism, and ongoing patriarchal violence is everywhere, but the difficulties of cobbling together this interview is a reminder that it is concentrated on southern ground. For my comrades to take time out to speak despite the precarious conditions of life itself reflects the steely commitment socialist feminism requires in Pakistan.

Through this interview, two kinds of interventions are made possible. First, as revolutionary Left politics in the Global South gains ground within academic institutions as a legitimate topic of scholarship, writing these histories remains stubbornly separated from the political practice of actually existing movements. This interview is a step towards bridging this gap. Second, a host of books are emerging in both Urdu and English accounting for the Pakistani Left. This literature reproduces a tenacious attachment to the biographies of big men in the telling of its history,[1] reflecting a practice of identifying parties through the name of male leaders.[2] By entering the biographies, experiences, analyses and theorisations of four socialist feminists, this interview actively disrupts a history and politics of the Left too long tethered to men.

—Mahvish Ahmad, January 2023, Lahore

Mahvish Ahmad (MA): I want to start with your autobiographies, as a route into telling a feminist history of the Left – and introducing the WDF. How were you politicised as socialist feminists? Why form, or join, the WDF?

Marvi Latifi (ML): The question of women's place in society emerged for me in 2006, though not in the way you might suspect. I was initially conservative, a bit of a fundamentalist, and started wearing an abaaya and destroying pictures of myself to follow strict ideas of Islamist modesty. It was only once I was quite deeply involved that I began to feel a restriction in my mobility, I was told I can't go here or there, so I began to think about gender.

I also experienced restrictions from my family. I come from a lower middle-class family so they let me study and go to school. But they also tried to stop me from political work, from going to study circles and protests, preferring I pursue personal interests like getting married early. Sometimes, their attempts to stop me turned violent.

I arrived at socialist feminism through the Left. A philosophy professor introduced me to the class question, the differences between rich and poor, around the time of the 2011 floods. The readings he introduced me to – classics like *The Germany Ideology* – combined with my own experience of watching the unequal effects of ecological devastation turned me towards questions of class oppression. As I got more deeply involved with the Left, by around 2014, I joined others in forming study circles. We went to villages in Sindh, some cities too like Sanghar in Nasirabad, with the main aim of understanding what gendered roles exist in our society, what kind of oppression women face. We read Kamla Bhasin's *What Is Gender?*

and Gerda Lerner's *The Creation of Patriarchy* and started the very first socialist-feminist magazine in Pakistan, *Nariwaad*, in Sindhi and out of Hyderabad. In a country where Urdu is the dominating, national language and Sindhi is minoritised – and where feminism has for so long been associated with liberal, urban upper-class women who speak Urdu – this was a big achievement. It builds on a long history of women's organising in Sindh, for instance, in the work of Sindhiani Tehreek, a women's peasants movement founded in the 1980s.

My route into the WDF came through the AWP, where I was a member. Here we had formed a woman's group called Naari Jamhoori Mahaz. We were very successful, the Sindh branch of the AWP mobilised women at a level noticed by leftists across the country. A few years later we felt it necessary to organise a separate front for women, so we established the WDF.

Ismat Shahjahan (IS): I'd like to first question the definition and boundaries of feminism. If the definition is too narrow, there is little space left to include my struggle or broader struggles that I consider part of feminism in Pakistan. Typically, resistance against patriarchy is defined as feminist struggle. But, coming from a socialist-feminist background, I, and the WDF, believe that the struggle against colonialism, class oppression, women's oppression, and national oppression are all feminist because half of humanity is formed by women.

On my involvement with the Left: I was born into a family of Khudai Khidmatgars, a non-violent, Pashtun anticolonial movement formed in the early twentieth century by Khan Abdul Ghaffar Khan. My grandfather's family were part of the Indian National Congress and deeply rooted in anticolonial struggles: My father's uncle was killed by colonial forces.

I grew up on the Left of the National Awami Party (NAP), which was formed in 1957. It brought together socialist, nationalist, and feminist forces. The Anjuman Jamhooriat Pasand Khawateen or the Democratic Women's Association (1950–2005) took part in the establishment of NAP. As a young girl, my father used to take me and my younger brother to a Marxist study group, run by his comrade, the communist leader Sarfraz Mehmood. I started my political journey at age 19 and became a student leader in 1983. I first joined the Pashtun Students Federation, a nationalist organisation, and then the Democratic Students Federation, a communist group, before finally joining the Communist Party of Pakistan (CPP). I participated in the very last election of student unions in Pakistan, before they were banned by the US-backed, military ruler Zia ul-Haq in 1984. I also joined the Qaumi Inqilabi Party, a mainstream leftist party which was formed after the dissolution of the CPP in 1989. I eventually became a founding member of the AWP, and later a founding member of the WDF. In 2018, I also joined the Pashtun Tahaffuz Movement (PTM). The PTM is a continuation of the struggle of progressive Pashtuns against imperialist war in the region, and one of the most important grassroots movements against militarised violence in Pakistan today. It emerged from Pashtuns displaced by the triple violence of the Pakistani military, religious militancy, and US American drones in the former Tribal Areas.

On developing a feminist consciousness: I was born to a mother who was a forcibly converted Muslim; she was among many Hindu and Sikh girls left behind in the chaos of Partition. She suffered from many kinds of oppression and was always supporting women in my village. That was how I developed my initial social consciousness. But critical political consciousness emerged during my work with the CPP. The CPP was banned and operated under the cover of the Awami National Party (ANP), so most Pashtun communists including myself were members of the ANP. After a split in the CPP, Pashtun communists believed we may need a national democratic revolution. Pashtuns were and remain an oppressed nation in Pakistan and gun fodder in an ongoing Great Game. Their oppression mirrors that of the Baloch and the Sindhis – as well as the Bengalis who seceded from Pakistan in 1971. Pashtuns specifically are racialised as violent and backward, suspected of harbouring loyalty to Afghanistan, and hounded by the military apparatus as terrorists. As Pashtun leftist women, we decided that we wanted to have an autonomous organisation, not only autonomous of political parties but also autonomous from Punjab and Pakistan level socialist-feminist configurations, like the Anjuman Jamhooriat Pasand Khawateen. So, we formed the Democratic Women's Association Pakhtunkhwa or DeWA (1987–94). That was the first socialist-feminist organisation that I worked with and I actually founded it myself in 1987. It was one of several democratic women associations throughout the world during the Cold War.

As far as the WDF is concerned, it emerged from broader efforts in post-Cold War Pakistan to rebuild the Left. I am the founding president of the WDF. As part of this effort, the AWP, of which I am also a founding member, was formed in 2012 in an effort to merge three left-wing parties. In addition to centring the agenda of women's emancipation in party politics, we decided to have an autonomous platform for women with a commitment to socialist feminism, one that saw all feminists and leftists as allies. Today, the WDF has its own flag, its own constitution, and its own manifesto.

Our aim is to bring together struggles of women along class and national lines, and also to create a space for women, who live amidst feudal or tribal formations, as well as working-class women in cities, where conservatism and class oppression is growing. In both places, we face extreme forms of religious fundamentalism and violent patriarchy. We are children of a war that has used extremism and fascism as its main instruments.

Tooba Syed (TS): My introduction to socialist feminism was more in terms of my own lived experiences rather than an introduction to feminist or socialist texts or movements. Like comrade Marvi, I was born into a lower middle-class family. My father had leftist leanings, but he was associated with the Pakistan People's Party during his youth, a mainstream, social democratic party.[3] I learned so much through his encounters. Both of my parents were leftists, but only my father actively participated because it was easier for him to do it as a man.

On my more formal engagement with politics – when I moved to Islamabad during my teenage years, I read in the newspaper that there was a protest against the rape of Mukhtar Mai[4] and I realised this was something I could join. It was a coincidence ... I just walked over. It was liberating to know that something I couldn't talk about in the confines of my home was suddenly made possible in public – we could say it all in the streets. So as a young girl, I joined protests, mostly against sexual or domestic violence. Then, in 2013 when the Baloch missing persons march led by Mama Qadeer was arriving in Islamabad, I reached out to the AWP. I met women comrades with whom I went to the march.

It became clear that there was space for all kinds of struggles from the platform of the AWP. This became one of the most important spaces I have belonged to. Yet, it was clear that changes were needed in the Left. Comrades in Sindh were already organising socialist-feminist fronts, so we came together to discuss the extension of their work, to talk about the formation of WDF at a national level.

MA: Thank you so much comrades. I asked you this first question because I see each of you as historical subjects participating in and shaping the history of the Pakistani Left. You are Left-feminist history in the making right now.

I'd like to now build on where each of you left off, at the moment you came to socialist feminism, and joined the WDF. What kinds of challenges have you faced in efforts to promote a socialist feminism? What kind of criticism or pushbacks have you had to grapple with from broader political formations, especially other progressives who you'd otherwise think were your comrades?

TS: In my experience, we faced pressure from various different organisations or collectives. Of course, there was some pushback from the Left because, for them, it was an argument about women and men working together instead of forming a separate autonomous organisation, so we had to first convince our own comrades. The party at large believed in the formation of either a woman's front of the party or women working within the party, they did not understand why an autonomous organisation was important for the political work of the Left in the country. However, we also received support from some male comrades on the Left. But there was a pressure that I didn't foresee coming, which was from within the feminist movement, or the mainstream feminist movement as we know it. I realised that many of us were not welcome in traditional feminist spaces, primarily because most feminists associated with other organisations – who might have socialist leanings but did not call themselves outright socialist feminists – were not very comfortable with our existence. We were not welcome in a lot of feminist spaces; we were never invited in discussions, we were never asked to come to seminars initially, I'm talking 2018, 2019. When we tried to organise the women's march, even though WDF was autonomous, we were still seen as women fronting for men of the Left. But we were women fighting the men of the Left at the same time.

ML: I totally agree with comrade Tooba. When we established WDF in Sindh, it was ironic that at a regional level Naari Jamhoori Mahaz was welcomed by Left and progressive circles. Yet, once we inaugurated the WDF at a federal level we faced challenges in Sindh and within the party – once we became autonomous at this level, we were criticised. In Sindh, WDF was also not welcomed in a number of other feminist organisations, because we address class as well as gender issues. Even now, as we are organising relief work in Sindh – one of the worst hit provinces in Pakistan after the floods – we again face a number of challenges. Liberal feminist organisations say that we take orders from our male comrades of the Left, and they dismiss us as a feminist organisation. But I think we are creating a kind of revolution and organising at the grassroots level.

IS: As the president of a feminist-socialist organisation in a country which has been ridden with military dictatorships, wars, extremist patriarchy, national oppression, state repression, and religious fundamentalism, it has been a nerve-breaking experience for me taking all these pressures and coordinated attacks. As my comrades have mentioned, a section of the Left thought that the woman question should be resolved within the class struggle only and that by establishing an autonomous organisation we are dividing the movement.

There are ideological issues between sections of the Left and the WDF, but WDF is the leading organisation theorising a socialist feminism in Pakistan. We have had to take a position on debates on labour theory, relations of production, social reproduction, and current debates on the new faces of capitalism, for example the social care debate. We have also broadened the ideological frontiers of feminism and included national liberation struggles into its framework.

The biggest challenge we face is from the state itself. Armed and political groups that had the patronage of the state attacked us, they attacked our rallies, and some of us had to go underground. There was an ongoing campaign against the Aurat Azaadi March. The liberal feminists organised the Aurat March (Women's March) and the WDF together with the Left organised the Aurat Azaadi March (Women's Emancipation March). As organisers, WDF had to face court cases, fake charges of blasphemy and so forth. I personally received threats from all sides, from the state, from religious militant groups. There was a coordinated attack on us from the media, there were court trials. Building a socialist-feminist movement in Pakistan is highly revolutionary work. At any moment anything can happen to you and all the frontline leadership of the WDF remain under threat. We had to raise self-defence groups in Islamabad to guard the movement ideologically and guard the movement physically. And whenever we take a rally, we do drills, and we figure out: From which side will they attack us?

MA: I'd like to ask you to scale up and think about socialist feminism in the region and around the world. To think, in other words, about international solidarity and difficulties you face in being part of a global conversation – also in terms of building a socialist feminism that crosses over to Afghanistan, Iran, India and China. What are some of the ideological and practical difficulties in building transnational solidarity?

IS: The socialist-feminist movement had a very close association with the Women's International Democratic Federation (WIDF) which was established in 1945 and was a global association, a platform of socialist women and outfits around the world. With the collapse of the Soviet Union and the collapse of many communist parties around the world, the WIDF did not continue as an active body. It was the forum where all socialist-feminist organisations in the world did international solidarity work. Today, there is no international platform of socialist-feminist organisations, that is a major issue.

Another issue is that in mainstream Pakistani politics the centrality of the anti-India cause is a big barrier for us to establish any relationship with our Indian sisters in struggle. As far as regional solidarity exchange is concerned, I used to work closely with the Revolutionary Association of the Women of Afghanistan (RAWA) way back in the 1980s and 1990s, but this organisation was crushed and its revolutionary leader Meena was assassinated here in Quetta in Pakistan. In Afghanistan the Left has been crushed, in Iran the Left has been crushed fully. Most of the feminist solidarity work in Pakistan and in India is through NGO forums which I don't prescribe to so I have not been actively pursuing these networks. It involves a lot of co-optation. In terms of international solidarity we have not been able to do much. We have established a brief relationship with the Kurdish movement, and we established some communication with the Communist Party of Iran. I feel that from the day the socialist internationals and the WIDF collapsed, we haven't found any platform, and the war with Afghanistan and very problematic relationship with India limit our abilities.

There is one view within the organisation, and I personally am also of this view, that we have to build an organisation *here*. WDF is a very small organisation on that account. We believe: Think internationally, or globally, and act locally. We want a home-grown, organic movement rooted in our own history and our own society first, and then we will find the right connections for international solidarity.

TS: WDF is still only four years old so I feel much of our time has been invested in grassroots organisation building. We've been so mired in local dynamics, state repression, internal dynamics we have here because of being a socialist-feminist organisation within Pakistan. Almost an entire year went into dealing with the court cases of the Aurat Azaadi marches.

We are part of Progressive International, we are founding members, but there aren't many socialist-feminist member organisations. Not much has happened on the feminist front within the Progressive International. If we have to form transnational or international feminist solidarity, I think we should prioritise the South Asian region because it is very important that we talk to each other right now given the floods, climate change, and the rise of authoritarianism across the region. So, I think that starting there and perhaps reaching out to other organisations in the Global South is what should be on WDF's agenda in the coming years. However, I agree with comrade Ismat. Our priority remains to first build our own organisation in the country.

MA: Let me return to the theme of this volume: the dominance of men in written histories of the Left, and the erasure of women. What would it mean to write the histories of women and feminist movements, or female figures in progressive politics or other kinds of political struggles? When you think about the histories of political struggle that you have grown up with and have heard about throughout your life, what have they looked like? Why do you think that women are made invisible in the history of the Left and political movements?

ML: In the history books we hardly find women's resistance or what role women have played. When women are at home, they provide services to male comrades or partners to allow them to do their political work, without women, men would not be able to do that work! And it's not only women at home but women outside who are made invisible. I want to talk about a character named Mai Bakhtawar, a daughter of Sindh.

When we organise, we don't bring the portrait of Mai Bakhtawar forward, but we have portraits of other male comrades or other peasant or Marxist leaders. We are trying to familiarise our co-workers to talk about all those who have played a role in peasant or other resistance movements. In the history of Sindh we have a number of peasant movements, be it Hyder Bux Jatoi's movement or other movements in Jhuddo and Sangar. There are a number of peasant movements in Sindh, but again, we have a lot of work written or mentioned in terms of Hyder Bux Jatoi, but it was because of Mai Bakhtawar's sacrifice that there was a Sindh Tenancy Act, which now secures peasant ownership of their own crop yield. Mai Bakhtawar is considered a brave daughter of Sindh.

During the colonial period, before partition in 1946, and even today, it was common in Sindh for landlords to arrive with armed men at the time of the yield and take most of the harvest, leaving little for peasants. This happened in Tando Bago Tehsil where Mai Bakhtawar lived. In 1946, there was a conference in the village of Jhuddo and many men went. Mai Bakhtawar was the only person securing the harvest on her land. When the men arrived, she resisted and stood against feudal landlords to protect her harvest. In that moment, she is remembered to have raised the very slogan later familiarised by Hyder Bux Jatoi, and which is heard spoken by peasant movements across the country: *Whoever sows, shall reap!* The men shot Mai Bakhtawar and she died. Because of this remarkable, revolutionary moment – Mai Bakhtawar's sacrifice – the Tenancy Act was passed by the Sindh Government in 1950. Mai Bakhtawar opened a path for women to be part of the peasant resistance, and women of Sindhiani Tehreek remember and are inspired by Mai Bakhtawar's struggle.

There is another recent character of Mai Jindo, a peasant in Tando Bahawal. In 1992 Major Arshad Jameel kidnapped and killed nine villagers. They included the sons and sons-in-law of Mai Jindo. The army said that they were terrorists, but this was false and they had been involved in a land dispute. Mai Jindo stood against Major Arshad Jameel's claims, and argued that they were fighting for their rights. She won the court case against him, and is today a symbol of resistance in a patriarchal Sindh, against the army.

These are not the only women. Women students from the University of Sindh took part against the One Unit Policy, protesting for the right to Sindhi in an Urdu-dominated Pakistan, and the restoration of provincial rights. Sindhiani Tehreek, a women's peasant movement, took part in the Movement for the Restoration of Democracy (MRD) against General Zia ul Haq.

TS: I think in feminist scholarship, the invisibilisation of women within the larger political context has happened because women who were not identifying as feminists or fighting for the causes of only gender-based oppression were never seen as having a legitimate voice or struggle that contributed to the feminist movement. In WDF we want to blur those clear distinctions between what is a feminist movement and what does not get categorised as a feminist movement by feminist scholars. Within the wider Left, historically, the Left was not as conscious of women's oppression as it is today, and I think that has another role to play as well. Only workers were seen as the true subjects of a class-based politics and revolution, and women workers are still not remembered nor recorded in these histories. I think that is changing now, we see the need for women in these movements and the need for women to be visible. There are a lot of women one can see in the photo archives, but you don't know their names.

IS: Generally, whatever is written in Pakistan does not even include the resistance against colonialism. Pakistan's history has been enforced through a state narrative that starts from 1947, August. And there are so many lies. I recently presented a paper for WDF's school and made the point that Bangladesh's entire struggle for freedom has been erased, including the rape of Bengali women at the hands of the Pakistan army. Most scholarship is coming from the Pakistani diaspora and they are writing from the framework of Muslim nationalism. The anti-nationalist and anti-class or bourgeois lens based on a state narrative has also excluded entire movements. Meanwhile, feminist scholarship marks an artificial line between women's movements and feminist movements, the former is not seen as part of the latter. But when you define feminism in these terms, you exclude women's movements in other progressive and connected struggles.

I believe one aspect of critical political work which we need to do is to build socialist-feminist scholarship in Pakistan. We do not think that patriarchy is the *only* structure of oppression. There is class, religious, and national oppression. For us, the national struggle, class struggle and the struggle for secular democracy is a part of the feminist struggle. We need to make a new socialist-feminist scholarship which recognises how these oppressions and movements are intertwined and interlocking.

Another problem also exists, we don't know who the characters in these histories were and what their role was. When the entire struggle is lost, even if you find a few of those characters, it doesn't really solve the problem. We need to look at broader resistance movements and women's leading and non-leading roles.

The fight to be seen, to build our scholarship is a critical area for us and we plan to open this debate but not at the cost of fracturing feminist solidarity or our solidarity with the Left. But we are opening this up and are determined to continue doing this.

MA: Thank you so much everyone, your answers have raised new and important questions. What are some of the methods for WDF's theorisation and its intellectual arm, in what kind of ways can we address the issue?

ML: First-hand experience is a must, it is necessary. It will only be possible when we connect people with the living experience of facing oppression right now with theorising. Language is also a barrier when we are trying to write these histories. These women are remembered in their own languages, not Urdu. There is also the question of how to articulate experience into broader theory, because women living in repression can find it hard to articulate what they are facing or going through.

TS: In my opinion histories can only be rewritten if you are doing something today towards change. My problem with the writing of history is that it is primarily written by people who are not part of the movement within the country. We need to change who gets to write and who doesn't get to write. I think it can only happen if organic scholarship or the people who are actually invested in this politics themselves start writing and I think it's only in the process of politically organising or working that you see what is missing and what has to be unearthed. Me and another comrade of mine who is part of WDF are trying to write. We don't know if we will ever finish, it's still a practice we are doing simply because we personally felt that there are gaps. There are a lot of missing archives, there are a lot of missing voices or missing movements. We're working on questioning this binary of what is and is not scholarship, what is and is not feminism. This is one of the main issues in terms of scholarship produced in or on Pakistan. Rewriting is important but it has to come from one's own political work and grounded-ness.

IS: Reclaiming or rewriting history is not an option for me. Change the history instead of rewriting it – this is my political position. Of course, we cannot be ahistorical in our struggle, we should remain in continuation with analysis and resistance. We do not need to engage in modernist or post-modernist tendencies of reconstructing texts, or the philosophical view that objective truth does not exist. We need not assume a break with the past, from history. But, we must focus on changing our objective realities, the structures of oppression which surround us, which are the condition of our politics.

I also believe that rewriting history projects can be meaningful but who rewrites them is an important question. We must think about standpoint. We should archive our own work and we have started doing so in *Nariwad*. A lot of researchers have contacted us, but when they publish they write something other than what we tell them. They do commissioned research projects they are paid for, and sometimes it becomes knowledge they break up and sell, knowledge but not truth grounded in struggle. So, I think it's better to not even get involved in these kinds of history projects. Instead, we want our organisation to write. We have to combine our struggle with our history, and have a historical approach to struggle.

A lot of this scholarship is in English but most of the working class in Pakistan can't understand English. We have some people in our own organisation who are not even able to read. So we must translate and also create texts in our own national languages including Pashto, Balochi, Sindhi, Seraiki, Punjabi, Pakistan's lingua franca, Urdu, as well as other languages.

TS: In a way, we end up writing our own history the very moment we stand on the frontlines of this struggle.

NOTES

1. Many books are biographies or autobiographies – one might even say hagiographies – of communist men. Take Sajjad Zaheer's *Roshnai* (Model Town, Lahore: Prime Time Publications, 2006), a book written from the perspective of the founder of the Communist Party of Pakistan about the Progressive Writers Movement or, more recently, Abid Hassan Minto's compilation of essays, speeches and interviews in *Apni Jang Rahe Gi* (Lahore: Sanjh, 2016). Or books like *Chale Chalo Ke Manzil Abhi Nahin Aai* (Lahore: Jumhoori Publications, 2017), penned by Nuzhat Abbas and Ahmad Saleem on Jam Saqi, the former general secretary of the Communist Party of Pakistan, who later joined the Pakistan People's Party, from Sindh. Though other writings on the Pakistani Left have a more capacious reading of Pakistani Left history – Saadia Toor, *The State of Islam: Culture and Cold War Politics in Pakistan* (London: Pluto Press, 2011), for instance, thinks deeply with progressive feminist poets – this remains a dominant genre of left-wing history-writing.
2. The AWP is, for instance, known as Abid Hassan Minto's party. A split in the now defunct National Awami Party led to the creation of one NAP associated with the Abdul Wali Khan and another with Maulana Bhashani. This reflects broader tendencies in Pakistani political parties and is not limited to the Left – the leading Pakistan Muslim League, Nawaz, is identified through the name of its male leader, Nawaz Sharif. Nevertheless, it does show us that the Left is not above reducing party politics to the identities of male leaders.
3. The Pakistan People's Party was formed by Zulfiqar Ali Bhutto, from a feudal background himself and a minister in the first military ruler's government, who eventually took up the mantle of Islamic socialism in Pakistan, with the support of long-time communist political workers.

His legacy and that of the PPP is checquered, and he and his follow-ers have been accused of both making a Left imagination possible on a mass scale through slogans like *roti, kapra, makaan* (bread, clothes, shelter) and of destroying any hope of a mass-scale Left movement.

4. In June 2002, Mukhtar Mai was targeted in a gang-rape sanctioned by a tribal council which ruled that it would constitute a revenge of honour. Mukhtar Mai went against local custom, which would expect her to commit suicide, and instead took the rapists to court. Her case became famous across Pakistan and the world.

Contributor Biographies

Mahvish Ahmad works on the material legacies of anticolonial and Left movements, archival practices in sites of disappearance, fugitive organising under conditions of war, and the shifting techniques of imperial and sovereign violence, especially in Pakistan. She's a co-founder of Revolutionary Papers, which studies anticolonial journals (with C. Morgenstern, K. Benson), a Trustee of the Islamabad-based South Asian Research and Resource Centre which holds 40,000 items on Pakistan's socialist and democratic movements, Archives of the Disappeared, which investigates archive in sites of annihilation (with M. Qato, Y. Navaro, C. Morgenstern), and *Tanqeed*, an English-Urdu magazine of the Left in Pakistan (with M. Tahir). She's an Assistant Professor of Human Rights and Politics at the London School of Economics.

Maurice J. Casey is a Research Fellow in the School of History, Anthropology, Philosophy and Politics, Queen's University Belfast. He received his DPhil in History from the University of Oxford. His research interests include queer history, histories of radicalism in the Irish diaspora and histories of political migrants in the inter-war Soviet Union.

Evyn Lê Espiritu Gandhi recently received tenure and promotion to Associate Professor of Asian American Studies at the University of California, Los Angeles (Tovaangar), effective 1 July 2023. She received her PhD in Rhetoric from University of California, Berkeley. She has published *Archipelago of Resettlement: Vietnamese Refugee Settlers and Decolonization across Guam and Israel-Palestine* (University of California Press, 2022), co-edited with Vinh Nguyen *The Routledge Handbook of Refugee Narratives* (Routledge, 2023), and written on topics including Asian American and Asian diaspora histories, transnational feminism, settler colonialism and Indigenous liberation, queer studies, and Cold War and Third World solidarities. She also hosts a podcast *Distorted Footprints* through her Critical Refugee Studies class.

Kanwal Hameed is an inter-disciplinary historian with a background in Middle East Studies, and currently a Visiting Postdoctoral Fellow at the Orient Institut Beirut. She received her PhD from the Institute of Arab and Islamic Affairs (IAIS), University of Exeter. She has published 'One Struggle, Many Fronts: The National Union of Kuwaiti Students and Palestine', in Sorcha Thomson and Pelle Valentin Olsen (eds), *Palestine in the World* (Bloomsbury, 2023), 'Toward a Liberation Pedagogy', co-authored with Katie Natanel and Amal Khalaf, *Kohl Anticolonial Feminisms* (January 2023), and *The Quiet Emergency: Experiences and Understandings of Climate Change in Kuwait*, co-authored with Deen Shariff Sharp and Abrar Alshammari, Kuwait Programme Paper Series, LSE Middle East Centre (13) (2021).

Karen Buenavista Hanna is an Assistant Professor of Gender, Sexuality, and Intersectionality Studies at Connecticut College. She has published over a dozen academic and popular essays including in *Amerasia*, *Hypatia*, and *Hyphen Magazine*. Her experiences as a New York City public school teacher and community organiser prior to her doctoral studies inspire and shape her pedagogy and research. She is currently writing her first book manuscript, *Revolutionary Intimacies: The Makings of a New Filipina/o American Left*.

Jehan Helou was born in Haifa, Palestine, in 1943. Her family was uprooted to Lebanon during al-Nakba in 1948. She was involved in the Palestinian national and women's liberation struggle for more than 20 years. She was a member of the Executive Committee of the General Union of Palestinian Women, head of its international relations, and a member of the Palestinian National Council. She became the director of Tamer Institute for Community Education in Palestine (2000–06) and is currently the president of the Palestinian national section of the International Board on Books for Young People.

Yatta Kiazolu is an Assistant Professor of Global and International Studies at the University of California, Irvine. She received her PhD in History from the University of California, Los Angeles. Her research interests meet at the interstices of twentieth century US and African American history, women and gender studies, and contemporary Africa and African diaspora studies. She is currently preparing a monograph which examines African American women's organisations and the range of Black feminist solidarities with African decolonisation from the post-war years through the 1980s.

Kebotlhale Motseothata is a scholar, writer, researcher, poet, human rights defender and journalist. She obtained her Bachelor of Arts Degree in African Literature and Theatre and Performance at the University of the Witwatersrand. She holds an Honours degree and an MA in African Literature both from Wits. She obtained her National Diploma in Journalism at Boston Media House. Kebotlhale is a member of the Golden Key International Honour Society. She is a MMUF and the South African History Workshop Fellow. She has been published by the South African Human Rights Commission, *The Kalahari Review*, Poetry Potion and the Mail &amp, and the *Guardian*. She has previously worked with the Feminist Republik and has also worked for the New Age newspaper (*Afro Voice*). Her work centres gender and culture in the liberation movement. Her research interests include the cultural narratives produced by the women of Umkhonto we Sizwe (MK), as well as the representation of women in the posters of the Medu Art Ensemble.

Thy Phu is a Distinguished Professor of Race, Diaspora, and Visual Justice at the Department of Arts, Culture, and Media at the University of Toronto. She is author of two books, *Picturing Model Citizens: Civility in Asian American Visual Culture* (Temple University Press, 2012), and *Warring Visions: Vietnam and Photography* (Duke University Press, 2022). She is also co-editor of *Feeling Photography* (Duke University Press, 2014), *Refugee States: Critical Refugee Studies in Canada* (University of Toronto Press, 2021) and *Cold War Camera* (Duke University Press, 2022).

Jeremy Randall, with a PhD in History, is the Associate Director of the Middle East and Middle Eastern American Center at The Graduate Center, City University of New York. He is a historian of leftism in the Middle East with a focus on Palestine as well as leftist critiques of sectarianism and capitalism in postcolonial Lebanon via intellectual and cultural productions. He is currently preparing a monograph on the alliance between the Popular Front for the Liberation of Palestine and the Japanese Red Army as an example of internationalism and solidarity with the Palestinian Revolution in the 1970s and 1980s.

Sara Salem is an Associate Professor in Sociology at the London School of Economics. Her research interests include postcolonial studies, Marxist theory and global histories of anticolonialism. Her recently published book is entitled *Anticolonial Afterlives in Egypt: The Politics of Hegemony* (Cambridge University Press, 2020). A selection of published journal articles include: on Angela Davis in Egypt in the journal *Signs*; on Frantz Fanon and Egypt's postcolonial state in *Interventions: A Journal of Postcolonial Studies*; on Gramsci and anticolonialism in the postcolony in *Theory, Culture and Society*; and on Nasserism in Egypt through the lens of haunting in *Middle East Critique*. She is currently thinking and writing about ghosts and anticolonial archives.

Roba Salibi has recently completed her PhD in Cultural Studies from the University of Exeter. She is currently a Postdoctoral Fellow at the University of Oxford.

Elif Sarican is a writer, editor, curator and translator. She has lectured at and collaborated with a number of cultural institutions including Haus der Kulturen der Welt, Künstlerhaus Mousonturm, Zürcher Hochschule der Künste, HAU Hebbel am Ufer and universities across Europe and North America. Elif, a researcher and archivist, collaborates with artists in the exploration and preservation of visual depictions showcasing Kurdish life both in Kurdistan and across the diàspora. She is guest editing a special issue of Barnard College's peer-reviewed S&F Online journal titled, 'Rage, Struggle, Freedom: Politics of Hope and Love', publication due in 2024.

Marral Shamshiri is a PhD candidate in International History at the London School of Economics. She is interested in the histories of socialism and internationalism, Third Worldism and the global cold war. Her current project looks at the history of the Iranian Left, focusing on the transnational and political connections between Iranian and Arab revolutionary movements in the long 1960s and 1970s. She holds an MPhil in Modern Middle Eastern Studies from St Antony's College, University of Oxford, and was a visiting researcher at the University of California, Berkeley, in 2021. She is Managing Editor of the journal *Cold War History*.

Madina Thiam is a historian of West Africa in the nineteenth and twentieth centuries. Her work explores the circulations of West African people and ideas; social histories of Islam in the Sahel; race-making in the Atlantic and Saharan worlds; Malian women's histories; and pan-Africanism. She received a PhD in History from the University of California, Los Angeles, and is currently an Assistant Professor of History at New York University. She also helps manage the *Projet Archives des Femmes* (PAF), an archival collection and digitisation initiative based in Bamako, Mali. PAF preserves thousands of endangered documents belonging to Malian women who undertook anticolonial struggles in the 1950s, and women's rights projects in the following decades.

Sorcha Thomson is a PhD Fellow at the University of Roskilde, Denmark, in the project 'Entangled Histories of Palestine and the Global New Left'. Her research explores the history of solidarity with anticolonial and anti-imperial movements. She is co-editor of the book *Palestine in the World* (Bloomsbury, 2023), an Editorial Fellow of *History Workshop*, a radical digital history magazine, and an Associate Research Fellow at Birkbeck, University of London. She holds an MPhil in Modern Middle Eastern Studies from the University of Oxford.

Molly Todd is a US-based historian specialising in modern Central America, refugee experiences, historical memory, and transnational human rights and solidarity movements. She holds degrees from the Universities of Wisconsin and Texas, and Reed College. Her publications include the monographs *Beyond Displacement: Campesinos, Refugees, and Collective Action in the Salvadoran Civil War* (University of Wisconsin Press, 2010) and *Long Journey to Justice: El Salvador, The United States, and Struggles against Empire* (University of Wisconsin Press, 2021), the textbook *Undergraduate Research in History: A Guide for Students* (Routledge, 2022), and numerous book chapters and articles. Her research has been supported by the National Humanities Center, the Whiting Foundation for the Humanities, and Fulbright and Mellon-Sawyer fellowships. She is a Professor at Montana State University, where she directs the Public History Lab and teaches courses on Latin American history and historical methods.

Women Democratic Front (WDF) is an autonomous socialist-feminist political organisation and resistance movement of women in Pakistan. More information about the organisation can be found at www.wdfpk.org.

Donya Ziaee is a former PhD candidate in Women's Studies at York University in Toronto. She left her academic studies to work as a radio journalist for the Canadian Broadcasting Corporation (CBC) and is currently a researcher for the Council of Canadians, a grassroots organisation that fights corporate power and influence in Canada.